Children

✗

Children:
A Multi-professional
Perspective

Dominic Wyse

School of Education and Community Studies
Liverpool John Moores University, UK

Angela Hawtin

School of Health
Liverpool John Moores University, UK

A member of the Hodder Headline Group
LONDON

First published in Great Britain in 2000 by
Arnold, a member of the Hodder Headline Group,
338 Euston Road, London NW1 3BH

http://www.arnoldpublishers.com

British Library Cataloguing in Publication Data
A catalogue record for this book is available from the British Library

ISBN 0 340 70061 0 (pb)

1 2 3 4 5 6 7 8 9 10

Commissioning Editor: Fiona Goodgame
Production Editor: Wendy Rooke
Production Controller: Iain McWilliams
Project Manager: Paula O'Connell

Typeset in Palatino by J&L Composition Ltd, Filey, North Yorkshire
Printed and bound in Great Britain by J.W. Arrowsmiths Ltd, Bristol

What do you think about this book? Or any other Arnold title?
Please send your comments to feedback.arnold@hodder.co.uk

Contents

Contributors

All the contributors are members of the childhood studies programme team at Liverpool John Moores University.

Robert Banton is a senior lecturer in child health and has carried out research in the area of child protection; he is co-author of *Keeping Kids from Harm*, produced in collaboration with the 'North Mersey Community (NHS) Trust'. He has recently been researching children's concepts of health. Previously he has worked as a health visitor and paediatric nurse.

Geoff Fenwick has worked in primary schools in the UK and overseas. His research and publications have reflected his expertise in the area of literature for children. His recent work includes examination of the importance of child-centred approaches to reading in primary schools. He is currently a research fellow at the School of Education.

Angela Hawtin began her career as a paediatric nurse working in cardiology, intensive care and community nursing. She undertook a law degree and, following further training, qualified as a barrister in 1995. Her main areas of teaching, research and publication have been focused on child law and social welfare; children's rights; and child protection. She has undertaken consultancy and teaching in these areas in Tanzania, Jordan, Kiev and India. She is currently Deputy Director of the School of Health.

Russell Jones is a senior lecturer in primary education. His previous work as a teacher – including work in an advisory capacity – and lecturer included strong emphasis on child-centred approaches through the arts. His recent research has looked at racism in predominantly white schools and this work has been published in *Teaching racism* by Trentham Books.

Nicola Leather is a principal lecturer and Head of Child Programmes at the School of Health. Her qualifications are in psychology with special emphasis on child development and stress. Research interests also include the relationship between complementary therapy and Western medicine. Previous posts have included clinical nursing posts in paediatrics, nurse teacher and senior lecturer within the area of child nursing and psychology.

Nicholas Medforth is the programme leader for the childhood studies programme. His qualifications include foci on psychology and sociology. His previous posts included work as a nurse specialist in paediatrics. His recent research has included an examination of the social construction of childhood and psychological aspects of children's pain experiences. He is currently involved in collaborative projects with children's organizations in the voluntary sector and has contributed to the multi-professional child protection project in Jordan.

Nell Napier is a senior lecturer in childhood studies at Liverpool John Moores University. She has been a childcare worker in the voluntary sector – working with children with disabilities – a nurse, and a primary school teacher. She is currently engaged in a PhD that is looking at the training of nurses and teachers.

Dominic Wyse is a senior lecturer in primary education. As a teacher he worked for three Local Education Authorities and taught from reception up to year six and had management and co-ordination responsibilities. His most recent book was a child-centred view of the teaching of *Primary Writing* published by Open University Press which has been enthusiastically reviewed. His recent research looked at children's rights in English schools. Consultancy work has included multi-professional initiatives to support children's rights in developing countries, where he collaborated with Angela Hawtin.

Preface

The interdisciplinary nature of work concerning children and childhood has become extremely important in recent years, with 'multi-professionalism' a significant part of this trend. This has been underpinned by a wide range of theoretical and practical action. In practice, multi-professional collaboration has taken some significant steps forward, and, in the UK, this has in part been prompted by the Children Act 1989. Academically, there are some exciting examples of interdisciplinary work. In 1996, the Children's Rights Centre at the University of Ghent held its first 'International Inter-disciplinary Course on Children's Rights'. The Norwegian Centre for Child Research publishes the journal *Childhood* which takes an 'international, cross-disciplinary view of the culture, economics, language, health and social networks of childhood and children'. In the UK, dissemination of the Economic and Social Research Council's multi-disciplinary programme 'Children 5–16: growing into the twenty-first century' continues. However, overall, academic progress towards interdisciplinary thinking and action in relation to the study of childhood is still in its infancy.

At the outset, it is important to say that this book is not intended to be a manual or handbook on multi-professional working practices. The reason that the title of the book refers to a multi-professional perspective is primar-ily related to the process of writing, although, as you will see, there are times when the book does explicitly discuss multi-professional work for children: for example, Chapter 5 looks at multi-professional practice in the child protection system and Chapter 6 includes an example of multi-professional work in Jordan.

The rationale for the book developed from a number of key ideas. One of these was that much of the publication of books and articles in the field of childhood studies does not involve interdisciplinary collaboration in the writing process itself. The result is that you tend to get publications that are either written by one or two authors, or edited collections with contribu-tions that are related primarily because they are collected together within one book. Our recognition of this resulted in a multi-professional approach to the writing of this book. Each chapter has several contributing writers who have different specialisms in relation to children and childhood. These specialisms include both practical and academic expertise in nursing, teach-ing, management, advocacy, research, the arts, psychology, social welfare, law, education, health and language.

The writers all teach on a childhood studies programme that is jointly owned by two university schools (health and education) and which includes colleagues from a range of other schools in the university. Multi-professional philosophies were established from the inception of the programme and this led to team-teaching which includes jointly planned and jointly taught residential components. The collaborative approach to the development of the programme was extended in the planning for this book. The book as a whole was planned by the team, and a mixture of contributions was agreed. The initial drafts were then provisionally edited and sent back to the team for further work. Following comments from two anonymous reviewers, the chapters were re-edited.

As you can probably imagine, our ambition to write in a multi-professional way created a number of challenges. One of these related to the fact that modern life is resulting in ever greater specialization in a wide range of fields, and yet there is still a pressing need to maintain a coherent overview; this is certainly true for the study of childhood. Childhood studies students need general understandings of the field itself but also need to understand in-depth individual aspects of the disciplines that contribute to the study of childhood. The book reflects this so that each chapter usually starts with general material, which is followed by specific accounts of related issues. This is a realistic recognition of the different levels of expertise that any group of professionals brings to a project: general knowledge is mixed with areas of extended specialization. In our desire to tackle specific subjects in greater depth, we are aware that this will make demands on the non-specialist reader, but we have endeavoured to account for this. We have not attempted the almost impossible task of comprehensive coverage, and so inevitably you will find omissions in the book.

Another challenge is part of a much older one: combining theory and practice. The study of childhood is underpinned by a wide range of competing theories once again coming from different disciplines. Since the 1970s, sociologists have had a significant impact on theories of childhood and have played an important role in developing theories of childhood that are interdisciplinary in nature (James et al., 1998), but we should perhaps continue to be wary of ownership of the study of childhood primarily in any one discipline. Developmental psychology has a longer track-record in theorizing but this has tended to be restricted in its focus on children. Flekkoy and Kaufman (1997) suggest that theories of children's rights can be traced back to the Ancient Greeks' thinking on democracy. There has also been significant theorizing on other historical aspects of childhood. Most of the chapters in the book include accounts of relevant theories, and these are balanced by specific practical examples and issues.

In order to clarify some of these examples and issues, and to facilitate your reading, it is perhaps useful to offer a 'map' of these significant features of the book (see Table 0.1).

The book is aimed to support specific modules on childhood studies programmes. Each chapter in the book relates closely to modules that are part of many such programmes. We have illustrated how the book differs from others in relation to the writing process; it is also different in its focus on the ages of childhood. There is already a wealth of literature related to early childhood. In the light of this, the book defines childhood as from pre-birth to age 18: the content is a reflection of this, and our advocacy of rights for children.

Table 0.1 Summary of chapters

	1: Images of childhood	2: The developing child	3: Children and assessment	4: The family	5: Children at risk	6: Children's rights
Disciplines	Sociology, arts	Psychology, education	Psychology, health, education	Sociology, politics, law	Law, social policy	Law, health education
Theory	Constructs of childhood	Development	The 'self'	Functionalism and feminism	Causation of violence	Empowerment
Practical example	Children's literature	Children's age and the law	Health screening	Family life today	Child protection system	Work in Jordan
General	History of childhood	Theories of development	History of assessment	Definitions of family	Empowerment and the law	UN Convention on the Rights of the Child
In-depth focus	Picture fiction	Experiences of black children	Educational assessment	Family breakdown	Teacher's role in child protection	Children's rights in four schools

Images of childhood

Nicholas Medforth, Geoff Fenwick
and Dominic Wyse

What is childhood? When asked this question it is likely that most people will
not have too much difficulty in offering some response. After all, childhood is
something which we have all experienced first hand, even if our experiences
differ from individual to individual. Some ideas of childhood include popular
contemporary definitions, such as a time of growth and development, innocence and freedom from responsibility, naïvety, dependence upon adult care
and protection, a time for play and education, a time to treasure, and so on.
Defining where the boundaries between childhood and adulthood lie causes
a little more difficulty. Can they be defined biologically, perhaps with the
onset or ending of puberty? Can they be defined legally where there is some
inconsistency between what age a young person might be permitted to marry
without parental consent, be convicted of a criminal offence, leave school, join
the armed forces, or vote in local and general elections?

In this chapter we establish one of a number of theoretical perspectives
that underpin our thinking about childhood. In 1988, Leena Alanen wrote
that 'the study of children is either totally absent in sociology or is treated
within very limited contexts'. The limited contexts that Alanen referred to
included the family and the school. Both these areas have generated much
research and theory, but, particularly in the case of schooling, this has tended
to be rather narrow in focus. It is our view that the sociology of childhood
offers one promising way of pulling together a range of issues that confront
people who work in the area of childhood. One of the key ideas that
sociologists have addressed is the way that childhood is defined and conceptualized. The realization that childhood is not a fixed and mutually
agreed concept is an important initial step on the way to having a more
coherent view of children and childhood.

The first part of the chapter uses some key ideas that can be found in the
literature on the sociology of childhood. The re-examination of history offers
some important insights on constructions of childhood. The discussion of
visual images of children throughout history and the impact of the printed
word lead to questions about the status and 'the disappearance of childhood'. The final section of this part speculates on current notions of
childhood. A number of these contemporary constructions of childhood
underpin the discussions covered in other chapters in the book.

The second part of the chapter develops one of the many important
concrete aspects of images of children: literature. The sociological influence
recurs particularly in relation to the seminal work of the Opies. This analysis

of nursery rhymes and chants is contrasted with fairy tales and modern picture books. The chapter concludes with investigations of autobiographical work, stereotypic characters and children themselves as authors.

Creating an image of childhood

The Western cultural concept of childhood is so familiar to us at the end of the twentieth century that it is easy to assume it to be a universal state: a phenomenon that has always existed historically, a natural state of human existence which cuts across class, geographical location, culture, gender and political and economic boundaries. Many commentators, however, would argue that the definition of childhood is part of a dynamic process rather than a fixed state and is a concept which is culturally constructed and therefore very much a product of its time and location. One such writer is H. Hendrick (1997) who identified a number of constructions and reconstructions of British childhood from 1800 to the present day. Before we explore such definitions of childhood in a little more detail it is perhaps worth considering what is meant by the term 'social construction' in this context. Hendrick reminded us that

> The term has nothing to do with the cultures that children construct for and between themselves. During our period 'childhood' – both the institution and the construction of – was composed by adults, usually those of the professional middle class. This is not meant to sound conspirational. No attempt is made here to suggest that children's condition is entirely devoid of a biological dimension, nor to deny the effects of physical being, though the nature of the consanguinity between the psychological and the biological is extraordinarily problematic.
>
> (Hendrick, H., 1997: 35)

Hendrick goes on to argue that different understandings of the nature of childhood have existed to express a desired state of childhood from an adult perspective. This forms part of a larger philosophy: one which seeks to support cultural and political commitments to the family, to control children, to promote a perception of childhood as a universal and natural state, and to underpin a particular social order.

Cox (1996) offers some further explanation of how such a process might occur by taking a Foucauldian approach to the concept of 'discourse'. Cox explains that

> at its simplest, a discourse is a social process in which, through language (used in its broadest sense to include all semiotic systems) we make sense of the world around us, but also the process by which the world makes sense of us (O'Sullivan et al., 1994). Discourses, thus construct society by constructing objects of knowledge, social subjects

and forms of 'self', social relationships and conceptual frameworks (Fairclough, 1992: 39) . . . . As children we are born into something which resembles a primordial soup of discourses; these represent the world to us and at the same time position us as individuals within that world.

(Cox, 1996: 6)

The idea that language and discourse actually help to *create* notions such as childhood can be uncovered through the examination of 'texts' which transmit the cultural meaning of experiences. These texts might include stories, letters, historical documents, legal papers, recordings of songs, conversations, plays and poems, paintings and photographs, newspaper and magazine articles, literature, film, television, or fashion. Some discourses may be less enduring than others, fluctuating in popularity and constantly competing alongside others for dominance; however, some may become deeply embedded into popular culture to the extent that they often go unchallenged or escape critical analysis. It is our view that for most people, including those who work with children, the concept of childhood has remained unsubjected to critical analysis.

Gittins (1998: 109) suggested that imagery (particularly visual imagery) plays an important part in 'representing and reconstructing reality in order to produce a separate and free-standing, universally recognizable form'. Arguably, the sheer number – the deluge – of images of children has helped to create the myth of a universal child and a universal childhood. Images of children are invariably constructed *by* adults to convey messages and meanings *to* adults. The meanings that are used to convey childhood change and vary, although there are certain recurring and central themes: dependency, victimization/helplessness, loss, nostalgia, innocence, danger and nature.

The history of childhood

Philippe Aries (1962) can be considered to be one of the first theorists to analyse discourse on childhood from an historical perspective. In his seminal text *Centuries of childhood*, Aries drew on the evidence of medieval paintings of children, their clothes, games and social relationships to argue the controversial position that childhood, like the family, is a product of modern Western society and as such did not exist in the pre-modern age. Children of the time were distinguished from adults only by the fact that they were smaller, and Preformationism (the view that children were miniature adults inhabiting an adult world) can be evidenced in paintings of infants and children from the period.

In mediaeval society the idea of childhood did not exist; this is not to suggest that children were neglected, forsaken or despised. The idea of childhood is not to be confused with affection for children; it corresponds to an awareness of the particular nature of childhood, that particular nature which distinguishes the child from the adult, even the young adult. In mediaeval society, this awareness was lacking. That is why, as soon as the child could live without the constant solicitude of his mother, his nanny or the cradle-rocker, he belonged to adult society.

(Aries, 1962: 128)

Aries was not necessarily describing the way that everyday experiences were devoid of a childish quality, rather highlighting the idea that the concept of childhood as a separate social space to adulthood (and consequently the concept of the child) could not have existed in people's minds at that time. According to Aries the concept of childhood was created from the end of the thirteenth century onwards and became more obvious during the sixteenth and seventeenth centuries. Aries saw the emergent concept of childhood as initially restricted to the professional and property owning classes and being characterized by two distinct dimensions. The first was the 'affective' dimension involving a definition of children as playthings to be coddled and indulged by adults who derived pleasure and amusement from them in return for their care and protection. Coexisting was the 'developmental' dimension, which resulted from ideological processes which asserted childhood as a time for social, physical and intellectual growth (deMause, 1974). Boundaries according to class and gender were also identified. For example, as late as the seventeenth century, some girls were married and running households at 14, whilst middle-class boys of the same period were being educated, and working class boys of the same age were sent to work.

Aries has not been without his critics on methodological grounds as well as on the basis that various forms of childhood – some of which were expressed through affectionate relationships akin to contemporary childhood experiences – existed even in medieval times. Critics have also suggested that there *was* a recognition that children had needs different from those of adults (Pollock, 1987). Nevertheless Cox (1996) suggested that Aries' work is important for a number of reasons. First, it raised the idea that childhood is a socially constructed phenomenon which could be subject to change, possibly for the better. Secondly, that childhood is a complex process not entirely governed by biology and one which results in a variety of lived experiences for children. These may be difficult to examine as they are not universal and are governed by social status, power relationships, economic factors, culture and geography.

One of the central points that Aries made was that medieval children largely inhabited an adult social world, working, playing and interacting with adults in an uncensored and unrestricted way. This idea was followed up by Postman (1983), in *The disappearance of childhood*, who linked the separation of childhood and adulthood with the emergence of widespread literacy and the development of a sense of 'shame' which accompanied it. Postman argued that the invention of the printing press in the fifteenth century separated children from adult knowledge, information, status and discourse, and redefined children as 'innocent'. Children were now required to occupy a social space which was separate, primarily because adults could read and write and children could not. This change in adult–child relations, according to Postman, allowed adult society to begin to control and regulate children, by determining exactly what kinds of knowledge they would gain access to and how and when they would have it.

Thus we return to H. Hendrick's (1997) contention that childhood during the nineteenth and twentieth centuries has been controlled from an adult perspective which sought to identify an ideal and universally approved childhood. This resulted in a battle for supremacy between different constructions of childhood which often coexisted and overlapped, as romantics, evangelists, social reformers and psycho-medics struggled to redefine childhood according to their particular ideological agendas. This of course always occurred against the backdrop of the social, economic, religious and political challenges of the era.

The legacy of several of these constructions and reconstructions of childhood can be located within contemporary discourse surrounding children, so it is worthwhile briefly considering the particular constructions identified by Hendrick before moving on to explore how his list might be extended as we move towards the end of the twentieth century. Incidentally, some of these constructions and reconstructions might be easily identified through a visit to a local art gallery or flicking through the pages of a newspaper or magazine. By treating historical paintings of children or contemporary photographs and articles as the texts of their period, it may well be possible to unravel particular ideologies surrounding childhood through an interpretative activity similar to that carried out by Aries.

THE ENLIGHTENMENT PERIOD AND BEYOND

Hendrick (1997) refers to a new world for children at the beginning of the eighteenth century which was underpinned by a new, less punitive approach as a result of the ideas about human nature expounded by philosophers and developmentalists of the Enlightenment. Up until this time children had often been regarded as the 'inheritors of original sin' and therefore in need of authoritarian adult control and correction through physical punishment in order to bring their will into line with the will of God. As Hendrick explains: 'The eighteenth century social construction of childhood, though much more recognizable to western society, emerged fragmented and equivocal, torn as it was between the notion of "innocence" and a pessimism born of evangelical and political anxieties' (1990: 37). The period saw a debate emerging about what constitutes the nature of the child. As we describe in Chapter 2, John Locke, an English philosopher writing towards the end of the seventeenth century, had proposed an early environmentalist position, seeing the child as *tabula rasa* or blank slate, born neither innately good nor bad, but waiting for life's experiences to write his personal history and shape his personality and character. Rather than breaking the child's will, Locke suggested that adults should listen to the child. By recognizing innate curiosity and rewarding learning through praise and rewards it would be possible to encourage children to become virtuous members of society through the provision of good adult role models.

The Swiss philosopher and educationist Jean Jacques Rousseau, writing during the early eighteenth century, agreed that children were different from adults but captured the imagination of his time by advancing a position of romantic naturalism in which the child was affectionately regarded as a kind of 'noble savage'. In his seminal text *Emile* (1762), Rousseau saw the child as a 'little human animal destined for the spiritual and moral life' who should be educated not through control and coercion, but instead should be allowed to follow an innate natural process of development which recognized that 'nature wants children to be children before they are men'. This point heralded the beginnings of an appreciation of childhood as a period in the life-cycle which had its own intrinsic value rather than simply being a process to be undergone before adulthood might be achieved.

Children were invested with a new sensitivity and this idea was picked up by poets and writers of the period such as Blake, Coleridge and Wordsworth whose Romantic aspirations involved the rediscovery of the nature of the self through an exploration of childhood 'innocence' perhaps as a reaction against the constraints, materialism and rationalism of adult society. Wordsworth, for example, saw childhood as the 'seed-time for the soul' and in *Songs of innocence and experience* Blake suggested that as children 'we are put on the earth a little space, that we must learn to bear the beams of love'.

Hendrick pointed out that the Romantic construction of childhood as innocent and a period invested with a natural sensibility was restricted to a narrowly confined elite and was in fact short-lived. Nineteenth century industrialization, the demands of a political economy and fears of social disorder which emerged as a result of the French Revolution led to the emergence of a very different set of reconstructions of childhood. These proposed a markedly less optimistic understanding of childhood and its place within the development of society. Children's needs were subordinated to the needs of adult society: 'notions of freedom were barely tolerated as democrats, trades unionists, labourers, women reformers and others fought for food, political representation and the right to free opinion' (James and Prout, 1990).

THE NINETEENTH AND TWENTIETH CENTURIES

Nineteenth-century social forces led to a series of competing constructions of childhood identified by Hendrick (1997: 39) and shaped by the characteristics of their age. The first was the 'evangelical child', which, fuelled by counter-revolutionary fears and a desire for social control in the ruling classes, led to a redefinition of children by popular evangelical writers such as Hannah More who suggested that they were lacking in natural goodness. Rather than having small but forgivable weaknesses, More suggested that children brought an innate evilness and corruptness into the world which adults had a moral duty to correct through education. Coexisting were the 'factory child' and the 'delinquent child', direct products of demands for free labour during the Industrial Revolution. These reconstructions led to the location of working class and unemployed children outside what leading reformers saw as the domestic ideal of the family. This meant that children were relocated into a world inhabited by adults, treading a fine line between innocence and experience. Their experience meant that they knew 'too much' about the survival skills needed to get by in existences dominated by work in factories and life on the streets. Such children were perceived by reformers of the time as needing to be cared for, protected and 'turned back' towards a state of innocence and religious conviction.

The mechanisms that supported this change in views of children were legal reforms such as the Factory Act 1833 and the requirement for children to be schooled during the last quarter of the nineteenth century. These measures had the result of creating a redefinition of childhood as a time of dependency, ignorance, separation from the adult world, protection and subjection to social control. The reforms also served to attempt to universalize childhood through schools, by providing a national experience of childhood which went some way (however partial) to cut across geographical, class and gender divisions, but also reinforced dependency and disempowerment for many children who had previously been responsible for their own lives and well-being.

During the early part of the twentieth century a number of constructions re-emerged. Hendrick identified the rise of the 'psycho-medical child' as a result of the rediscovery of poverty and health concerns in Edwardian England: the child as subject of scientific study with the rise of developmental psychology and the 'child study' movement. The 'psychological child' emerged as a result of psychoanalytic theory and the setting up of child guidance clinics. The 'welfare child' resulted from attempts to protect children from abuse and neglect through the Children Act 1908 and the setting up of school medical inspections and health visiting services. Final constructions identified by Hendrick in the post-war period are the 'family child' and the 'public child'. These saw the child in a 'natural' family, as a response to Bowlbyism and attachment theory, and the reinforcement of the family's role in child care, guidance and emotional support through provisions of the Children Act 1948 and the Children and Young Persons Act 1969.

THE PRESENT DAY

Let us now move on to consider some possible contemporary reconstructions of childhood which overlap to inform today's popular understandings of what childhood means as we move towards the millennium. In thinking about contemporary reconstructions it is perhaps worthwhile reminding ourselves of some of the key themes which have emerged so far:

- the packaging and universalizing of childhood through popular culture;
- a separation of childhood from adulthood through restricted access to information and cultural products;
- an understanding of childhood as a natural period of innocence and innate beauty;
- a view that children need to be controlled, corrected and shaped into responsible citizens in order to remove a potential threat to the social order;
- an argument that childhood constitutes a period of particular vulnerability which warrants adult protection and statutory advocacy or intervention;
- a perception that childhood is a time of growth and development towards adult competencies; and
- a feeling that childhood should be a special, magical time in which children should be supported through adult (family) affection, love and nurture perhaps in return for a later responsibility towards parents and society.

The reader may be able to identify some of these ideas, and perhaps tensions between them, as the basis of some of the contemporary formulations we propose here. It is well beyond the scope of this chapter to examine them in any critical detail; however, they are worth raising in the hope of stimulating further exploration. We are unable to consider all of them here, and some are addressed in other chapters such as the child as citizen with rights.

The first contemporary reconstruction is the 'charity child', very much popularized during the 1980s by television events such as the BBC's *Children in Need* appeal, or ITV's *Telethon* and iconized through graphic images of starving African children during the pop concert *Live Aid* or in charity relief appeals. Others include pictures of street children in Latin America or graphic news reports of the children whose lives have been torn apart by war. At the same time, children – through their perceived natural innocence – may also become a yardstick against which adult corruption, insanity and inhumanity may be contrasted or measured. Such a representation of children, carrying with it implicit messages about children as disempowered, innocent and passive victims, is often reinforced by 'mercy missions' as diverse as those designed to provide care and improved facilities for children in Romanian orphanages and dream holidays for children with life-limiting medical conditions. The phenomenon of the charity child re-emerged against the backdrop of the politics of individualism associated with Thatcherism and the New Right. This brought with it a denial of a collective responsibility to take care of the more vulnerable groups of society, and attempts to relocate the child within the traditional family.

Another contemporary phenomenon is the 'hurried, processed, developed, tested and assessed child' which results from political attempts to universalize childhood educational experiences through pre-school provision, the imposition of National Curriculum and statutory school testing schedules, and attempts to engage parents in the education process. Such attempts by the state to universalize and process children are not restricted to the field of education. For example, in the field of health, consider targets for uptake of immunizations and involvement of parents in child-health record keeping (the assessment of children in these settings is covered in more depth in Chapter 4). The media frequently demonstrates a keen interest in this particular construction of childhood through celebrations of exam successes of young children who have achieved results to be envied by young people twice their age.

The culture of promoting development may also be evidenced through a visit to one of the many high-street stores which recognize an insatiable market for toys and books which are designed primarily to aid children's learning. This has had the effect of inculcating fears of delayed progression bordering on paranoia in some parents, and perhaps contributed to initial reactions of horror to the now almost universally popular and innocuous children's TV programme *Teletubbies* which generated much initial discussion about potential harmful effects on children's language development.

This point leads us towards considering the instantly recognizable 'marketer's dream child'. With many children having access to a consumable income unprecedented in previous generations, children have become subject to a relentless pressure from advertisers, particularly where advertising is interspersed between children's TV programmes. Here, even children with very limited material resources can find no escape from advertisers who not only tap into children's dreams, but actively construct and cultivate them, as may be clearly identified in the Disney phenomenon which is now busily establishing itself in the fantasies of children in the developing world as well as the West. The fashion industry has also capitalized on children's susceptibility to the dream factory, with many children's clothes indistinguishable in style or price from those of adults.

The media provides the text for much of modern culture, so it is unsurprising that our next reconstruction is that of the electronic child identified by Gill (1996). Children increasingly have access to unlimited, uncensored, and uncontrollable information through a barrage of media including radio, terrestrial and non-terrestrial TV, video, computer games and the internet. Much discussion has been generated surrounding the potential benefits and harm to children which might arise from such developments. A particularly disturbing area of concern has been the uncontrolled promotion of child pornography on the world-wide web. This highlights a formerly more covert representation of children as sex objects, which might previously have found more legitimate, but no less discomfiting, expression through child beauty pageants or in implicitly sexual representations of children in art and advertising.

Our discomfort with such representations of children, closely aligned to a separate world of adult sexuality, perhaps mirrors some still intensely voiced reactions to Freudian ideas about childhood sexuality. They challenge constructions of childhood as a period of innocence and need for protection which are deeply embedded in our collective consciousness. This point brings us back to the idea that childhood emerged as a separate social space to adulthood at a particular point in history. Postman (1983) argued that suddenly, through the written text, adults had access to information and a mode of communication and discourse which children were not afforded. This served to exclude children from the adult world which they had previously inhabited. According to Postman, however, this process has been reversed by the invention and almost universal availability of television and the electronic media resulting in the disappearance – or what Jenks (1996) describes as the 'strange death' – of childhood.

The idea that childhood is declining or receding raises some interesting questions for the reader to consider. To what extent is childhood a socially constructed phenomenon? Can we accept that childhood exists as a universal biological or developmental reality which crosses cultural boundaries? Is childhood rather a historical or political process which is constantly evolving as different representations of childhood emerge and recede in response to social and economic forces? Is childhood as we know it in real danger of disappearing and to what extent might we be prepared to accept or resist such a loss?

All of these questions have relevance to the practitioner working with children as the answers they formulate will inform their personal understanding of what childhood is about and consequently their preconceptions about, and expectations of, the children with whom they interact. Perhaps the most important question contemporary society needs to consider is how far can the practitioner or policy maker go in allowing the child access to rights, information, resources and services which might previously have been reserved for those who inhabit the world of adulthood.

As we have seen, images of children and their culture come from a wide array of sources. One such source is the area of literature and language where some particularly significant aspects of childhood are reflected. The following sections of this chapter illustrate the images of children from nursery rhymes, oral accounts, contemporary picture fiction and classic longer fiction, and the chapter concludes with a short account of children as authors.

Literature for children

Literature for children has become a profoundly important area for many people who work and interact with children. Many childcare and education settings use books and particularly stories in a variety of ways. However, the choice of such texts remains a problematic area for many people, particularly in the light of the explosion of choice that has occurred in the latter part of the twentieth century. The importance of literature for children is sustained by a unique partnership between author and reader. Authors attempt to portray particular images of children, and readers respond to these images.

The study of literature for children presents readers with insights into children's behaviour as observed or imagined, in written and pictorial form.

Children's lives, portrayed in a variety of situations and settings, reflect changes in the relationship between society and children. Often books which were highly successful in their day become subject to criticism because attitudes have changed. For example, the brutal treatment of the hero of *Tom Brown's schooldays* (Hughes, 1856) may have raised a storm of protest had its setting been in the twentieth century. Conversely, Victorian society would have been outraged by the irreverence of Astrid Lindgrenn's (1945) girl hero, Pippi Longstocking.

As society's values change, so must children's literature. Ten years ago, *Dennis the Menace*, without much doubt the most famous cartoon character in British children's comics, was regularly bent over his father's knee and beaten with a slipper. Now, this no longer happens. In its day, Stowe's *Uncle Tom's cabin* (1852) was regarded as a powerful literary weapon in the campaign to abolish slavery. During the late 1960s, the ways in which black people, both young and old, were portrayed in this book were subject to severe criticism and Uncle Tom himself was regarded no longer as a dignified, gentle, influential representative of his race but as someone who had sold out to white dominance, hence the derogative use of the term 'Uncle Tom'.

We have already mentioned the relationship between author and reader. An aspect of the reader's response is the onlooker/participant factor (Benton, 1978). The writer surrenders absolute ownership of a book in terms of interpretation the minute it is published. Readers will make their own unique interpretations even though the differences between many of them will be slight. As the reader takes ownership of the text, a character might engender empathy so strong that in some cases the reader becomes not just an onlooker or observer but, in mind at least, a participant in the story.

At times a child's empathy with particular situations or characters in a book might well become therapeutic. That is, what a reader experiences in real life might be seen as similar to the happenings in a book and this might create comfort or even inspiration. A reader once informed us that he had read *David Copperfield* at the age of 4; his statement caused initial disbelief. Further discussion revealed that he had been evacuated from Manchester to North Wales in the early part of the Second World War. A small child with only adults for company in a gloomy vicarage in a little town, he had found Dickens' novel in the library and identified with David Copperfield at once. Already a good reader, his motivation had appeared to sharpen his skills yet more. Bibliotherapy has been used for many years in clinical psychology. Recent developments (Doll and Doll, 1996) suggest that its use is being extended by librarians: there seems no reason why it should not be used, in a less scientific way, by parents and teachers also. The beginnings of such an approach have been reflected in the publication of texts that explore particular issues such as death or divorce.

In the immediate post-war period children's books were in short supply. The problem for many teachers was whether the number of books available to their pupils in class libraries would be sufficient to last out the school year. In many homes also, books were few in number. The situation began to change for the better in the early 1960s as cheap paperback editions became available. Within 10 years, 3000 new children's books were being published annually. Now, in the late 1990s, that figure has doubled. Furthermore, during the last 50 years, the appearance of books has improved immensely. Now virtually every book cover is illustrated in colour, and modern technology has made illustration much more sophisticated.

With more high-quality books, the situation might seem to be almost ideal. Ironically, such an abundance creates several problems. The identification of good books becomes more difficult and many go out of print before they have had time to make an impact. This is not a problem for established children's classics, those books which have stood the test of time. Nor does it create difficulties for authors who are already well known. The sheer volume of books being published today, however, makes it extremely difficult for new writers of talent, and new books of quality, to be identified.

Many of the books considered here are children's classics, either old or relatively new. Others are well on their way to achieving this status. The majority are readily available. All of them have children and young adults as their main characters. It must be remembered, of course, that outstanding children's books do not necessarily require this. They may be concerned mainly with adults; they may be about animals, anthropomorphic or otherwise.

CONSTRUCTIONS OF CHILDHOOD IN LANGUAGE AND STORY

Stories and rhymes have represented children and aspects of their culture since human beings first began to communicate. What started as an oral tradition (spoken, acted and sung) has continued as an oral tradition but has been added to by the additional genres of television, film and the printed image. The genre that often catches children's imagination first of all is the nursery rhyme. In order to examine nursery rhymes, it is useful to consider the work of the Opies.

Iona and Peter Opie carried out the most extensive period of work in the area of children's rhymes, games, chants and sayings. The process of collecting and classifying left a legacy that offers a rich picture of one aspect of children's culture. The Opies looked at children's culture in a number of ways and published three key books: *The Oxford dictionary of nursery rhymes* (1951); *Children's games in street and playground* (1969) and *The lore and language of schoolchildren* (1959).

In the *Oxford dictionary of nursery rhymes*, each nursery rhyme is accompanied by historical analysis in terms of the origins and the various versions that exist.

Ring-a-ring o' roses
A pocket full of posies,
A-tishoo! A-tishoo!
We all fall down.

For example, they suggested that *Ring-a-ring o' roses* only relatively recently became standardized. This was not the case prior to 1898, when a collector called Lady Gomme found 12 versions with only one being similar to the one above. In New Bedford, Massachusetts, during 1790 the following was being sung:

> Round the ring of roses,
> Pots full of posies,
> The one who stoops last
> Shall tell whom she loves best.
>
> (Opie and Opie, 1951: 364)

The Opies offer the following information about *Ring-a-ring o' roses*:

> The invariable sneezing and falling down in modern English versions has given the would-be origin finders the opportunity to say that the rhyme dates back to the days of the Great Plague. A rosy rash, they allege, was a symptom of the plague, posies of herbs were carried as protection, sneezing was a final fatal symptom, and 'all fall down' was exactly what happened. It would be more delightful to recall the old belief that gifted children had the power to laugh roses (Grimm's *Deutsche Mythologie*). The foreign and nineteenth-century versions seem to show that the fall was originally a curtsy or other gracious bending movement of a dramatic singing-game, and the present writers have on several occasions gathered from the oral tradition a sequel rhyme for the players to rise on their feet again,
>
> > The cows are in the meadow
> > Lying fast asleep,
> > A-tishoo! A-tishoo!
> > We all get up again.
>
> Lines similar to these last are also known to the Irish Celts.
>
> (Opie and Opie, 1951: 365)

It is now widely recognized that nursery rhymes do have an important part to play in early learning. One example of this is their contribution to children's phonological awareness, which helps with reading. However, nursery rhymes offer a wide range of other learning opportunities such as music and movement awareness, moral understanding, the learning of numbers and letters, the social enjoyment of chanting rhymes and so on. As Whitehead (1993) suggests, we should be careful not to undervalue the wider value of nursery rhymes at the expense of falling in line with the politically convenient notion that nursery rhymes are good for phonics.

Nursery rhymes are part of the oral tradition of most societies. They continue to change and evolve, often through the collaboration of early childhood educators and children. If we take *Ring-a-ring o' roses* again, it is now common to add the following second verse:

Down at the bottom of the deep blue sea
Catching fishes for my tea
With a one, and a two, and a three!

Another example of this evolutionary process comes from the experience of a father and his daughter of 2 years and 4 months. The daughter attended a nursery two mornings a week. The father realized that his daughter's singing of *Baa baa black sheep* had changed to include a second verse that sounded something like this:

Want to make a jumper, want to make a skirt
(made up words and sounds) . . . a woolly shirt
Thankyou to the master, thankyou to the dame
Thankyou to the little boy who lives down the lane.

As you can see, the child had made up words that she was not familiar with. The father asked the nursery nurse where the extra verse had come from. In reply she said that she thought that the new verse had evolved during the singing sessions. However, discussions with other nursery nurses revealed that the second verse was also known to them.

One to make a blanket
One to make a skirt
One to make the little boy
a woolly woolly shirt

'Thankyou' said the master
'Thankyou' said the dame
'Thankyou' said the little boy
who lives down the lane.

Nursery rhymes are one example of the way the oral tradition continues to influence children. However, they are very much jointly owned between children and adults, with the balance of power perhaps initially lying with the adult. When a child is very young, it is usually the adult who teaches the rhymes to the child. Often though, it is the child who then wanders round the room singing, chanting and creating his or her own versions that sometimes sound like gobbledegook. Further experimentation often results in deliberate changes to the words for humorous (often rude!) effect. This reflects the child's innate motivation for learning and a strong desire to control his or her world. As the children get older, the rhymes they sing are owned much more by the children themselves and disseminated through their informal networks.

A teacher collected the following chants and rhymes from the children in her class:

All the girls in Spain wash their knickers in champagne
All the boys in France do the Hula Hula dance
and the dance they do is enough to tie your shoe
and the shoe they tie is enough to tell a lie
and the lie they tell is enough to ring a bell
and the bell they ring goes ding a ling a ling

In pin seventy pin
In pin out
If you are a locker bocker
Please step out

Eany meany macka racka
rah ray dommi knocker
lollipop, hom pom push

Racing car, number nine
Losing petrol all the time
How many gallons did it lose?

The question of where children's chants and rhymes come from is difficult to answer. To this day, they are passed down from generation to generation. The examples above have a number of features that are common to many chants and rhymes. *All the girls in Spain* is a skipping or clapping rhyme and this is evident from the strong rhythmic and rhyming structure. Part of the enjoyment comes from the nonsense implied by the words: the Hula Hula dance is actually a Hawaiian women's dance. The other examples are 'dipping' rhymes which usually are used to decide who is 'it' or 'on' for a game of 'tig' or 'tag'.

The significance of rhymes and chants in relation to the images of childhood that they present is difficult to establish. One possible idea is that the context, purpose and structure are more important than the semantic aspects. The universal importance of play, dance, rhyme, rhythm, games, and so on is more important than the particular words, which are subject to periodic change and updating.

Over a period of 8 years, the Opies collected a wealth of material related to the *Lore and language of school children*. The blurb of this book offers a useful précis:

It is a record of his [sic] strange and primitive culture, including seasonal customs, initiation rites, superstitious practices and beliefs, innumerable rhymes and chants (800 are given here in full), catcalls and retorts, stock jokes, ruderies, riddles, slang-epithets, nicknames, and the traditional juvenile argot which continues to flourish in street and playground, largely unknown and certainly unheeded by the adult world.

(Opie and Opie, 1959)

This idea of childhood as a primitive culture and separate haven is addressed by James *et al.* (1998) who identify a tension between a mythical past and a modern present. Their observation that the Opies accepted that children's lore and language are constantly subject to modern influences is one that is taken up by Boyes (1995). Boyes also identified the important methodological consideration of 'gatekeepers' in the Opies' research. She offered evidence from Iona Opie that 'knickers' was about the strongest language that the publishers would allow in print. As adults tend to act as gatekeepers in order to censor material, this can restrict awareness of aspects of children's culture. Children quickly conceptualize the micro-politics of censorship and when asked to remember jokes or rhymes will self-sensor their material according to their perceptions of what the adult wants to hear. The humorously crude and inventive distortion to a well known 'dipping' rhyme heard in a playground by a teacher illustrates that there is perhaps more to learn from children's rhymes: 'Ip dip dog shit, fucking bastard you're not it'!

The tension created by the construct of the 'tribal child' is developed by James *et al.* (1998). Like many commentators, they recognize the 'magnificent' contribution that the Opies made, but also remind us that the negative reductionist interpretation of the language of children was challenged by other researchers who, like the Opies, recognized the positive aspects of interacting with children directly in order to better understand their lives. Towards the end of their book *Theorizing childhood* James *et al.* (1998: 215) offer a more optimistic possibility for the tribal child by acknowledging that the construction may offer a potential for 'resistance to the normalizing effects of age hierarchies, educational policies, socialization theories, and child-rearing practices'.

THE CHILD IN FAIRY AND FOLK TALES

All cultures have their traditional stories, for example the Anansi stories of African culture, Greek myths and legends, European tales influenced by the Grimm brothers and Hans Christian Andersen, and so on. The move from the oral tradition towards printed versions of these stories is a relatively recent phenomenon, but, even within this short time span, many printed traditional stories have gone through a number of changes.

Fairy and folk tales are likely to be the first form of literature which children become familiar with, often before they go to school. Many of them come from an oral tradition and were not originally intended for children in particular. Their conversion to print has resulted in some of them becoming much more child-orientated and rather more gentle than they were originally. It is a mistake to think, however, that their contents are watered down so much that they lack suspense and excitement. Nor can it be assumed that they are so mild that they should be confined to a very young readership. In *The red shoes* for instance, the main character becomes so obsessed with her footwear that it dances away with her; the situation can only be terminated by cutting off the shoes as well as the feet within them. This story and many others indicate that fairy tales and folk stories can be the province of older children also. The best known collections of fairy tales are those compiled by the Grimm brothers, Hans Christian Andersen (1974), Charles Perrault (1696) and, in the UK, Andrew Lang (1973). Many of the best known tales are common to all four.

How do child characters behave in those stories? By and large, the girls tend to be passive. Thus, Red Riding Hood depends upon the intervention of the woodcutter to save her from the wolf, Cinderella needs her Fairy Godmother, the Sleeping Beauty requires the help of her prince and Thumbelina must wait patiently for her frog to become human before she can experience happiness. Generally, an air of passivity clings to these characters: by suffering adversity with grace they are rewarded. Even the tragedies of the girl in *The red shoes* who has her feet removed and *The little match seller* who freezes to death are ultimately rewarded by their elevation to heaven.

There are, of course, some exceptions. Both Hansel and Gretel are more in control of their fate than some of the characters already mentioned and it is Gretel, the girl, who shoves the witch into the oven and slams the door. And after the saintliness of so many of the other young female characters, the wilfulness of Goldilocks is refreshing. One can even feel some sympathy for Rumpelstiltskin despite the extremity of his demands. After all, the young queen who outwitted him owed him her life three times over. Generally, boy characters, although they are fewer in number, tend to be more enterprising, depending upon trickery to defeat brute strength, such as Tom Thumb and Jack in *Jack and the beanstalk*.

More recently, alternative versions of some of these classic tales have challenged the stereotypic roles of the characters. Babette Cole in *Princess Smartypants* (1986), for example, creates a princess who makes it hard for her suitors, rejecting them all, even the craftiest. Roald Dahl in *Revolting rhymes* (1982) has Red Riding Hood shooting the wolf, he also depicts Goldilocks as a juvenile delinquent who gets her come-uppance. The changes to traditional stories are made for a variety of reasons. Often publishers try to simplify the language of traditional stories. Unfortunately this sometimes leaves them so bland that they lose the magic and power that have kept them alive for so long. The continuing power of the American film industry has resulted in some Disney films having a book of the film; or perhaps we should say book of the film of the book of the oral tale. The relentless pace of more and more complex effects for book covers and presentation also necessitates changes to original stories. Making more money often seems a good enough reason to revamp a traditional story. On a more positive note, some authors have ingeniously altered traditional stories, and, in the process, create something new and original that is still clearly linked to the traditional version. Examples of this include *The stinky cheese man and other fairly stupid tales* by Jon Scieszka and Lane Smith (1992) where the absurdity of some traditional stories is highlighted; *The boy who cried wolf* by Tony Ross (1985) where the wolf ends up eating most of the people in the village just for fun, then after a change of mind decides to eat the boy and comments 'C'est la vie'; *The practical princess and other liberating tales* (Williams, 1978) which attacks the sexism and stereotypic nature of many traditional stories; and *The true story of the three little pigs!*, again by Jon Scieszka (1989), which gives the wolf's side of the story because he was misrepresented by the press, of course!

CHILDREN IN PICTURE BOOKS

There have been immense changes in this form of children's literature over the past 30 years. This is not to deny the impact of talented illustrators before then. With few exceptions, however, they usually used their talents to assist the efforts of writers. Some of these combinations were so effective that the work of artist and writer become inextricable. Who could envisage *Alice in Wonderland* without John Tenniel's magnificent illustrations? Indeed, the popular visual image of Alice is, inevitably, that which Tenniel created. Similarly, A. A. Milne's Winnie the Pooh stories owe much to E. B. Shepard. And although not so well known, Thomas Henry was responsible for the image of Richmal Crompton's William Brown.

One reason for illustrators subordinating their talents was probably because, like fairy tales, picture books were seen to be primarily for young children. Now, many picture books are just as appropriate for older children. Many illustrators who start out working with authors eventually produce the words themselves. One of our most famous illustrators, Raymond Briggs, has been doing this for many years. Ironically, *The Snowman*, a book about a young boy who builds a snowman who comes to life, contains not a single word, yet is not in the least obscure, such is the talent of this illustrator.

Children created by modern illustrators tend to challenge the world of adults, although at times they are glad to depend on it for security. Perhaps the best example of this comes from Maurice Sendak (1967). In *Where the Wild Things are*, Max is sent to bed, but escapes through the window of his imagination to visit the Wild Things, grotesque but benign monsters, only to return to find his supper waiting for him. At times, children appear to be independent of adults, sometimes scoring points off them. In *Enchantment in the garden*, a recent book by Shirley Hughes (1996), which is probably one of her best, Valerie copes independently with mystical happenings. And in *Tarzana*, Babette Cole's (1991) character frees the animals from a zoo, rescues the president from gangsters and persuades him to return the animals to their proper environment. David McKee's (1980) *Not now, Bernard* makes a telling comment on parents who do not listen to their children. John Burningham (1987) in *John Patrick Norman McHennessy: the boy who was always late* ends with the headteacher, who always disbelieves his pupil's bizarre reasons for lateness, being cornered in the rafters by an angry gorilla. John Patrick chooses not to believe the head and mimics his repetitive refrain: 'There are no such things as gorillas in the roof Sir . . .'

So, there has been an explosion of the range and quality of children's picture fiction over the last 20 years. There also continues to be much picture fiction that is poor quality. We recognize that high quality is a potentially subjective description, but it is possible to identify some general characteristics of such fiction. The issue of quality is an important one and potentially difficult. People who work with children clearly want them to get the maximum benefit from the texts that they are exposed to. Too often the picture books on offer are of questionable quality: an examination of the books in most supermarkets, many book shops, some nurseries and schools highlights this view. Children themselves reveal their preferences through their enjoyment of particular texts; however, there are a number of dilemmas that exist when using children's judgements. Sometimes their ability to choose can be limited by their lack of experience of a range of texts and a lack of opportunity to reflect on the issues.

High quality picture fiction offers children a unique opportunity to connect with the author's imaginary world. Often this can be a particularly personal and intense experience. The features of books that often generate such experiences include a stimulating text and brilliant illustrations. However, although the best picture books offer artistically effective illustrations which themselves often contain a number of subplots (for example when Lily takes a seemingly peaceful walk but her dog is subjected to a range of nightmare visions conjured by ordinary features of the urban landscape; Kitamura, S., 1987), it is possible to exaggerate the importance of the pictures over and above the special resonances that text can create. High quality fiction operates on a number of semantic levels. The reader can read between the lines, utilize higher order thinking, and adult readers find things that appeal to them at their level. This is necessary because adults often read many times with children and the book needs to retain their interest as well as the child's.

If we take the classic picture book *The very hungry caterpillar* by Eric Carle (1970), this semantic sophistication can be illustrated. Young children enjoy the story of the growth of a caterpillar from egg to butterfly. The huge amount and bizarre range of food that the caterpillar eats appeal to the child's imagination. The sequential ordering through the days of the week and the list of foods to be eaten on Saturday engage the child's desire to count, list and sequence. For the adult reader, the historical importance of the book's technology is perhaps of interest: Carle's book was one of the first to use cut-away pages and has holes for little fingers to poke through and follow the caterpillar's path. This has led, some 27 years later, to the breathtaking technological aspects of some of today's books. Indeed, Johnson (1990) has developed this tradition by showing children how they can include book technology in their own writing and bookmaking. The adult reader also appreciates the importance of using scientific language such as 'cocoon' and perhaps the implications for diet as evidenced by the caterpillar feeling much better when he goes back to eating 'one nice green leaf'. Structurally, the first page ('In the light of the moon a little egg lay on a leaf') seems to act as a preface to the second page which is the beginning of the story proper ('One Sunday morning the warm sun came up . . .'). Similarly, the last three pages might be seen as a coda as the caterpillar progresses from fat caterpillar to cocoon to 'a beautiful butterfly'. This kind of structural sophistication provides an interesting story for the child and an analytic focus for the adult.

Not now, Bernard by David McKee (1980) takes a typical phrase that an adult may say to a child and develops a story around it ('"Hello, Dad," said Bernard. "Not now, Bernard," said his father'). The common language of adult–child interactions has been a rich area for authors of children's fiction as it allows them to tap into the culture of childhood. In *Not now, Bernard* the author taps into what must be a frustrating experience for children at best, and one that could amount to neglect. The illustrations have uniqueness, simplicity and cartoon-like humour. Bernard's attempts to speak to his parents lead to a series of minor disasters followed by the monster that Bernard's parents think is fictional ending up eating Bernard. The parents are so obsessed with their own lives that at the end they fail to recognize the difference between their own son and what he has now become, a purple monster with horns! Although children can empathize with Bernard's predicament, the story can also encourage adults to reflect on their own interaction with children.

Authors of children's fiction find a variety of ways of rooting their work in children's culture. Janet and Alan Ahlberg's most important contribution to children's literature was in the ways that they weaved children's stories and nursery rhymes within one text. A good example of this is *Each peach pear plum* (Ahlberg and Ahlberg, 1978a). The text is structured in rhyming couplets with each double page having one couplet and an accompanying illustration. The rhythm and rhyme of the text appeal to young children and aid their memory of the text. The book also draws on the game 'I spy' as each couplet includes those words; for example, 'Baby Bunting fast asleep I spy Bo-Peep'. As you have probably guessed, a whole range of nursery rhyme characters populates the story, culminating in a picnic with plum pie:

Three Bears still hunting
THEY spy Baby Bunting
Baby Bunting safe and dry
I spy Plum Pie
Plum Pie in the sun
I spy . . .
. . . EVERYONE!

(Ahlberg and Ahlberg, 1978a: 24–31)

Anthony Browne's work is notable because of the way that his books often focus on important issues while maintaining genuinely interesting stories. Examples of such issues include sexism – *Piggybook* (1989); self-esteem and bullying – *Willy the Champ* (1990); one-parent families – *Gorilla* (1983); class – *A walk in the park* (1977); and gender and sibling rivalry – *The tunnel* (1992). All his books are accompanied by mesmeric illustrations that seem to derive from surrealism.

The final author we want to examine in this section is Trish Cooke. Her book *So much!* is more recent than some of the previous examples, as it was published in 1994. Although prizes are a notoriously unreliable way of judging books, on this occasion the Smarties Book Prize, the Kurt Maschler and the She/WH Smith awards were justified. Indeed, Anthony Browne is quoted on the back of the book: 'It is always a delight to see an established artist taking risks, breaking new ground and succeeding brilliantly.' *So much!* explores an aspect of black British children's culture and like many children's books has a *naturally* repetitive structure:

They weren't doing anything
Mum and the baby
nothing really . . .
Then,
DING DONG!
'Oooooooh!'

Mum looked at the door,
the baby looked at Mum.
It was . . .

(Cooke, 1994: 7)

As can be seen from the extract, the text encourages children to predict what will happen next; this helps to develop an important reading strategy and recognizes children's enthusiasm for guessing and problem solving. The illustrations show accurate and positive images of a British Afro-Caribbean extended family, and as each character arrives at the house, they first want to do something with the baby, such as squeeze him (Auntie Bibba), kiss him (Uncle Didi), eat him (Nanny and Gran-Gran), fight him (Cousin Kay Kay and Big Cousin Ross):

And they wrestle
and they wrestle.
He push the baby first,
the baby hit him back.
He gave the baby pinch,
the baby gave him slap.
And then they laugh

and laugh and laugh.
'Huh huh huh!'

(Cooke, 1994: 28)

The language of the book brilliantly uses some of the rhythms and repetitions of African English which links it with other writers such as the Ghanaian poet John Agard. Once again, one of the core features of the book reflected in the title is based on a common childhood experience: the adult and child game 'How big's baby?' or 'How much do we love you?'.

CHILDHOOD REMEMBERED

There is a great deal of literature which recalls individual childhood. Much of it is autobiographical. Laurie Lee (1952) wrote evocatively of his early childhood in a Cotswold village in *Cider with Rosie* as did Flora Thompson (1945) in *Lark Rise to Candleford*. The background for such material need not, of course, be rural. Helen Forrester's (1974) *Twopence to cross the Mersey*, for instance, is an account of a childhood amidst urban poverty in Liverpool during the 1930s and *Somebody up there likes me* (Graziano and Barber, 1956) traces a boyhood spent in the East Side of New York at about the same time. Graziano was a champion boxer; his sport, like many others, and particularly cricket, has consistently attracted publishers in search of best-selling autobiographies. Many such books mention the childhood years of their authors, but in many cases the accounts are routine and lacking in interest. Indeed, both biographies and autobiographies of many celebrities often contain no more than a token mention of the early years.

Many writers make use of their own childhood experiences in one way or another without necessarily writing autobiography. Nina Bawden (1973), for example, used her own experience of war-time evacuation to give authenticity to *Carrie's war* and there is little doubt that a great deal of Dickens's work owes something to his own childhood experiences.

Children's lives recalled in diary form are also interesting. Two outstanding examples are *The secret diary of Adrian Mole aged 13³/₄* (Townsend, 1982) and *The diary of Anne Frank* (Frank, 1954). The former is fictitious, but obviously owes a great deal to Sue Townsend's knowledge of family life with particular reference to teenagers. The latter is a true autobiography and probably one of the most poignant diaries of young adulthood ever to be written.

The unpublished versions of ordinary people's childhood can be invaluable. Much work of this kind is oral history. For example, students who have recalled accounts of school experiences, sometimes from previous generations, often realize that they have stumbled on fascinating material which can be developed well beyond the essays for which they did their research. Working with mature students some 25 years ago, it was possible to build up a picture of war-time Merseyside and what it meant to children at that time. There was the school which had a memorial in its hall to 60 of its former pupils killed in the First World War; the girl in trouble in the 1940s because she looked for her cat when the siren sounded; families whose houses were destroyed four and five times during bombing raids; the boy who picked up a bomb on the recreation ground; the collapsed barrage balloon at the bottom of the street and the hundreds of people killed by a direct hit as they sheltered in the cellars beneath a school.

The following longer account from a mature student raises a number of issues. The current concerns with constructions of childhood perhaps under-play the positive sense of a childhood universal to all people irrespective of their age, culture, class, gender or race. One feature of contemporary British society is the problems to do with meaningful integration between adults and children. Yet many children experience the particular excitement gener-ated by oral accounts of real events in the lives of much older friends and family.

Buglo was a small boy with freckles and dark, penetrating eyes. We had met at infant school but our ways had parted at the start of the junior school. We came together once more when we were placed in the same class in Junior 2. Buglo saved the place next to him for me.

The teacher in that class was probably well into her sixties but had been retrained because of the shortage of classroom practitioners due to the war. There were more than 50 of us and the routine was much the same day in, day out. We had register, religion, arithmetic and English each morning. For arithmetic you did countless sums about shopping, like calculating the price of half a stone of potatoes and two pots of jam and adding up the total. Quite apart from the fact that two pots of jam was a mouth watering piece of wish fulfilment in those days of rationing, it was not particularly riveting. All you did was write the answers down in your book alongside the occasional bit of working out.

Our solution to arithmetic was to attempt some of the first examples and then simply write down the numbers of the others. After that we began the lesson under the desk which was concerned with two sub-jects which fascinated us – war and history. For some reason we had developed an interest in the Boer War, perhaps because the uniforms and weaponry were similar to those of the small lead models of toy soldiers and guns which we collected. Buglo brought in several leather bound tomes which chronicled the campaign and we pored over their maps and sepia pictures below the desk while our arithmetic books on top acted as a cover. When the teacher called out the answers we emerged from our studies of Kruger, the Karoo, Ladysmith and Mafeking to fill the answers in and mark them correct. Our history blossomed, our arithmetic declined.

Buglo's anarchy extended well beyond the classroom. In those days there were no school dinners. Children either went home for lunch or brought sandwiches. Buglo arranged a nice compromise. We could say we were going home and then eat our sandwiches as we wandered the streets and alleyways of the town. Our explorations were educational though sometimes hair-raising. We watched the slaughter of animals from the abattoir wall, purloined the odd foreign stamp from the second hand shop, discovered where the undertaker kept his coffins and, purely by mistake of course, turned on the tap of a tar boiler.

Our greatest adventure was the saga of the tumble-down house. It was our den, made more attractive by the fact that the military dumped their spent cartridge cases and used bullets there. This was where we held meetings with our gang most nights after school.

One evening we had a visit from a captain of the newly arrived regiment. We were not to use the house any more he told us, it was army property. As he left Buglo looked at us. 'We're not letting that bugger tell us what to do, are we lads?'

We agreed and Buglo at once took a lighter from his pocket and applied it to the many curled up strips of wall paper in the room. Within seconds, billowing smoke was everywhere and as we fled down to the alleyways we could hear shouts and the sound of military boots drumming along the pavements. But the members of the new regiment were unfamiliar with the terrain and we escaped.

Buglo stayed away from school the next day. The rest of us went through agonies all morning. But the Head never mentioned the incident in assembly nor were there angry visits from the police or soldiers. At lunch-time we crept as near as we dared to the old house. A tank stood sentinel nearby. The house had not burned out. Evidently it had been just too damp. And that episode was the high point of Buglo's campaign against adulthood. Thereafter, our exploits were never quite so exciting.

The authenticity of such accounts, even when compiled by professional writers, is often challenged. H. E. Bates's account of the activities of a lively relative in *My Uncle Silas* (1939) was greeted with incredulity by many readers. Yet Bates claimed that, had he *not* watered down the truth, the book might never have been published.

CHILD CHARACTERS: CONTROL AND COERCION

It might appear that the noble savage is a term better reflected in the depiction of boys in classic literature. Certainly, it appears that girls in literature took some time to achieve some semblance of independence. This particularly applies to American books. Jo in *Little women* (Alcott, 1868) demonstrates her strength mainly by supporting her mother in a home where the father has been removed by war. Katy in *What Katy did* (Coolidge, 1872) is an early example of a tomboy. She influences her friends, causes trouble at school and presents problems for her aunt who takes over the running of the household when Katy's mother dies. Thereafter, however, Katy is swamped by the didacticism common to children's books of the day.

She becomes handicapped for a time and the experience gives her the responsibility to take over her father's house when her aunt dies. Similarly, Anne in *Anne of Green Gables* (Montgomery, 1908) is an orphan who rebels against her new home until its security allows her to settle down.

If these early examples appear to be somewhat staid, it should be remembered that Lewis Carroll's *Alice in Wonderland* was first published in 1863. Admittedly, Alice belongs to fantasy rather than the family environment of the American books. Nevertheless, considering the constraints of Victorian England, Alice's independence is remarkable. This is not gained in a 'tomboy-like' way, being far more cerebral than physical. Alice confronts the absurdities of the Queen, the Dormouse and the Mad Hatter with equanimity, challenging them with a logic which mirrors that of the author who was a mathematician. With Alice, the constraints of the didacticism were loosened; girls in literature could now challenge adult values, even if these were disguised as those of bizarre characters of fantasy. Though not quite as effective as Alice, Johanna Spyri's (1881) *Heidi* is also an independent character. Going to live with her reclusive grandfather as an infant, her straightforward approach to life eventually results in family reconciliation.

As attitudes changed, girl characters became more varied and more physically active. Yet, for this to happen, the tomboy approach hinted at in *What Katy did* and *Heidi* was more accentuated. George is undoubtedly the leader in Enid Blyton's (1942) *Famous Five find a treasure island* and in all of that series. Yet it appears that she must shorten her name from Georgina if she is to be credible. Much later, Gene Kemp (1977) adopted a similar ploy in *The turbulent term of Tike Tiler*. Tike, much less genteel than George, is an independent spirit who creates havoc at primary school. In a clever twist in the plot, her identity is only revealed near the end of the book when she climbs onto the school roof and a teacher shouts 'Come down at once Theodora Tiler, you naughty girl'. Rather more lively than George, Tike nevertheless must appear to be a boy before she is accepted. An alternative view is that Gene Kemp deliberately obscured Tike's identity to illustrate that girls can be as active and mischievous as boys.

Is such subterfuge necessary? One might think that following Astrid Lindgrenn's (1945) *Pippi Longstocking* it was not. Not subtle, though much more physical, Pippi might be seen as the modern equivalent of Alice. Orphaned though affluent, she appears in a small Swedish town and, in a mixture of fantasy and family life, she repulses criminals, questions the logic of schooling, lifts a horse over her head, avoids being placed in an orphanage and copes single-handed with a conflagration. After Pippi, girl characters should never have been the same again. Roald Dahl (1969), as iconoclastic as Lindgrenn, produced a character not unlike Pippi in Matilda. Matilda is more involved with fact than was Pippi and possesses no superhuman qualities. But she combines physical and mental agility to outwit librarians, teachers and her parents. Although the book contains some of Dahl's typical crude insensitivity (Matilda's father, a second-hand car salesman, being the subject of much ridicule), it at least provides us with a girl who does not need to be disguised as a boy in order to be original and active. Since the mid

1980s it would appear that there is less need for girl characters to justify themselves. Margaret Mahy's books, for example, provide us with characters who confront strange situations with calmness and competence.

Boys in children's literature have never needed to struggle so hard to achieve prominence and power. Mark Twain's *Tom Sawyer* (1876) and *Huckleberry Finn* (1884) remain classics not only of children's fiction but of American literature in general. They have survived accusations of racism and sexism, mainly because of Twain's incisive portrayal of two boys suspicious and, at times, weary of adult authority who involve themselves in adventures which, set against the background of the Mississippi in the nineteenth century, are exciting, dangerous and realistic. Another classic, *Treasure Island* written by Robert Louis Stevenson (1883), takes a similar approach. Jim Hawkins' exploits are always on the brink of danger and disobedience.

More recent examples have involved younger boys in less demanding situations. The main character in Erich Kästner's (1929) *Emil and the detectives* is a young boy who enlists a gang of children in Berlin to bring the man who has picked his pocket to justice. And in a series of books commencing with *Just William* in 1926, Richmal Crompton created a boy whose constant battles against the authority of adults in general and parents in particular entertained children for several decades. William does not seem to have had a successor, at least not within the pages of a book. Today's 10-year-old noble savage is to be found in *The Beano* comic. Dennis the Menace has been tweaking the nose of adult authority for over 40 years now. Like William, he wins more often than he loses.

William Brown and Dennis the Menace, like Peter Pan, have never grown up. They are perpetual 10 year olds. Adolescent characters, perhaps the most natural source of resistance to adult demands, have continued to be created, although their background now tends to be urban. One of the finest examples has, perhaps, not received the acclaim it deserves. The central character in *Pennington's seventeenth summer* by Peyton (1970) is a secondary school rebel who is tolerated by his teachers only because he is talented musically. A series of misdemeanours is eclipsed when he wins a local music competition, despite hands made painful by a caning from his form teacher. His headmaster, exploiting the about-to-be-expelled Pennington to the full, requests that he plays some of his winning pieces at morning assembly. In a climax which resonates with adolescent defiance, Pennington plays *Tannenbaum (The red flag)* which is loathed and detested by his form teacher. Pennington cares nothing for the consequences, he has been offered a university scholarship.

The image of children and childhood in language and literature is a partial one. The role of adults is again powerful and yet, like any text, they must appeal to their audience – namely children themselves. The historical longevity of a text is one measure of its popularity with children and adults. Once again this raises contradictions. Surveys of children's preferences (Children's Literature Research Centre, 1996) often reveal a narrow range of authors as favourites such as Roald Dahl and Enid Blyton. However, it is possible that such surveys tell us more about the authors that children can remember than about the ones who are their preferences. For example, the *Point horror* and *Goosebumps* series have been best-sellers in recent years but their authors remain less well known.

To conclude, we will take a brief look at children themselves as authors for another glimpse of childhood.

CHILDREN AS AUTHORS

Fairly predictably, children's writing tends to be less accessible than children's literature written by adults. Until recently, writing done in class-rooms rarely found its way out of pupils' exercise books except when some of it was displayed on the walls. Newer approaches to the teaching of English encourage children to create their own books, often for a wider audience (Graves, 1983; Wyse, 1998 and Johnson 1990), although the current developments in literacy once again threaten this. So it is possible these days, although rare, to see more examples of children's writing in school libraries and reading areas alongside the usual commercially published material. In addition, school magazines are now much more common and word processing gives them a much more professional appearance.

Beyond school, however, examples of children's writing are fairly sparse, mainly because they are rarely viable commercially, but there are exceptions. Both in the UK and the USA there are periodicals which consist entirely of children's writing and occasionally the collected work of children becomes popular in book form. A fairly recent example of this is *To Dad* (Exley and Exley, 1973), which became a huge success. With flair and imagination, it seems, children's writing in published form could become much more common than it is at present.

The vigour and freshness of much of what children write quickly become obvious to those who take the trouble to study it. That is not to say that it is always original. Many stories are modelled on the work of popular authors such as the late Enid Blyton. And Ian, aged 8, in his witty short story *The very bad robber* was obviously borrowing from a previously read detective story when he wrote:

> If you want to see your son again come to the Old George tonight at midnight with a thousand pounds.
>
> Signed
>
> The Bad Robber
>
> P.S. Alone please, and in cash.

Much of what children write contains details of their personal experiences, and it is here that their writing is often at its most lively and interesting. The late Robert Westall, a distinguished writer for both adults and children, remained as a teacher of secondary school boys at the same time as being a popular author. It enabled him, he claimed, to ensure that his writing about teenagers retained its authenticity. On one occasion, dismayed by the routine nature of some of his pupils' essays, he asked them to write about some of the more interesting aspects of their lives, assuring them of confidentiality. Their writing at once became more lively and expressive, less 'safe'. Some of their accounts were hair-raising and perhaps prone to exaggeration. Yet when one boy related how he sometimes burrowed into sand dunes until a creaking sound warned him that the roof was about to collapse it was possible to recall a real-life situation where a boy had disappeared in similar circumstances.

Younger pupils often express a desire to write about some of the more unconventional events in their lives. Philip, aged 9, when asked about his truancy, responded in writing as follows:

> I heard something rattle on my window. It was Simmo throwing gravel. I opened it and he said 'Are you wagging it today then?' I jumped out of the window and we went down the street. There was a driver delivering bread and Eccles cakes from the van. Then we went to our den under the main street. Then we went for a walk and I was sick, 'That is God punishing you for nicking the Eccles cakes' Simmo told me.

At times children's oral descriptions can be yet more vivid. A collision with the corner of a desk one day resulted in a large gash above George's eyebrow. He returned to school the same afternoon clutching a substantial sum of money which his mother had given him as a reward for not crying when the stitches were inserted. Not long afterwards, he was discovered fighting. When it was suggested that he would not like to be hurt in that way he at once described the worst pain he had ever experienced. Later he wrote about this.

> Last November we was chumpin' (collecting material for a bonfire) and we found an 'owd mattress. We brought it back an we was doin' duffs jumpin off the toilet roof onto it. Then me mates duffed me to jump wi me 'ands tied be'ind me back. Me ankle got caught in the springs and a tripped ower on me face hit the pavement. It were right painful.

Stories such as these, whether oral or written, are usually produced voluntarily. Their creators seem to be searching for an audience. But it is not the sort of writing to be displayed on the classroom wall. Confidentiality like that promised by Westall is paramount. James Britton (Barnes *et al.*, 1986) claimed that the teacher's role as a sounding post for children's stories was one which could be sub-divided. One of the divisions he described as 'the trusted adult' is one which needs to be taken seriously.

From time to time, collections of children's writing occur in academic volumes devoted to the subject. One of the most interesting was compiled by Clegg (1964). His approach was partly developmental for, in some cases, he provided examples of an individual child's work over a period of years. In addition his study was spread across the whole range of compulsory schooling. Here is the writing of a 6 year old, excited to be describing an experience from his own world, so excited in fact that one can sense the headlong manner in which he tackled the work. His thoughts appear to be running ahead of the difficult task of recording then in writing. Certainly the spelling and punctuation lack accuracy, but there is scarcely a word which cannot be understood fairly quickly. One wonders just how much of this story might have been lost had the writer slowed down so that his work could be more technically accurate.

'When i grow up'

I like to be a barber cose you Get a Rayt Lot of Moniy and in your shop you Get a Rayt Lot of PePel in your Shop. Theyav bayds I will Put bill krim on thar her. I like to cut mashtasase Sum men will brinG ther little boys to ave ther little boys her Kut. I like to Put sheyvinsowp on ther fayses and sheyv it off. I want to be a barber Naw I will Giv then shotbackandsayd krowcot,sqerneck i sel rasebLads, shavinsowp and biLcriym i shaL chath the Men 3 shiLig and boLd men 2 shiLig and boys 6 Pans.

Another distinguished commentator on children's writing collected the work of slow-learning pupils in a secondary school. Holbrook (1964) found that despite the disadvantages they suffered, the writing of the 15 year olds he taught could be both powerful and expressive. Who works harder, the child who writes fluently and with ease, or the one who has to struggle to attain coherence? The work of a 15-year-old girl of very low school achievement might help to solve this question.

I am writing a story about what I do in the summer holiday when it is hot. I go swimming and when it isten so hot I go to find some wild insexs last year I had some frogsporn. Is have some evry year and only a few diy. I is quite had to find a place for I keep my frog sporn under nethe that tank where it is very cool it thak about 3 monsth to get hast first they get long then they grow their finse and after a few weeks they get bigger and bigger but last year their whant very meany eggs aroudn I went to the moat fast there whernt any ther so I wnet downw the lane but nere the wit bridg there was ony about 50 eggs. I got down and piked them up with my hands and put them in a big gare with some sea weed they must have a large tin or they have not mush room to move. I use a big paint tin to put my frog sporn in and at the end of my garden their is a stream I clime down the back and flop the frogs in the water and you can just watch them swim away. it is best to tipe the frogs away when they jush loos their tail then you know there will live and jus one other thing help them glean hard there sea weed every week and they will like a bit of raw meat to chew and that will keep them orren.

Had this girl been asked to write something beyond her own experience it is unlikely that she would have revealed the depth of knowledge which is evident in this passage for all her obvious difficulties with spelling and punctuation.

Overall, children's literature, like so many other images, perhaps tells us more about adults' perceptions of children than offering a realistic portrayal of children and their lives. Although the depictions are often stylized, partial, generalized and escapist, this does not imply that the texts are without value: the enjoyment that children take from a wide range of texts provides powerful evidence of merit. To make meaning out of such images of childhood one needs to link interdisciplinary perspectives with in-depth foci in specific areas; however, the search for a particular childhood may be illusory as children's individual experiences and stories will always confound attempts to construct generalizations.

The developing child   2

Nicola Leather, Angela Hawtin, Nell Napier,
Dominic Wyse and Russell Jones

Theories of development

Western societies did not systematically study child development until after
the Industrial Revolution in the nineteenth century, although childhood had
long been recognized as an important, distinct period in the human life-cycle.
People have many assumptions about the nature of development: some
assume that children become what we make them, that their development
is in our hands. This learning theory view is shared by many psychologists,
but we could look at development from another angle – how do children
grow and develop on their own, utilizing their inner needs to seek out certain
types of experiences and activities at certain times of life? This approach is
identified as developmental and is also shared by many theorists.

Child development theories have had a significant impact on society's
perceptions of children and childhood. For that reason the first part of this
chapter includes an account of the major theories of child development. It
concludes with one example of the application of stage theories. The close
link between theories of development and education forms the rationale for
the second part. The significance of play in relation to development and
learning is followed by reflections on the importance of child-centred education. The chapter concludes by looking at some of the issues related to the
education of ethnic-minority children.

FOLK FOUNDATIONS OF CHILD DEVELOPMENT

Initial studies of child development were based on the 'folk' model, emphasizing common-sense explanations of observed behaviour. For example, the
British philosopher John Locke (1632–1704) thought that the child was born
as a *tabula rasa* (blank slate), whose every characteristic was moulded by
experience. Locke proposed that children were neither innately good nor
innately bad, they were nothing at all (Crain, 1992). This view placed emphasis
on explanations concerning the child's acquisition of knowledge, and tended
to deny that innate factors have a part to play. Locke argued that whatever
the child became was the result of learning and experience. His principles of
learning – association, repetition, modelling, rewards and punishment –
have become the basis of learning theory (as we will see later).

In contrast, the Swiss philosopher Jean Jacques Rousseau (1712–1778) took
a more naturalistic view of child development. Rousseau agreed that

dren were different from adults and felt that they had their own modes of
king and feeling. Children needed to be allowed to perfect their own
capacities and learn in their own ways. He considered that children were
naturally good, requiring little or no moral guidance for normal development. This theory focused on how children grow and develop on their own,
and was less impressed by the influences of others teaching and moulding
children. Rousseau proposed that development proceeds according to an
inner, biological timetable, which unfolds fairly independently from environmental influences (Crain, 1992). These general views influenced the debate
concerning the relative merits of 'nature and nurture' to the development of
the child.

NATURE/NURTURE DEBATE

The debate over nature versus nurture is present throughout psychology.
Many theorists seek to explain human behaviour in terms of either inherited
factors or life experience. In truth, all individuals are a product of their own
genetic makeup and of their nurture. An individual's genotype is his or her
particular set of genes, whereas the phenotype is his or her actual behaviour.
What we observe is the phenotype and is a product of nature and nurture.
An individual's genotype predisposes him or her to certain developmental
outcomes, which could be within a genetically determined range, for example
height. The actual resultant development (for example the measured height
of the individual), is determined by the environment.

One of the main differences between the 'folk' or common-sense understanding of development and a scientific understanding is the extent to
which theories are subjected to systematic testing. The scientific study of
child development began in the nineteenth century with Charles Darwin's
(1809–1882) study of evolution. After studying medicine and theology,
Darwin was selected to travel on the world-wide voyage of the HMS *Beagle*,
during which he made observations that led to his theory of evolution.
Darwin concluded that many species had a common ancestor; newer species
developed by a process of adaptation to the changing environments. Darwin
believed that natural selection applied to both physical characteristics and to
behaviours. He has been called the first ethnologist – a biologist who studies
animal behaviour from an evolutionary perspective (Crain, 1992). Ethnologists seek to understand and explain behaviour in terms of its adaptive or
evolutionary value, that is the extent to which the behaviour contributes to
the survival of the individual and thus the species as a whole. Ethnologists
have introduced some important concepts into the field of child development, such as imprinting, instinct and critical or sensitive periods.

John Bowlby (1907–1990) stated that we can understand human
behaviour only by considering its environment of adaptedness, the basic
environment in which it evolved (Bowlby, 1982). In the 1930s, he became
interested in the disturbed behaviour of children raised in institutions,
including their apparent inability to form loving relationships themselves.
He concluded that this inability stemmed from the lack of a permanent,

loving mother–child relationship in early life. Bowlby extended his work to include children who were separated from their mother for long periods, whilst still living at home. His work emphasized the importance of the mother–child bond. In order to gain protection within a species, children need mechanisms to keep them close to parents. Thus they have evolved attachment behaviour, the gestures and signals that promote and maintain proximity to caretakers. Attachment behaviours are basically innate, have a fairly typical pattern in all members and are of value to the species.

STAGE THEORIES

Another way to think about child development is to divide life into stages or phases, a process utilized by Piaget and Erikson among others. All stage theories utilize the same theoretical structure:

- they are based on qualitative changes in behaviour over time and age;
- they describe an invariant sequence of development, the rate may differ but the order is always the same;
- each stage has structural cohesiveness; in other words, the behaviour described within each stage should be consistent and coherent; and
- stages form a hierarchy, because each subsequent stage builds in some way upon earlier stages.

Stage theories rely on the concept of maturation, a biological process which is modified by evolution.

The twentieth century has been dominated by grand theories which have attempted to interrelate nature and nurture, along with the biological and social factors that influence development. Although grand theories are no longer perceived to be appropriate (with the emphasis now moving to detailed examination of particular phenomena), the study of these theories introduces the ideas and principles that have shaped current study.

Jean Piaget (1896–1980) is considered to be one of the most influential early theorists within developmental psychology and his influence is still strong today. Piaget was originally a biologist (paradoxically his views often have a biological basis rather than a psychological one) who regarded himself as a genetic epistemologist (someone who is interested in the growth and development of knowledge). He based his theory on the observations he made whilst working in Binet's laboratory on the first intelligence tests to be developed. Piaget noted that children of the same age tended to make the same mistakes and that these appeared to relate to their underlying under-standing of the problem being considered, rather than pure error.

The basic concepts of Piaget's theory are the functional invariants of organization and adaptation. He perceived cognition as a process of adaptation in which the young child adapts to the environment and makes sense of the world. This adaptation has two characteristics: 1) assimilation – taking in information, thinking, noticing; 2) accommodation – to cope and mould self to the situation, to change the way we perceive as a result of the information assimilated (*see* Fig. 2.1).

Assimilation   Accommodation

Figure 2.1 Piaget's cognitive theory of adaptation

This is the method children use to organize their behaviour patterns. For example, when babies are weaned from the breast or bottle onto more solid food, one of the experiences that they have to adapt to is the way the food is presented to them, on a spoon rather than via a nipple. The baby must assimilate the new situation to the behaviour already used, namely sucking. As the process of taking food from a spoon is different from sucking, the baby must accommodate his or her behaviour to this new situation. In doing so, the baby is said to have made some cognitive progress by developing a new scheme, or schemata, to cope with this new situation.

Piaget's view was that children increase in knowledge because of bio-logically regulated cognitive changes. Self-discovery and self-motivation are perceived as being critical in the development of intrinsic satisfaction: 'Each time one prematurely teaches a child something he could have discovered himself, that child is kept from inventing it and consequently from under-standing it completely' (Piaget, 1970: 715). As will be shown later, Bruner and Vygotsky subscribe to a different view, feeling that cognitive development depends on the guidance of those with greater knowledge.

Piaget's theory had four main stages: 1) sensori-motor; 2) pre-operational; 3) concrete operational; and 4) formal operational. In common with other stage theorists, he described the stages as sequential, hierarchical and qualitatively different. In addition to the four main stages there are many intermediate sub-stages related to particular concepts. Piaget's method of experimentation is often commented upon, as initially he observed the behaviour of his own three children, and then extended his work to other children. It was a naturalistic approach, so there was no laboratory equipment and no experimental controls; the children were observed in their natural environment.

Stage 1 Sensori-motor period (approximately birth to 18 months)

Piaget suggested that infants are born with innate reflexes such as sucking and grasping. These are innate schemata which progressively develop in response to experiences, leading to the formation of new schemata by accommodation. When a schema matches the experience, new information is assimilated into the child's knowledge. The infant is busily discovering relationships between sensations and motor activity. Piaget considers that the most important aspect of this stage is that the child starts off being completely egocentric, and, in the course of the sensori-motor period, learns to distinguish self from the rest of the world, whilst learning that people and things continue to exist even when they are not visible to the child. This is the concept of object permanence, and it usually develops at around the age of 10 months. By the end of the sensori-motor period, the child is beginning to think symbolically, as demonstrated by the use of early language devices.

The sensori-motor period comprises of the sub-stages/characteristic behaviours indicated in Table 2.1.

Stage 2 Pre-operational period (approximately 18 months to 7 years)

Whilst the child is now able to distinguish between self and objects, he or she is not able to conceive the idea of experiencing objects from a viewpoint other than his or her own. For example, when relating a story, the child does not make any allowances for the fact that the listener needs all the information that the child already knows, the child will just relate the incomplete interesting points. Piaget describes this inability to perceive something from another's point of view as failing to decentre, and used the well known 'three mountains experiment' to illustrate the problem. In the experiment, a three-dimensional papier-maché model is constructed of three mountains, each with distinguishing features (*see* Fig. 2.2).

Piaget placed a doll in various positions to see the mountains from different angles. The child was then asked to point out a picture of the view that the doll will see from various angles. Usually children cannot conceive what the doll will see, and choose the view that they themselves can see. Piaget sees this as evidence that the child is failing to consider something from another point of view (decentre), that he or she is utilizing an egocentric bias and he demonstrated that this egocentrism is present throughout the child's thought.

Other experimental tasks that Piaget utilized at this stage are often called conservation tasks. These illustrate that the pre-operational child is unable to consider two aspects of the same situation at the same time, does not

Table 2.1 Sub-stages of sensori-motor period

Sub-stage/characteristic behaviour	Age
Reflex actions, e.g. sucking	birth–1 month
Primary circular reactions, repetitive actions, e.g. smiling, kicking	1–4 months
Secondary circular reactions, repetitive actions with an external object	4–8 months
Co-ordination of secondary schemes, schemata used to solve problems, object permanence develops	8–12 months
Tertiary circular reactions, experimenting with action	12–18 months
Symbolic problem solving, beginning of use of language	18 months plus

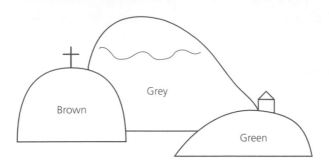

Figure 2.2 Piaget's 'three mountains experiment'

consider the transformation that is occurring and demonstrates irreversibility. Adults are often surprised to discover that young children believe that the amount of a substance is changed when the shape is altered, for example from a ball to a sausage. The procedure for a variety of conservation tasks is shown in Fig. 2.3.

The most frequently considered conservation task is the conservation of liquid. This experiment asks the child to consider two identical glasses of liquid. The experimenter ascertains that the child agrees that there is the same amount of liquid in each glass. The liquid from one glass is then poured into a third glass of a different size, and the child is asked whether there is still the same amount of liquid. Children appear to be inclined to ignore the way in which the change took place – the transformation procedure – and this leads to a false judgement about amount and a failure to conserve. This lack of consideration about before and after states, and transformations, is the main reason why children are so gullible to magic, disappearing and conjuring tricks.

The pre-operational child appears to learn most effectively by using repetition, and does not tire from seeing the same film, hearing the same book/story, or attempting the same problem or learning task.

The final concept to be considered in relation to the pre-operational child is that of reversibility. Piaget demonstrated that pre-operational children do not understand that mathematical and logical problems are reversible: for example $2 + 3 = 5; 5 - 3 = 2$. Thinking at this stage can easily be disturbed, and a child can often be misled. Pre-operational thought may be described as intuitive: things are as they seem to be, rather than as they are.

Stage 3 Concrete operational stage (approximately 7 to 11 years)

This third stage characteristically relates to the junior school years and shows a more integrated and stable pattern of thought. Piaget sees operations as essentially mental tasks. As children have now decentred and are able to conserve, they are able to consider a wide variety of problems, but they do appear to be able to function best when they have concrete knowledge of the problem under consideration.

Type of conservation	Child sees	Experimenter then transforms	Child is asked conservation question
Length	Two sticks of equal length and agrees that they are of equal length	Moves stick over 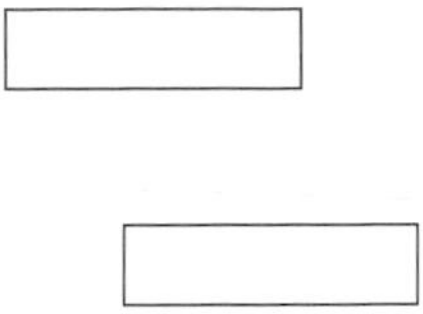	*Which stick is longer?* Preconserving child will say that one stick is longer. Conserving child will say that they are both the same length.
Liquid quantity	Two beakers filled with liquid and says that they both contain the same amount	Pours liquid from one glass into a taller thin glass, so that the level is higher	*Which glass has more liquid?* Preconserving child will say that the taller glass has more liquid. Conserving child will say that they have the same amount.
Substance amount	Two identical balls of modelling clay and agrees that the two are made of equal amounts of clay 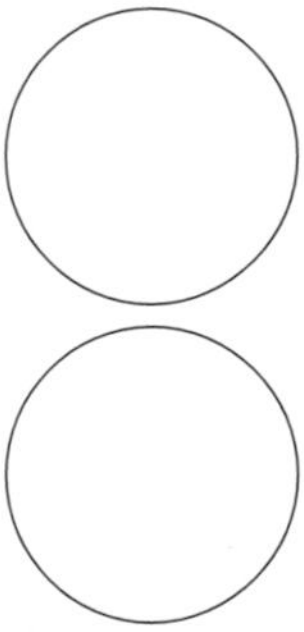	One ball rolled out into sausage 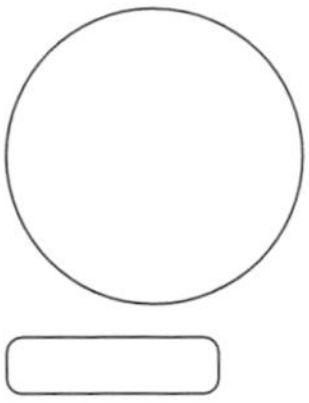	*Do the two shapes have the same amount of clay?* Preconserving child will say that the longer piece has more clay. Conserving child will say that they contain the same amount.

Figure 2.3 Procedures of Piaget's conservation experiments

A well known Piagetian task to illustrate the difference between pre-operational and operational children is known as the 'class inclusion' problem. The children are shown a picture containing, for example, a number of red cars and a number of differently shaped vehicles of a different colour – this may consist of four small blue vans and ten larger red cars. All children will tell you that these are all motor vehicles and that there are more cars than vans. But when asked if there are more cars or more vehicles, pre-operational children will respond 'more cars'. They fail to sort out the whole relationship between cars and vehicles – they appear not to realize that one class (vehicles) can include another (cars). The concrete operational child is not centred on the dominant class, and is unable to handle hierarchical concepts and classifications.

Stage 4 Formal operational stage (approximately 11 years plus)

According to Piaget, this is the final stage of cognitive development, during which abstract, logical thought develops. The child is able to form and test hypotheses, theorize and criticize, without necessarily agreeing the content of the argument. Purely verbal problems that can cause difficulties for the concrete operational child can now be solved, such as: Paul is fairer than Robert; Paul is darker than Neil – who is the darkest?

A Piagetian task for distinguishing between concrete and formal opera-tional thinkers is to try to solve scientific problems. The important aspect of the problem is not the answer obtained, but the use of the hypothetico-deductive method of reaching the solution. An example of such a problem is as follows: an individual is given four weights, a piece of string and a hook. The task involves constructing a pendulum, using the string attached to the hook, and suspending the weights from the variable length of string, and then discovering what influences the swing of the pendulum. What is interesting is not so much a final answer but more the way in which the child sets about discovering the answer.

NON-STAGE THEORIES

The consideration of non-stage theories leads us to a different way of con-sidering development, in terms of experiential rather than maturational factors. A non-stage approach does not identify changes that occur at a particular age, but focuses on factors which lead to certain outcomes. Thus development is described in terms of influences rather than as a progressive sequence, and includes ideas related to social learning.

During the 1960s and 1970s, Piaget's tests of operational competencies were constantly used by developmental psychologists and educators. How-ever, a distinctive strand of research, focusing on the social context of cognitive testing, had begun to offer an important new dimension to the debate about the development of operational competencies.

McGarringle and Donaldson (1975) studied the judgement of 4-year-old and 5-year-old children on number and length conservation problems. They utilized two experimental conditions, which differed only in how the trans-formation of materials was handled. In the standard condition (following Piaget), the rearrangement of the materials, after the child's judgement of equality, was made quite deliberately and openly by the experimenter. In the modified condition, the same rearrangement was achieved, but this time by a 'naughty' teddy bear. The toy bear 'escaped' from his box and rushed about causing chaos, including rearrangement, until recaptured. The rearrangement was represented as accidental, rather than deliberate. In the standard condition, 16 per cent of the children were able to conserve, in the modified condition 63 per cent were able to do so (other studies have shown similar findings). A question that must be considered is whether young children fail to conserve because of misleading features in the procedure.

The experimenter, in drawing the child's attention to his own actions in rearranging the materials, is giving implicit cues to the child as to what to expect next. Thus, if the experimenter lengthens or shortens one row of counters relative to another, the child may interpret the ensuing question as having to do with length, whereas in fact it has only to do with the number of counters. The experimenter's actions refer to one dimension, and the questions to another and the child's incorrect response may simply reflect confusion. Having the transformation performed by an errant teddy bear may go a long way towards removing the confusion.

Donaldson (1978) argued that the child's cognitive abilities will only be revealed in situations which make sense to the child. In an attempt to create a less ambiguous situation, Light (1986) designed a conservation test in which the transformation of materials would appear to be merely incidental to some other activity. Children aged 5 and 6 years old were tested in pairs. In the standard condition children watched as two identical beakers were filled up with pasta shells to the same level. When they had agreed that they were equal, the contents of one of the beakers was tipped into a larger container. They were then asked (in turn) to judge whether or not the amount of shells was still the same. In the incidental condition, the pairs of children were first shown grids into which the shells could be inserted – they would be playing a game. Shells were then put into two beakers and judged to be equal (to be fair to the game). The experimenter then 'noticed' that one beaker had a sharp broken rim, with some suitable non-verbal signals, the experimenter 'found' another (larger) container and tipped the shells in. The usual conservation questions followed, and since social influence within the pairs could amplify the result, only the answer of the first child was noted. In the standard condition only 5 per cent of the children were able to conserve, but in the incidental condition 70 per cent were able to do so. The reason given by Donaldson (1978) for this increased conservation is that the task makes sense, that transformation took place because of an 'accident', and therefore was not considered to be important by the child. The question was asked in order to confirm that the children still felt the game to be fair.

As far back as 1974, researchers have been considering the relationship between the language used in the tests and conservation. It is normal for most children to answer the first question in a standard conservation task correctly, as it is usually an obvious question. But when the question is put for a second time (after the transformation), young children characteristically change their response. One possible reason for this could be that the repetition of the question by the adult/experimenter may lead the child to suppose that the first answer was incorrect. This issue has been addressed by having the questions asked by two different people. The experimenter has to leave the room after the transformation and another experimenter enters, who continues with the task by asking the second question.

Sociocultural perspective

Before addressing the influence of Vygotsky, we briefly refer to an important sociocultural consideration. Cross-cultural studies can help us to identify behaviour that may be universal and perhaps innate, and behaviours that seem to be due to experience. They remind us that our own view of development is essentially an ethnocentric one. Any account of development is necessarily culturally based, but it is important to remember that the understanding of human behaviour is not universal. What is true for middle-class white Europeans is not necessarily true in other classes or cultures of the world. One important dimension along which cultures vary widely is individualism versus collectivism. Most Western cultures emphasize individualism, while Asian, Latin and African cultures are more likely to emphasize collectivism. This variation must be considered when observing children in their natural environment, and when designing tasks to assess ability. The importance of culture in relation to development and learning is something we return to at the end of this chapter in a section on the experiences of black children in Britain's schools.

In contrast to Piaget's theories, a theory which emphasized social and cultural influences was that of the Russian theorist Lev Vygotsky (1896–1934). After a degree in law and work as a teacher of literature, he began work in the area of child psychology and education. During his short life, despite poor health, he worked intensely and productively. Yet much of his work was censored or hidden by colleagues out of fear. His published works were banned by the Stalinist regime because his ideas ran contrary to the preferred theories of Pavlov. Vygotsky's work has a strong political theme and supports the Marxist ideal that the only way to bring about change is by altering social conditions. His work was generally unknown in the West until it began to be translated in the 1960s and 1970s.

Vygotsky perceived cognitive abilities as being formed and built up in interaction with the social environment, rather than as internal and individualistic entities: inter-psychological before they become internalized and intra-psychological. Children develop sophisticated cognitive competencies despite starting with fairly basic ones, because more experienced people are available as teachers and models to guide the child repeatedly through the behaviour to be learnt. Thus the more expert person provides a context or 'scaffold' within which children can act, assisting them to demonstrate competence and reach the solution successfully. As the task being learnt becomes more familiar and more within the child's competence, the adult can leave more and more for the child to do, until at last the child can undertake the whole task successfully.

Vygotsky's emphasis on social interaction implies that more complex cognitive functioning may be possible in a dialogue between co-operating individuals than is possible for those individuals alone. Thus the level of functioning of any individual may depend upon the social support available. In addition he saw the capacity to learn from the instructions of others as a fundamental feature of human development. Vygotsky coined the term 'zone of proximal development' (ZPD) to refer to the difference between the child's actual level of development and his or her potential level of development under the guidance of others. 'What children can do with the assistance of others might be in some sense even more indicative of their mental development than what they can do alone' (Vygotsky, 1978: 87).

The ZPD is perceived as being critical in leading and directing cognitive development. Thus, Vygotsky argued that learning is the result of the social interactions between the growing child and other members of the child's community, which enable the child to acquire the tools of thinking and learning.

Bruner's ideas drew on the work of both Piaget and Vygotsky. In common with Piaget, he believed that 'action' was the starting point for the formation of symbolic, abstract thought. In common with Vygotsky he valued the role of instruction and social interaction in cognitive growth. Bruner described the structure of thinking in terms of categories which are hierarchically organized.

Enactive representation

This refers to perceptual motor actions and is similar to Piaget's sensori-motor period, but Bruner argued that this mode of thought is not limited to infancy and is involved in many familiar activities. It could be thought of as learning by doing, practical intelligence at a physical, muscular level.

Iconic representation

This is the use of our imagination to represent a past event or plan for a future one. The task involves use of memory and past experiences, as well as perceiving an experience not yet undertaken, by the use of mental images which may be based on sight, hearing, smell or touch.

Symbolic representation

Symbols are powerful, abstract, arbitrary ways of representing ideas, that bear little or no resemblance to the object or notion; symbolized by things such as words, letters, numbers and equations.

Bruner pointed out that although the primary mode of representation utilized will change with age, all three types of representation will continue to be used throughout life. The practical importance of Bruner's theory is his development of Vygotsky's concept of expert intervention. Bruner used the idea of the expert providing the 'scaffolding', enabling the learner to take small steps; the process of discovery learning. The intervention of an expert, as described by both Vygotsky and Bruner, enables children to fully exploit their current capabilities; without it, the process of learning and development would, at the very least, be slower.

Behaviourism and learning theory

From this perspective the focus is placed upon the observable behaviour rather than the internal processes. Behaviourists explain behaviour in terms of how it is learnt, rather than in terms of innate factors, with learning taking place through conditioning, reinforcement and shaping. Learning may be perceived as a framework for understanding development, and almost all types of behaviour may be explained using behavioural concepts. As has been noted previously, learning theory emerged from the Lockean tradition. The major theoretical components of learning theory will now be discussed.

Pavlov (1849–1936) became interested in innate learning and described what has become known as classical conditioning. In this form of learning, a reflex action becomes conditioned to respond to a new, formerly neutral, stimulus. The following well known experiment was described by Pavlov. A dog was placed in a dark room with a light turned on. After 30 seconds some food was placed in the dog's mouth, initiating the salivation response (unconditioned stimulus). The procedure was repeated several times, and each time the presentation of food was accompanied by the light (conditioned stimulus). After a period of time, the light elicited the salivation response by itself, the conditioned reflex (Crain, 1992). The experiment was repeated many times, utilizing different reflexes and conditioning stimuli, with the same results. Pavlov was the first scientist to conduct strict experiments related to learning theory, and although he dealt with only a few innate responses, he started the work of trying to prove that the theory of learning was effective.

Watson (1878–1958) was the first major psychologist to apply the principles of learning theory to problems of child development. Watson was a strict behaviourist, who only studied overt behaviour. One of his prime interests was the conditioning of emotions, with his major (if ethically rather worrying) experiment being the conditioning of fear in an 11-month-old boy who he called Albert. The boy was initially not afraid of rats, but by using conditioning techniques Watson was able to condition the child to show fear in the presence of rats.

Skinner (1905–1990) was a strict behaviourist like Watson, and therefore avoided any reference to intangible mental states such as goals, desires and purposes, confining his study to that of overt behaviour. He was particularly concerned with how the environment may control behaviour, so the approach taken was not Pavlovian, but described as operant (pertaining to how the animal operates within and on the environment). Thus, behaviour is determined by its consequences and is not invoked by simple conditioning. If the individual learns that the behaviour produces a positive effect, it is continued. Skinner's work led on to practical applications of operant conditioning, with operant techniques being used to correct behaviour problems. The technique has also been used to devise teaching/instruction programmes, which use small steps, active learning and immediate feedback.

The behaviourist theories considered so far are concerned with individual learning and behaviour. They do not account for whether the behaviour of the individual may be altered if it was taking place within the social setting. Bandura (born 1925) argued that in social settings the individual learns a great deal by imitation, learning more rapidly by observing the behaviour of others. Bandura stated that social learning is different from trial and error learning. Following a period of observation of a task being undertaken competently, Bandura described how it is possible to demonstrate the behaviour skilfully at the first try. This new behaviour is acquired through observation alone, thus the learning appears to have a cognitive dimension and must include cognitive variables. It is possible to undertake this type of learning from models of many different kinds – live models, those on television, in books, and via verbal instructions/descriptions.

This process of learning within the social environment has four component processes:

1. Attention – in order to imitate it is important that first we pay attention. Different methods can be used to obtain and hold our attention.
2. Retention – individuals remember actions in symbolic forms, usually visual representation with some verbal cues. Rehearsal may be used to maintain the image.
3. Motor reproduction – it is vital that the individual processes the required motor skills for the task in order to reproduce the behaviour.
4. Reinforcement and motivation – it is possible to learn a task/skill and not to use it. Performance is governed by reinforcement and motivational variables. The reinforcement may be direct, vicarious or by self.

The example most often used to explain social learning is the learning of aggressive behaviour by children (this is something we return to in Chapter 5). Bandura examined aggression in children and noted that children who observe aggressive behaviour notice how and when the behaviour is reinforced, and imitate accordingly. One of his experiments to explain this phenomenon is considered to be a classic. In the study (Bandura, 1965), children individually watched a film in which an adult male actor was involved in some moderately aggressive behaviour towards a Bobo doll (a large, inflated, rubber doll), including the type of behaviour often seen in cartoons. Each child was assigned to one of three conditions, which meant that each child saw the same film but with different endings.

• In the aggressive-rewarded condition, the actor was praised and given treats.
• In the aggressive-punishment condition, the actor was called a bully and attempts were made to hit him.
• In the no consequences condition, the actor received neither reward nor punishment for his aggressive behaviour.

Immediately after the film, each child was taken into a room containing a Bobo doll and other toys. The child was observed via a one-way mirror to see his or her behaviour towards the doll. Results indicated that those who had seen the actor punished exhibited significantly less aggression than the other two groups. In a second phase of the experiment, the researcher returned to the room and informed the child that there would be a reward if he or she could imitate the behaviour seen in the film. All the children were able to do so, indicating that they had all learnt the behaviour, but those who thought they would be punished had decided not to actually participate in the aggression.

Psychoanalytic perspective

The primary focus of this perspective is not motor or cognitive development, but the concepts of inner thoughts, fantasies and impulses, the emotional and motivational development. The principal founder of psychoanalytic theory was Sigmund Freud (1856–1939). Freud was basically a developmentalist, who believed that psychological change and growth were governed by internal forces and biological maturation. Freud considered the childhood stages as relating to different body zones at different ages, leading eventually to that of adult sexual gratification (see Table 2.2). Each of the earlier stages is outgrown normally, but in the event of arrested development (or fixation), some problems associated with an earlier stage persist.

Erikson (1902–1994) offered a modified Freudian view of the development of personal identity throughout the lifespan. He agreed that people are born with a number of basic instincts and that the personality has three basic components (the id, ego and super-ego). Erikson assumed that development occurs in stages (eight covering the whole lifespan), and that the child must successfully resolve the crisis or conflict at each stage in order to be prepared for the crises that may emerge in later life. He stressed that children are active explorers, who seek to control their environment, rather than passive creatures who are moulded by their parents, and that they are largely products of our society, rather than their own sexual instincts. Therefore, Erikson differed from Freud in giving more emphasis to social and cultural forces in development. At, or around, each Freudian stage he introduced concepts that gradually 'lead to an understanding of the most decisive, general encounter between the child and the social world' (Crain, 1992: 249) (see Table 2.3).

Table 2.2 Freud's theory of psychosexual stages

Psychosexual stages	Behaviours related to stage
Oral	Gratification through stimulation of mouth and lips, via feeding or thumb-sucking
Anal	Gratification through withholding and expelling faeces
Phallic	Gratification through fondling the sexual organs
Latent	Sexual interests no longer active, interest turns to other things
Genital	Normal heterosexual interest arises

Table 2.3 Erikson's psychosocial stages of childhood

Age (years)	Stage	Description of stage
0–1	Infancy	Trust vs. mistrust. Parents must maintain a nurturant environment so that the child develops basic trust in others.
1–3	Early childhood	Autonomy vs. shame and doubt. Child develops autonomy through bowel and bladder control.
3–6	Childhood	Initiative vs. guilt. Child must initiate own actions in a socially acceptable way.
6–14	Later childhood	Industry vs. inferiority. Child must learn to feel competent, especially in relation to peers.
14–20	Adolescence	Identity vs. confusion. Child must develop a sense of identity.

Erikson extended psychoanalytic theory by enlarging the stage sequence to cover the whole lifespan. He gave us an appreciation of how social factors enter into the various stages and interact with biological factors to influence the development of the individual.

An analysis of the key assumptions made about the major theoretical approaches is outlined in Table 2.4. In the final row of Table 2.4 we identify whether stage theory is part of various development theories. We would like to consider one example of the application of stage theory in practice. Stage theories have had a strong impact on the way that children are viewed and supported by society. For example, children's daily lives in a range of settings are controlled by the law; many of these laws are based on the notion of stage theories and in particular that age is synonymous with competence. To conclude the first part of this chapter, the next section will illustrate the seemingly arbitrary nature of some age-related laws by looking at the legal system in general and focusing on health provision as a specific example.

CHILDREN'S AGE AND THE LAW

In the UK and indeed in most Western societies the perceived stages of development of a child are used to frame legislation and policy and to make decisions about what a child is capable of doing, is expected to do, and is allowed to do. This can also be seen within the wider context of the amount and types of information which children are allowed to have about themselves and the world in which they live. Children in the UK are broadly defined as those under the age of 16 years old (in some areas 18 or 21 years old), and within this broad definition children are grouped, classified and defined according to their stage of development related to age.

Age-related norms in the law lead mainly to the exclusion of children from the legal process. The first example of this can be found in the fact that

Table 2.4 Summary of development theories

	'Scientific' theory	Cognitive theory	Sociocultural theory	Learning theory	Psychoanalytic theory
Prime influence on development	Biological	Use and processing of experience	Social environment	Nurture	Both nature and nurture
Quantitative or qualitative developmental change	Both	Qualitative	Qualitative	Both	Qualitative
Stage theory?	Sequences not stages	Yes	No	No	Yes

children under 16 years old have no legal capacity, that is, they are not allowed to be the plaintiff or defendant in a civil action and they cannot enter into a contract (except for essential services), this must be undertaken via a 'next friend' which must be an adult. They cannot make a will or hold a legal interest in land or property, though land and so on can be held in trust for the benefit of the child. This arbitrary age of 16 years old is imposed regardless of the actual capabilities of the child.

The age of criminal responsibility currently stands at 10 years old, below which a child is said to be *doli incapax* or incapable of forming the necessary intent for a crime. It used to be that between the ages of 10 and 14 years old, a child could be held criminally liable if the prosecution could prove 'mischievous discretion', that is, that at the time the child committed the offence he or she could distinguish right from wrong. This was usually decided by reference to the child's actions immediately before and after the crime was committed. This has now been abolished with the introduction of S34 of the Prevention of Crime and Disorder Act 1998 so that after the age of 10, a child can be held criminally responsible, but will be subject to a different approach to trial and sentencing from that used for adults.

Children taking part in the legal process itself as witnesses or victims giving evidence will be subject again to a decision as to whether they are 'competent'. All adults are presumed to be competent to give evidence unless and until it is proved to be otherwise. All children are deemed to be *incompetent* unless and until it is proved otherwise. The judge will make this decision based on oral examination of the child and, on the basis of the answers a child may give, will decide whether a child has sufficient cognitive ability to distinguish truth from lies and understands the implications of lying in a courtroom. This ability to so distinguish does not of course guarantee that the child will tell the truth any more than taking an oath will guarantee that an adult will tell the truth. There is, however, a belief that children are more prone to lie than adults, not to be able to distinguish fact from fiction, and are easily led. One of the main pieces of research that this belief was based on has been discredited, yet it still forms the basis of many approaches to children and the legal system. The approach appears to be to protect children by excluding them and to protect 'innocent' adults from the vagaries of children's evidence by making it extremely difficult to get it accepted by the court.

Within the health care setting, the stage of development which a child is deemed to have reached can be instrumental in decisions relating to the child's right of consent to medical treatment, the amount of information given to the child and, in extreme cases whether a child has the right to treatment at all.

It is the right of every adult of sound mind to consider the pros and cons of suggested medical treatment, and make a decision as to whether they will undertake it. No other person has the right in law to give consent on behalf of an adult and the information given to the person must be sufficient for him or her to make an informed choice. Legal redress is available where these rights are ignored. In an emergency 'life or death' situation where the adult is unconscious and unable to communicate, then medical treatment can be given without consent and the defence of necessity can be relied upon should an action be brought at a later date, that is, the medical practitioner must prove that the treatment given was necessary in order to save the patient's life. Unless information to the contrary is available, the medical practitioner will usually assume in making this decision that the patient would want to live, regardless of his or her long-term prognosis or resulting condition.

By virtue of infancy and lack of ability verbally to communicate wishes, consent for treatment for an infant is given by the person with parental responsibility. This can either be the biological parent or any other person to whom the court has given parental responsibility. This person can refuse treatment on behalf of the child even if the medical treatment is 'life saving' where the child is severely disabled and may have a lesser quality of life than the parents would wish for him or her. In some cases, the courts may be asked to intervene in these decisions but only where they are brought to their attention.

Despite evidence which shows that fairly young children are able to assimilate information and make strategic decisions based on personal survival and safety issues, there is a presumption that children under 16 years old are not able to understand the consequences of their decisions in the area of consent and medical treatment, and the law gives precedence to parental wishes unless and until the child can prove that he or she has the necessary understanding to make the decision him or herself. Children under 16 years are usually assumed to be unable to make these life-affecting decisions.

If children wish to have input into the decision making in this area they must be prepared to convince a court that they are 'Gillick competent'. This term arises from the case of Gillick v. West Norfolk and Wisbech AHA [1986] AC 112, [1985] 3 All ER 402 in which it was held that a child under 16 years old had the right to receive contraceptive advice and treatment without the consent of her mother as she was deemed competent to understand not only the immediate decision but also the consequences of that decision. Although the notion of Gillick competence could be useful if it was better understood and more frequently used, there are still problems. There may be many children under the age of 16 years who lack the necessary understanding to make these kinds of decisions; however, this should be considered in the context of the many adults who also lack such understanding and yet have the right, enforceable in law, to make whatever decision they want in relation to medical treatment, even if this means that they will die as a result of the decision made.

The first part of this chapter has outlined the major theories of development and has illustrated one aspect of their application in relation to health and the legal system. The influence of development theories has also been particularly strong in relation to learning and education. In this context 'play' is seen as significant because it is both a vehicle to support development and something that is subject to developmental theories. Play is also seen as an important feature of the educational process and as such has been much debated by educationists. The next section briefly revisits the views of some of the early theorists on childhood, development and learning. This is followed by the analysis of two key issues in relation to education: child-centred learning; and the experiences of ethnic-minority children.

Development and education

PLAY

Play means different things to different people. As Bennett *et al.* (1997) pointed out, the ideology behind the purpose of play is characterized by disparity rather than coherence. It can be seen as the opposite of work or it can be seen as preparation for life. In Western society today, it is assumed that all children play and it is often accepted that play is what children do naturally. Play is variously described as purposeful, purposeless, valuable, free, natural, innocent, or that which leads to children achieving full potential.

The study of play, although known from the time of Plato and Aristotle, brings us back to the folk foundations of development and Rousseau, who through his fictional character Emile advocated a free and natural life for children unrestrained from the need to study school subjects (as we saw in Chapter 1). His ideas were taken up by two people who had an important influence on learning and development: by Froebel (1782–1852), who started kindergartens where children learned through play; and by Montessori (1870–1952), who in her schools emphasized children learning through experience.

Spencer (1873) believed that the purpose of play is to expend surplus energy. Groos (1898) believed that both animals and humans use play to develop their skills. The work of Freud saw play as a way that children can escape the real world and engage in wish fulfilment, sometimes coming to terms with real-life anxieties. Millar (1968: 29) extended this idea by explaining the psychological coping strategies used by children in play. She pointed out that children can project their feelings onto dolls, so that the dolls might act maliciously. For example, a child might displace his or her feelings of jealousy for a new sibling by throwing a doll against a wall rather than harming a new baby.

Earlier in this chapter, we outlined the profound influence of Piaget and Bruner on the thinking about child development; both expounded views on play. Piaget believed that children use play to assimilate new experiences. Play was seen as an aspect of intellectual development following predetermined stages. During the sensori-motor stage children start by repeating acts such as hitting a dangling pram toy and by the end of this stage engage in active experimentation. At the pre-operational stage children engage in 'symbolic' or 'make believe' play. This play has the function of developing representational thinking and often involves role-play. From the age of 8 onwards, children engage in 'games with rules'. This form of play is consistent with children's more logical thinking. Bruner believed that play is crucial in teaching children the rules and conventions of society. For example, he believed that the 'peek-a-boo' game played with babies is an early introduction to turn taking in conversation.

There are also various views about the role of play in cultural reproduction. For example, the toys that children play with have been identified as agents of socialization. Barthes (1957: 53) maintained that 'toys literally prefigure the world of adult functions' and that they 'cannot but prepare the child to accept them all'. He wrote of the dolls which urinate and which children can feed and concluded that they are 'meant to prepare the little girl for the causality of house-keeping, to "condition" her to her future role as mother'. He maintained that 'toys always mean something and this something is always entirely socialised'. The issue of toys and their impact on learning and development is something that has been examined more recently.

Bob Dixon's (1990) study of children's toys and games and puzzles looked at the 'ideas, views and attitudes' which were presented to children through the materials. He looked at a wide range of very well known materials (Sindy, Action Man, He-Man, My Little Pony, Dungeons and Dragons, Monopoly, Death Race and many more) and how these were presented to children. He found that gender divisions and male aggression were reinforced, and that there was evidence of cultural imperialism. These findings indicate that the choice of toys is an important part of the role of the adult in providing quality play for children.

One concern that many parents have is that children spend so much time playing computer games and watching television. An important point about computer games is that although not all of them are solitary games, parents are often not involved in playing them. Perhaps parents sometimes look back with rose-tinted spectacles to a time when children spent many a happy hour reading or playing board games or hop scotch, when, even if adults were not around, the content of the games was known to them.

Are the new technologies (perhaps today's toys) something that adults should be concerned about? Do they add to the quality of play on offer to children or do they detract from it? Gunter and McAleer (1997: 6) reported that in 1994 children watched television for between 2. 7 and 2. 8 hours a day, the highest levels being between 4 p.m. and 9 p.m. on weekdays. They asked whether greater use of electronic media displaced activities such as reading. They found that watching television was engaged in simultaneously with other activities, and that, while it sometimes displaced functionally similar activities such as going to the cinema, children 'may be learning to identify the unique benefits and gratifications that can be derived from different media and divide their time between the many'. It was also maintained that television 'can bring them knowledge and other personal benefits which may be unavailable to them through any other source'.

However, Sanger et al. (1997: 169) reminded us that 'Screen based technologies are rapidly increasing.' Their research into young children, video and computer games left them very concerned about the type of experience which children were having. They were concerned that children were receiving little guidance at school or at home in the use of videos and computers because of the lack of knowledge that parents and teachers had of new technology. They were also concerned about the amount of time given over to these unsupervised and unmediated activities.

Summarizing their research Sanger *et al.* stated that 'The suggestion . . . is that parents and guardians who take a really active role in helping children to navigate screen based experience are uncommon.' They pointed out that children are being kept indoors more often for fear of what might happen to them unsupervised out of doors. They found that children still preferred to socialize rather than act alone, and that they often preferred to act physically rather than seek vicarious sublimation; however, they assert that 'social change and the place of the child as a virtual prisoner in the home, mean that the diet of the young is being constituted more and more by entertainment technology'. They were concerned about this state of affairs and stated that 'enabling the young to become critical consumers in the face of adult apathy, indifference or antipathy, and to develop control over the technology and authorship within it should be at the heart of education. It doesn't appear to be. '

New technology can enhance and widen the experience of children. But, for the developing child, a diet of video and computers is not going to be sufficient and there is no significant evidence that this is what children themselves want. Parents do need to become more conversant with new technology and to find ways to talk to children about how to get pleasure in 'acceptable' ways, but educational establishments have a big role to play in helping children to be discriminating about the use of new technology.

Children spend a great deal of time at school, and the debate about education and play has been long running. At its simplest, it could be said that play has been seen as a way of facilitating learning in a less painful way than the rote methods of the past. Play is not just a less painful way of learning, it also brings meaning to the learning context, and surely this is the most compelling argument for play being at the centre of the curriculum.

So what is the justification for play as part of formal education? As Bruner argued, children learn their culture through interaction with it, so that, for example, small children learn how to use cups and forks in the context in which they are used – during meal times. Bruner maintained that school is a very strange place for the transmission of the culture to take place. The task of the teacher is to make sure that the context for the transmission of culture is as meaningful as possible in the school setting. Play is sometimes seen as a way of doing this.

It is common for teachers to talk of structured play. Perhaps the word structured legitimizes play as part of school life. Both Froebel and Montessori advocated methods which were very much structured, and set up situations where children could learn through play. Nevertheless, play has had a very bad press since the Plowden Report of 1967 endorsed the role of play in early childhood education (later in this section we look at the Plowden Report in more detail).

One of the problems is that when play is put into practice it often does not match the high ideals claimed for it. As Bennett *et al.* (1997) pointed out, there is a gap between rhetoric and reality. They reviewed research from the late 1980s and found that play in nurseries and classrooms often lacked cognitive challenge, and did not live up to its promise to realize a constructivist approach to education. This was something that OFSTED had also found.

> In the poorer classes teachers over-directed work and under directed play. They used play as a reward for finishing work or as an occupational or holding device. By contrast in the effective classes, play was used positively to develop children's abilities across a wide range of activities.
>
> (OFSTED, 1993b: 10)

The Rumbold Report (Department of Education and Science, 1990: 11) set out conditions that need to be fulfilled in order for the value of play to be realized:

- sensitive, knowledgeable and informed adult involvement and intervention;
- careful planning and organization of play settings in order to provide for and extend learning;
- enough time for children to develop their play; and
- careful observation of children's activities to facilitate assessment for progression and continuity.

However, the challenge here is to allow for intrinsic motivation whilst at the same time 'carefully planning and organizing play settings'.

In trying to argue for the place of play in relation to the National Curriculum, Tyler (1991: 21) pointed out that there is an emphasis on a 'child's right to studies which are both broad and balanced'. He went on to assert that 'it is reassuring then that much of the content of that part of the National Curriculum designed for the youngest age group of children within compulsory education is consistent with the good practice of early years education in the recent past'. He quoted the Department of Education and Science: 'In the early primary stage, children are learning mainly through first hand experience about their immediate surroundings' (1988: 8). He argued that play is inextricably linked with the child's entitlement to childhood as well as education. This is a debate that has been rekindled recently in relation to the fact that children in the UK start formal schooling much earlier than in many other European countries.

Leslie Abbott (1994) used a case study to look at the usefulness of play in the current climate of National Curriculum, Attainment Targets and League Tables. She showed, using the illustration of a year 1 class turned over to a 'construction' site, how play can keep its integrity as child directed and still comply with the demands of the National Curriculum. She pointed to important factors such as ownership, children being involved in planning for play, children understanding the purpose of play, quality resources including adult involvement, and meeting curriculum requirements, including cognitive and affective domains and equal opportunities.

If educators want to live up to the principle of the right to play and to assert, as Tyler does, that it is linked to the child's entitlement to childhood, they must make every effort to maintain a high quality of play in educational settings and demonstrate the value of play for helping children to learn and develop. Abbott, as we saw, advocates the importance of ownership in relation to children and their education. Questions about ownership, empowerment and children's opportunity to participate are central to this book. Within education, they have at times become areas for intense debate. This debate has been at its most vociferous in relation to 'child-centred education'.

CHILD-CENTRED EDUCATION

The theories of Piaget, Vygotsky and Bruner have had an important impact on educational theory. Piaget's influence has been particularly significant in relation to the mathematics curriculum and the belief in hierarchical stages of learning. Vygotsky's work has found resonance particularly through the emphasis on collaborative, oral and apprenticeship modes of learning. Bruner's influence came mainly through his ideas on the 'spiral curriculum' where areas of learning are revisited at increasingly high levels of sophistication. His theory challenged the view that curriculum organization should be *dominated* by a linear and sequential assimilation of new knowledge. However, it was Rousseau's ideas that have had a more direct influence on child-centred education.

The child-centred ideas of Rousseau were built on by John Dewey. Kerry and Eggleston (1994) suggested that Dewey's emphasis on spontaneity and problem solving contributed to the phenomenon of 'topic' work in primary schools. This is the practice of organizing learning activities around themes such as 'water', 'ourselves', 'vehicles', and so on. The rationale for these links is that children's understanding of the world tends not to be organized around 'subjects'; their thinking tends to proceed by association from one related idea to the next. Ideas such as topic work, problem solving, discovery learning, teachers as facilitators, and so on became linked to the philosophy of 'child-centred education' which was one of the rare attempts by a small number of educators to genuinely involve children in their curriculum. Examples of the practice include building on the children's interests, involving them in the planning of work, reacting spontaneously to issues of interest, offering choices, engaging in discussion and decision making, and encouraging independent learning strategies.

The Plowden Report (Department of Education and Science, 1967) is a pivotal document in relation to the debate about child-centred education which has since been opportunistically vilified and has become deeply unfashionable. The attack follows similar lines to other criticisms of progressive practice and is based on the principle that such practice has been widely adopted: in fact, there is little evidence that this was the case. The current educational climate has a curriculum prescribed by government that must be followed by all children. Free-market economics with parents as consumers of the education system in part contributed to the idea that, if families were to have choice over schools, there was a need for all schools to be offering the same curriculum; the irony being that this was supposed to offer 'entitlement'. The quality of such entitlement is highly questionable when children are obliged to attend school and their curriculum is prescribed. We would argue that true entitlement is closely tied in with power and rights, not the simple access to uniformity. In spite of the demonstrable failures of centralized curricula (the third rewrite of the National Curriculum is due in 2001), the current move is to further unashamed prescription manifesting itself in the National Literacy and Numeracy strategies.

This fashion for centralized and prescriptive curricular is a far cry from the Plowden Report:

> The tendency is spreading to junior schools. Children may plan when to do the work assigned to them and also have time in which to follow personal or group interest of their own choice. In a few infant and junior schools the day is still divided into a succession of short periods. In the great majority, we are glad to say, there are longer periods and these can be adjusted at the teacher's discretion.
>
> (Department of Education and Science, 1967: 197)

The idea that children are able to follow their own interests or even to plan when to do work assigned to them is quite alien to the current climate. Similarly, the notion of the teacher as a professional with discretion to adjust the timetable to suit the children's needs and interests runs counter to the insistence on detailed subject time-tabling. Most primary schools currently run secondary style timetables, with the practice of children moving to other classrooms in ability groups (or sets) for certain subjects not uncommon. The comparison between current political opinion on education and the Plowden Report is startling.

> The idea of flexibility has found expression in a number of practices, all of them designed to make good use of the interest and curiosity of children, to minimise the notion of subject matter being rigidly compartmental, and to allow the teacher to adopt a consultative, guiding, stimulating role rather than a purely didactic one . . . . The topic cuts across boundaries of subjects and is treated as its nature requires without reference to subjects as such. At its best the method leads to the use of books of reference, to individual work and to active participation in learning.
>
> (Department of Education and Science, 1967: 199)

Unfortunately for current teacher education, students and newly qualified teachers, there can almost be disbelief that such practice is even possible.

Another theoretical strand to child-centred education is the notion that high expectations of children's capabilities lead to higher standards of learning. The idea of the 'self-fulfilling prophecy' was investigated in a famous study by Rosenthal and Jacobson (1968). The study used a test called the 'Harvard Test of Inflected Acquisition' which purported to be a predictor of academic success or 'blooming/spurting'. This particular test was used because the teachers in the study were unlikely to have seen it before and because in a school with significant numbers of bilingual children it was deemed to show basic learning ability, and did not rely on a high level of skill in literacy or numeracy. Although its approach was predominantly scientific, the study also used qualitative techniques to develop a welcome methodological eclecticism. One section of their book, 'a magic dozen', includes a series (admittedly limited) of 12 portraits of the children. Also, the use of Bernard Shaw's play (the book where the research is reported is called *Pygmalion in the classroom*) as a means to enhance the narrative pre-dates the current interest in genre and the writing of research.

The 500 or so children were tested and the teachers were informed about the children who the researchers deemed to be intellectually 'blooming'. However, the children concerned were not chosen on the basis of the tests, but through random means. When the children were re-tested, the younger children (American first and second grades) who had randomly been designated as bloomers had made statistically significant gains on the test.

The notion of expectation has become extremely powerful. The importance of high expectations is a common concern in educational discourse, even to the extent that it has been used politically to downplay the differences that exist in the education of children from a range of socioeconomic backgrounds. In the first part of this chapter, we raised the importance of cultural factors in relation to development and learning. The following account of a piece of research shows how culture and ethnicity are an important consideration in relation to education. The examples of institutional racism reveal troubling experiences for the children and adults concerned. They also raise the issue of the quality of training for people working with children.

EDUCATION AND ETHNICITY

A recently completed 3-year research project (Jones, 1997) undertaken in predominantly white primary schools revealed several concerns for people involved in educating children. It was found that student teachers found it difficult even to begin to address issues of ethnicity in the classroom. In conversation and in written tasks they would tend towards theoretical strategies to address these issues, but when faced with the violence and abuse of overt racism in schools, they felt powerless. First, because they had not been through a process which educated them towards the ways in which they might begin to deal with these realities, but also because they were concerned that in 'rocking the boat' they would endanger their own training and eventual qualification. In short, it became easier to avoid the issues than to deal with them, and this was a strategy students sometimes learnt directly from those immediately responsible for their training. One example of this highlighted a situation where an Asian girl was verbally attacked in school in the presence of some 70 other children, but out of sight of any teachers. In examining the ways in which this particular incident came to happen, and the ways in which similar incidents were dealt with by the school, it was found that the Head and staff were reluctant to begin to develop strategies for addressing racism for fear of 'creating a problem that wasn't there before'. This was not uncommon, and several other schools offered similar excuses for not dealing with these issues. When asked about the policies prepared in their schools, common replies were:

They don't need an equal opps policy here, it's an all female staff.

I didn't notice multicultural or equal opps policies. They seem to be kind of Christian oriented.

I shouldn't think there's a multicultural statement to be honest but I'll ask.

There is no multicultural policy as such. It's coming through on the RE because that's what the school inspector insisted.

They are trying to get them reeled off at the moment for the OFSTED.
(Beginning teachers)

I don't know if there is a policy or not to be honest. I think we've got a policy for just about everything. It must be in something somewhere. I don't know. Don't quote me on that. Ask me about special needs.

There is a draft equal opps policy and we have a separate multicultural education policy. I know there is one but when I asked to see it the Head said he had lost it.
(Mentors on school-based PGCE course)

We are looking towards writing a multicultural education policy.
(Head teacher on school-based PGCE course)

In the school where the attack took place, the staff were aware of racially motivated fights outside the school in the evenings, as gangs of white youths from nearby areas moved in to attack the Asian families who lived around the school. The ancillary staff were known to use derogatory terminology in front of the children (one cleaner said 'Oh Pakis, I can't be doing with them'), and the Head was reluctant to make any kind of written statement about the situation or the school's position within their community. Outside the school, a wall was spray painted 'Pakis Out', but the Head still insisted:

i I touch wood when I say this but at the moment that isn't an issue at
hool. There has been within the last three months an issue developing
e the school, not with our children, with the older children, with
gers . . . there have been quite a lot of disturbances at nights. That I
might well (pause) I think in twelve months, two years time, that it
well work it's way down.

rect avoidance of these issues became a common strategy observed
ughout the research, but it became clear that teachers were making
ormous judgements about ethnic minority children based on prejudices
about (for example) language acquisition, parental occupation and perceived
'social skills'. In another school, the one Asian boy in his class was repeatedly bullied. The beginning teacher said: '[He] gets some terrible stick. He is
a Pakistani lad and he is always crying. You know, he can't really speak very
good English anyway (pause) he gets very upset and the kids call him
"Paki", but what . . .? (silence)'. This beginning teacher did nothing about
the situation, first because she had been advised by her teacher to ignore it,
and secondly because, as she observed, 'He does give as good back. He's a
little pain.' An Afro-Caribbean boy in the same class was not regarded in the
same way by the teacher or the student teacher. The teacher stated: 'His
father is from Mauritius and his mother is Filipino but I don't know what
they talk at home. I would think English because father is a clinical psychologist, he's not stupid at all'. This suggested that the Asian boy was more
likely to fit into the 'stupid' category as he did not have professional parents,
and because his English was weaker. These attitudes had certainly been
transferred to the student teacher, who said: 'I don't think he's got any social
skills because he can't speak English properly.'

These examples are indicative of the ways in which questionable attitudes
towards children have been left unchecked because of education's lack of
involvement with cultural issues. It is understandable that children who
suffer overt and other forms of racism in school evident from the study
and who continue to suffer in the wider society (Childline, 1996) find learning a struggle. It is therefore unsurprising that many of the old stereotypes,
prejudices and misguided beliefs are beginning to become noticeable once
more (ignoring the assumption that they ever really disappeared). For
example, when we contacted the Department for Education and Employment (DfEE) and requested information on any circulars relating to the issue
we received a letter which began:

I have not found any circulars concerning multi-cultural education in
primary schools. I hope that the attached press notice is of some
interest/use, but please note that it is ten years old.
(Department for Education and Employment, 1996).

The 'Campaign for Racial Equality' claimed that the Department of Education and Science (DES) were being 'ostrichlike' in their refusal to address

'race' issues such as underachievement and ethnic monitoring (Pyke, 1996: 1), and several writers have expressed their concerns that teachers gain their qualifications and begin working in schools with little or no understanding about the needs of ethnic-minority children. Earlier forms of teacher education clearly linked through to these issues in compulsory courses in what was known as the 'sociology of education', but these kinds of courses have now all but disappeared from programmes of initial teacher education. When it is considered that many beginning teachers are now experiencing training which is primarily school-based, it is easy to imagine that ethnic-minority issues take even less of a precedence as these student teachers' priorities lie firmly in the acquisition of skills in classroom management, and the drive towards the effective transmission of knowledge via the preparation, delivery and assessment of National Curriculum requirements. Writers such as Hill (1994) and Newbold (1997) have claimed that teacher training has become a mechanistic process, producing mechanistic teachers who are skilled simply at the level of knowledge transmission, and who know little about the reality of childhood.

The reality of teacher education is that the vast majority of newly qualified teachers are white, have little or no opportunities to explore their own cultural status in relation to the children they are likely to meet on a professional basis and consequently have poor conceptions about the needs of ethnic-minority children. It is important, however, to remember that many of these newly qualified teachers will still find work in areas where there are no ethnic-minority children in the school, or perhaps there may be children present from a single black or Asian family. It has been argued strongly that it is these children (and their teachers) who are in the greatest need of multicultural education (Gaine, 1988, 1995; Jones, 1997). It is all too easy for educators in these social situations to claim that there is no need to address multicultural issues in their teaching because there simply are no ethnic-minority children in the school. It has been pointed out that this is precisely why there needs to be more of an emphasis on these issues, because if ethnic-minority children were present, then at least there are opportunities to open discussions into comparative beliefs and faiths, to explore cultural similarities and differences and so on. In the exclusively white school, these issues do not occur through the direct presence of ethnic-minority children and so often become lost completely in the drive towards meeting National Curriculum requirements. It is at this level that misconceptions, stereotypes and myths become pervasive, and this can reach from the local level of the classroom to national levels. For example, when the Teacher Training Agency (TTA) were contacted and asked for guidance on the place of multicultural education within initial teacher education we were told:

I've not heard of multicultural education. I am not aware that it is a particular requirement of the National Curriculum. I can see why it may be more appropriate in multicultural areas or you might find it linked to things like education about drugs.

Whilst of course it would be wrong to suggest that this is the formal line that any national agency would be keen to adopt and maintain, it is indicative of the way in which misguided notions of 'race' become part of educational dialogue. For this TTA representative the association was clear; multicultural education was something that needed to be done in areas where there were *more* ethnic-minority children (the implication being that it is *less* appropriate in predominantly or exclusively white areas of the country) and that there is a clear connection between teaching children about other 'races' and teaching children about drug abuse.

The poor treatment of black and bilingual children in the education system in part once again reflects the failure of society to genuinely involve children in their learning. Although small numbers of teachers and schools have committed themselves to involving children meaningfully in their learning, this will remain a minority until society and the state recognizes and acts on the need for participation. A truly child-centred and inclusive education system presents demanding challenges for all people involved with children's learning, but it is a challenge that urgently needs addressing if larger numbers of children are to develop and learn in positive and fulfilling ways.

3 Children and assessment

Nell Napier, Robert Banton and
Nicholas Medforth

We are all assessed and measured in a variety of ways, both formally and informally. Informal assessment may be based on our appearance, gender, age, and so on. Formal assessment is usually based on standardized measures such as examination results or can involve responses to other kinds of physical or psychological testing. Both formal and informal assessments can have a profound effect on our lives, our opportunities and the way we see ourselves. There is still a tendency to make judgements about groups rather than individuals based on informal assessments. For example, all women who dress in a certain way, all young men who attend football matches or all people over a certain age can have attributes ascribed to them merely by being part of a group.

Our view of ourselves, or self-concept, can therefore be seen to be the product of many different factors: how well we achieve measured by recognized standards of health, wealth or intelligence; how others assess us as individuals or group members based on societal norms of the time; and how we assess ourselves in relation to our own values and beliefs. Typically, professional people from a variety of settings have a duty to assess and record children's achievements and make judgements about their development; however, it is still rare to find examples where children are meaningfully involved in those processes. Quite often, the adult justification for such lack of involvement is the notion that children are not capable of understanding the issues involved.

This chapter begins by looking at the ways in which children assess themselves. This first section is important because it provides a contrast with the later sections of the chapter which focus on adult-determined assessment processes. It is followed by two short general sections that address the development of formal assessment in the UK and the kinds of definitions that inform assessment practice. These general sections and the remainder of the chapter focus on assessment in two important domains: health and education. It is in these areas that most assessment of children is carried out but the two systems have significant differences in their main practices and foci.

Informal assessment and children's assessment of themselves

Much of the literature examining the process of socialization and the way that children are integrated into the cultural context within which they live has portrayed children as passive actors shaped by adult influence. Currently researchers recognize that this it too simplistic a model and that children are very clearly and determinedly active participants in both their own socialization and cultural construction. This means that children constantly try to challenge and reshape adult influences according to their own personalities and goals.

Any observer of children, whether parent, professional, relative or neighbour, is likely to be aware that even very young children possess a developing insight into their social worlds. Research suggests that social awareness in children begins during early infancy. Developing children constantly assess themselves in terms of both their relationship with others, as well as their own achievement of social competence, mastery over the environment, self-reliance and personal attainments (Scaffer, 1997).

Most of us spend a considerable amount of time thinking about ourselves, and our own particular world view is developed from a subjective standpoint. We see the world in terms of how it affects us as individuals, how we might affect the world, who we are and where we might be going. In order to do this, children need to develop a sense of themselves as an entity, a self-concept. Bukatko and Daehler (1995) suggested that this involves the 'me' and 'I' aspects of the self; the child developing a growing realization that he or she is an independent, unique, stable and self-reflective entity with a set of personal characteristics.

One of the earliest tasks in this developing awareness begins with the child learning to distinguish his or her own face. At this stage, the self-concept is largely shaped by the perceptions and values children hold about themselves, rather than the characteristics identified by others. According to Damon and Hart (1988), infants are initially unable to differentiate themselves from the world around them and one of the central tasks for developing infants is gradually to develop a body awareness, realizing that their bodies are separate from their environment and are something which is unique to themselves.

Self-definition is not only restricted to the ways in which children describe themselves in physical terms. The objective part of the self-concept will also include classification in terms of easily observed categories such as age, sex, skills and abilities, possessions, friends and family and location during the early childhood years and this is termed as the 'categorical-self'. There is some considerable evidence to suggest that in the pre-school years children are also developing insights into their own psychological processes and social attributes (Damon and Hart, 1988) and this is likely to be supported by personal reflections – many readers will recollect small children describing themselves as happy, kind, lonely, silly, brave, good at telling jokes, and so on.

The establishment of a self-concept is important to the developing child as it will provide the basis for later development of a sense of identity as the child goes on to compare him or herself with parents, relatives, and other children, recognizing that others, too, are separate individuals. Children may, for example, view themselves as stronger than a brother, not as clever as mum, funnier than the girl next door, not as fast as dad, and so on. Bukatko and Daehler (1995) cite the work of a number of researchers whose findings suggest that this shift in emphasis in self-description from an inventory of skills, and physical, social and psychological attributes towards an emphasis upon comparisons with others occurs at around 7 years of age.

In Chapter 2, we outlined Piaget's theories related to greater awareness of the self and the link to a decline in egocentricity during the pre-operational stage. It has been suggested that self-attributes are logical, organized and generally consistent at this age, and that later self-knowledge becomes more abstract with a growing concern with how others might regard oneself. Thus the child's developing self-concept will be affected by numerous factors including self-examination of personal attributes and the perceptions of others. This is often linked with reflection on their physical characteristics such as body image, sense of strength and autonomy, perception of health, social values and roles children are likely to have.

Clearly, the way that children measure themselves in relation to their own characteristics and abilities, and compare and analyse themselves in relation to others, will not only influence the development of their own self-concept, but also the ways in which their social world relates to them. Differing schools of thought in psychology offer alternative explanations regarding the extent to which this particular aspect of the child's developing personality will be related to inherited or environmental factors, with behaviourists and social learning theorists emphasizing the influence of the social environment and maturationists emphasizing unfolding genetic patterns. However, most psychologists would now acknowledge the existence of an interaction between heredity and the social world. In this way, labelling children as intelligent, selfish, kind or stupid may well become self-fulfilling prophecies and have direct influence not only upon how children perceive themselves, but also determining the ways in which they are reacted to by others.

Children's self-concepts will always contain elements both of a sense of reality and a socially constructed ideal. However, as Hendrick (1997) points out, this is often not constructed by children but by adults. The child is likely to incorporate both of these features into a self-regulatory function, experiencing satisfaction when personal performance (as measured by self or others) is consistent with self-image and discomfort when achievement does not match an ideal. Some children may well need to maintain a consistent self-concept even when this is detrimental, as this is less threatening than attempting to challenge an existing perceived identity. For example, a child who sees him or herself as a failure at maths and has such a perception reinforced by teachers and peers may unconsciously sabotage his or her attempts to achieve good grades in this school subject. It has also been suggested that children's feelings of competence may be undermined by certain teaching practices which include the use of evaluative symbols such as stars and stickers as rewards, making public comparisons between children and ability groupings.

Scaffer (1997) reviews a range of research related to the self. Competence is very closely related to self-concept and self-esteem in children. One study he reviews found that children evaluated their competencies in numerous areas, and defined them into four broad categories: cognitive competence (doing well in school, feeling clever, remembering things easily, under-standing what they read); social competence (having lots of friends, being popular, being important to one's classmates, feeling liked); physical com-petence (doing well at sports, being chosen early for teams, being good at new games, preferring to play rather than watch); and general self-worth (sure of oneself, being a good person, being happy with the way one is). These categories were integrated into a self-concept questionnaire which was administered to over 2000 children. It was found that children perceived themselves in either favourable or unfavourable terms on each of these sub-scales by the time they had reached 8 years of age, and that they accurately reflected the ways in which they were perceived by teachers and peers. It was also found that children tended to recognize that competence could be context specific – that is, a particular child could be regarded as competent in the classroom, but not so on the playing field – and that some attributes tended to be more important than others. The children studied typically defined their self-worth in terms of their cognitive and social competencies. Other research reviewed in Scaffer's book confirms that children who enjoy the highest self-esteem are those children who have many friends and are high achievers in school.

Assessment of competence and popularity by peers becomes increasingly important to children during the middle childhood years when they move away from 'vertical' attachments to people who have greater knowledge and power, towards horizontal attachments to people with equal social power, where reciprocal skills such as co-operation, competition and social intimacy can be practised. Popularity amongst peers therefore has an increasing significance to children of this particular age group, a fact which was borne out by interviews with children carried out by another study. Initially researchers regarded popularity as an unidimensional continuum; however, more recently, subtle distinctions have been made. Researchers have offered behavioural profiles for three categories.

'Popular' children tend to be physically attractive, positively orientated, involved in high levels of co-operative play, are willing to share, able to sustain interactions with other children, tend to be seen as good leaders, are probably good at sports and exhibit little aggression. Conversely 'rejected' children tend to be argumentative, exhibit anti-social behaviour, be extremely active, talkative and disruptive, make frequent attempts at social approaches but also engage in inappropriate behaviour, and tend to engage in solitary activity, being unwilling to share or co-operate in play. A third category is 'neglected' children who also engage in a great deal of solitary activity, avoiding interaction with larger groups, tending to be shy and unassertive, rarely engaging in anti-social behaviour or aggression and tending to withdraw in the face of others' aggression. Scaffer (1997) also highlights research which suggested that rejected children may suffer the greatest difficulties, with an increased tendency to develop school problems, be excluded from school and engage in truancy and subsequently get into trouble with the police.

In Chapter 2, we outlined the views of Erikson. He regarded the development of a sense of self as culminating in the formation of an 'identity' during adolescence, a crucial step in the formation of personality at this particular stage of the life-cycle. Erikson argued that each stage within the life-cycle had its own challenges and crises to resolve. Whilst during earlier stages children will have been facing the challenges of developing a sense of trust in others, during adolescence, a sense of initiative and autonomy and the formation of an identity become essential. If the teenager has the opportunity to try out different roles and arrives at a positive path to follow which relates to a consistent sense of self, then a positive or healthy identity is likely to have been achieved. If this is not successfully achieved, identity confusion may result and may well persist into adulthood. Santrock (1990) offered an example of how a difficult search for identity may result when a child is confronted with a stereotypical cultural identity which is inconsistent with his or her own sense of identity. He described the views of Mary, a 13-year-old Innuit girl who lived in a small Arctic village. Whilst sympathizing with the views of those in her community who yearned for the old days and a traditional lifestyle, Mary also had contemporary Western interests, possessing a stereo and being interested in rock music, as well as aspiring to a city lifestyle. Some of these interests were, in fact, shared by Mary's grandfather, yet Mary experienced teachers who came to her village from cities such as New York and Chicago, who described Innuit culture as they thought it ought to be, rather than empathizing with Mary's life.

Trawick-Smith (1997) argued that culture plays an important part in identity formation, not only during adolescence, but also during the child's early years: feelings of competence, social acceptance, moral self-worth and control integrate with gender, ethnicity and family membership. Trawick-Smith highlighted that, despite early research suggesting that belonging to a cultural group which is perceived to be an ethnic minority led children to develop poorer self-esteem than those children represented by the dominant culture, more recent research suggests more optimistic findings. Children of historically under-represented groups have been found to base their self-evaluations on very different criteria than children of the dominant culture, and whilst recognizing that they face bias on the grounds of ethnicity, most acquire positive views of themselves through taking pride in their family, ethnic group and community.

Informal and formal systems of assessment are significantly different yet both have overlapping and dramatic effects on children. Because formal assessment plays such a large part in the lives of children, it is important that we ask ourselves what the rationale is for this type of assessment, what effect it has on children and whether it is fair.

The development of formal assessment

To find the start of mass formal assessment it is necessary to look to the nineteenth century. Before the nineteenth century, occupation was determined by birth, and schooling served the function of socialization for given roles (Broadfoot, 1996), therefore the necessity for assessment was limited. In the nineteenth century with increasing industrialization, assessment for competence became necessary. In 1868, the Taunton Commission advocated a system of inspectors to see that standards were being maintained in elementary schools. The Education Act 1870 saw the selection of children from elementary schools for secondary schools. This was expanded after the 1902 Act and the Free Place Regulations of 1907.

The first national exam was the School Certificate of 1917. Pupils had to pass five or more academic subjects to achieve it. In 1951, the GCE (General Certificate of Education) was introduced with Ordinary and Advanced Levels to be taken by grammar school pupils. In 1965, the CSE (Certificate of Secondary Education) was introduced giving secondary modern pupils the opportunity to have a school leaving certificate, the top grade being equivalent to O level. In 1988, the GCE and CSE were merged to make one examination open to all – the GCSE. The Education Act 1944 brought selection for secondary education for all. This was achieved by intelligence testing, whereby those who achieved the highest scores were selected for grammar schools and an academic education, and those who achieved lower scores being destined for secondary modern schools. This system was in place until the government became committed to comprehensive schools in 1965. The Education Reform Act of 1988 introduced National Assessment with testing at 7, 11 and 14 years of age being standardized across the country.

The nineteenth century also produced significant changes to health assessment. In the 1840s, evidence given to the Royal Commission stated that only 45 per cent of children born into poorer families would reach their fifth birthday as compared with just over 82 per cent of children born to the gentry. Major historical events such as the Industrial Revolution sparked a number of health concerns, and as a result, the middle to late nineteenth and early twentieth century was a period when considerable interest began to be shown in the issues of health and illness, and along with this there emerged ways of measuring health. The life chances of children, and thereby the future adult population, were seen as causing considerable concern.

Baistow (1995) suggests that:

> Public health and child welfare became issues of social concern calling
> for voluntary and state interventions, for the future strength of the
> nation was seen to lie in the good health of its children.
>
> (1995: 20)

Why was there such interest in child health and welfare? Could it be that the
plight of thousands of children had touched the hearts of policy makers and
caused the concern, or was it as the Royal Sanitary Commission suggested in
1871 that 'the constant relationship between the health and vigour of the
people and the welfare and commercial prosperity of the state required no
argument . . . public health is public wealth'. To put it simply, the country
could not afford to have a population who could not work in order to
produce goods and services which would create wealth.

The state of the adult population's health became obvious when recruits for
the Boer War were in such poor condition that they were not fit for service in
the army. Many individuals were not fit enough to work, and not fit for active
service for the Empire. These events and others were a major impetus for
government to act, and there followed a whole raft of pioneering legislation
aimed at improving the health of the nation. It is not the intention to discuss the
specific legislation and strategies, except to say that they were wide ranging
and covered just about every area of life from sanitation, housing, food
supplies, water systems and specific medical treatments and interventions:

> in order of importance the major contributions to improvements in
> health in England and Wales were from limitation of family size,
> increase in food supplies and a healthier physical environment and
> specific preventive and therapeutic measures.
>
> (McKeown, 1976: 6)

Along with these changes there was an emergence of new sciences to
identify and rectify social problems, and with this came new experts to
advise on how best to deal with these issues. Experts came from the newly
developing fields of sociology and psychology, along with the more traditional medical experts who now had a new tool with which to talk about the
health of the population (or rather ill health), namely epidemiology. Later in
this chapter we go into more detail about the importance of epidemiology.

We now take it for granted that formal assessment of children takes place
regularly throughout their childhood, but against what are we assessing them,
what standards are we using? There are a range of ways of defining what it is to
be healthy and/or educated and it is to some of these that we now turn.

Definitions of health and education

When we assess health just what are we trying to measure? In order to
effectively measure anything it must be definable: does health offer such a

clarity of definition? The definitions of health are numerous and cover a wide range of perspectives from the biomedical conception which views health as simply the absence of illness to more holistic views that see health as a positive force that allows us to achieve our goals in life. David Seedhouse (1996) in his book *Health: the foundations for achievement* provided a useful overview of differing conceptions of health and he believes that the major views of health could be condensed and combined to view health as a foundation for achievement.

However, Ashton and Seymour (1988) argued that attempts to define health are futile and ultimately de-energizing and have led to nothing but conflict. But this does leave us with a problem. If we are to measure the health of children, just what are we to measure? We could take the well known but dated World Health Organization (WHO) definition of health:

Health is the state of complete physical, social and mental well-being, and not just the absence of disease or illness.

(World Health Organization, 1946: online)

How would you measure a state of complete well-being? Can anyone really attest to feeling completely physically, socially and mentally well all at the same time? This conception of health is often identified as an ideal state, as it represents what an individual might aspire to, but all too often not attain. In terms of trying to measure the health of individuals, it raises a number of difficulties. The definition is unnecessarily subjective, which does not invalidate the concept, but it does make it very hard to quantify and use any measures in order to make judgements about the health status of the population, and any assessment of health needs.

Due to this critique and other emerging influences, the WHO updated its definition of health in 1984 when it stated that:

Health is the extent to which an individual or group is able, on the one hand, to realize aspirations and satisfy needs; and on the other hand, to change or cope with the environment. Health is, therefore, seen as a resource for everyday life, not an object of living; it is a positive concept emphasising social and personal resources, as well as physical capacities.

(World Health Organization, 1984: 2)

This definition is important for a number of reasons. Health is seen as being held not just by individuals, but also by groups, and is related to their ability to meet the needs they have identified. Health is seen as a resource that is used by individuals or groups to react to and change their environment. As a definition, it gives a strong and positive meaning to health, but still is very difficult to measure. For health professionals trying to assess the health of a population and plan services to meet their health needs, it is very broad and could encompass many areas of policy that lie outside their medical domain.

The nature of definitions is a question that can also be asked about education and how an educated person might be defined. The United Nations Educational, Scientific and Cultural Organization (UNESCO) has established a task force on education for the twenty-first century. The task force defines education – and by implication the things an educated person would be expected to know – by describing four 'pillars': 'learning to know, learning to do, learning to live together, learning to be' (UNESCO, 1999). 'Learning to know' is concerned with the mastery of learning tools more than the acquisition of structured knowledge. It is about understanding, knowledge and discovery. 'Learning to do' is partly about traditional training for the range of occupations that are available. However, there is also recognition that the types of work needed in the future may emphasize the importance of the knowledge components of tasks. 'Learning to live together' describes the importance of discovering other people and becoming involved in common projects. This is, in part, a recognition of the problems of conflict and violence around the world and the negative side of competitiveness. 'Learning to be' emphasizes the importance of complete development: mind and body, intelligence, sensitivity, aesthetic appreciation and spirituality. It is also about the development of independent critical thinking and the 'complete fulfilment of man in all the richness of his personality, the complexity of his forms of expression and his various commitments'.

Like the WHO definition above, UNESCO's definition of education is not just about individuals, it is explicitly related to the other people of the globe. It interestingly cites the potential problems with inappropriate competition, seeing this as a threat to the 'pillar' of learning to live together. This certainly raises questions about the competitiveness that is an inherent part of many Western systems of national assessment, not least in the UK. 'Learning to be' also makes some crucial statements about the educated person and gives a particularly rich description of such an education. It is important to consider whether the increasing narrowness of some national curricula is in the spirit of such a definition.

Health assessment

Why do we measure or assess the health of children? Parents may measure their children from birth: one of the first questions asked by most parents is often 'Is the baby OK?' Clearly this reflects parental concern that their child is going to be healthy and strong, and hopefully grow into a healthy adult. Professionals also ask the same questions and will begin to measure the child almost straight from birth. Measurements of the child's weight, head circumference, and length are made by the midwife, and shortly after, the paediatrician will conduct a more detailed head to toe medical examination of the child. This is to identify any deviation from the normal physiological functioning of the body in order to initiate treatment as soon as possible and correct, if possible, any disease or injury the baby may be suffering from.

This measuring of the child's health will continue throughout his or her school life and indeed into adulthood. Today, as a society, we assess, measure and collect more data related to health than ever before. Demographic and epidemiological data are collected in a variety of ways and are used to examine the health status of the population, the uptake of health services, as well as to plan future services and strategies aimed at improving the health of the population.

We can measure the health of children in two main ways. The health of an individual child can be measured, which tells us a lot about that individual, but nothing about the population of children as a whole. The child will be assessed by members of the primary health care team, namely the general practitioner and the health visitor. The assessments will be made against a series of psycho-motor developmental milestones and physical examination of the child. We can also measure the health of groups of children using an epidemiological approach.

Hart (1985) pointed to the fact that because of the absence of a universally valid measure of health, it has traditionally been measured in terms of its absence, that is, mortality (death) and morbidity (illness) rates. It is relatively easy to measure when health is not present in terms of when individuals are sick or even die, and then to argue that if morbidity and mortality rates decrease then the population must be more healthy. Clearly this approach views health as the absence of disease or illness. And it is this type of data, termed epidemiological data, which will be used to examine how children's health has been measured.

Epidemiology is the study of the distribution and determinants of disease in human populations. Epidemiological data come from a variety of sources, death certificates, registrations of births, medical consultations, registrations of illness and recordable diseases among others. Epidemiology seeks to answer three basic questions: Who gets ill? Why do they get ill? How can they be treated?

The first area consists of the description of patterns of disease in populations, and involves the measurement of mortality and morbidity. As epidemiology deals with populations, we cannot always simply count the number of people with disease x or y and make a comparison with other communities. Because of this, epidemiologists rely on statistical methods in order to make comparisons; data are expressed in terms of ratios, percentage and rates.

For example, the measurement of the birth rate is the number of children born in a year per 1000 of the population, or

$$\text{birth rate} = \frac{\text{number of births in year} \times 1000}{\text{mid-year population}}$$

$$\text{death rate} = \frac{\text{number of deaths in the year} \times 1000}{\text{mid-year population}}$$

MORTALITY MEASURES

It is relatively easy to count the number of individuals who have died, and even what they have died of. The data are not 100 per cent accurate though, because of errors such as filling in death certificates incorrectly, and misdiagnosis of the cause of death. The crude death rate is taken to be the total number of deaths in one year per 1000 of the population. The death rate is of limited use due to complicating variables such as the age of individuals or special circumstances, for instance the provision of a hospital in the area, which may mean that individuals from outside the area are counted in the statistics. Of more use are the specialized death rates:

- Stillbirth rate: the number of foetal deaths over 24 weeks gestation per 1000 total births.
- Perinatal mortality rate (PMR): the rate of all stillbirth deaths and deaths in the first week of life per 1000 live births.
- Neonatal mortality rate (NMR): the number of deaths in the first 4 weeks of life per 1000 total live births.
- Infant mortality rate (IMR): the number of deaths of infants under 1 year of age during the year per 1000 live births.
- Standardized mortality ratio (SMR): a very useful measurement which allows epidemiologists to make a number of comparisons. The general way it is derived is:

$$\text{SMR} = \frac{\text{observed number of deaths}}{\text{expected number of deaths}}$$

The figure is traditionally then multiplied by 100 to avoid a cumbersome fraction. SMRs of more than 100 indicate that the number of deaths in the population under study is higher than expected, that is, an SMR of 150 indicates that there were 50 per cent more deaths than expected. Conversely, SMRs lower than 100 indicate fewer deaths than expected, so if the rate is only 80 then we are observing 20 per cent fewer deaths than one would expect to see.

MORBIDITY MEASURES

In terms of measuring disease, there are a few problems that must be taken notice of when examining morbidity data. Death is relatively easy to count, but illness less so. Problems such as individuals not reporting illness, misdiagnosis of an illness and those who do not attend doctors but use complementary medicine make the morbidity data less than 100 per cent accurate. However, in the main these can be used to detect trends in the patterns of illness.

Some of the most commonly collected morbidity data for children would be the number of children who contract the so-called 'childhood illnesses' of measles, whooping cough, diphtheria and rubella. In England and Wales in 1995, there were only 7447 cases of measles, 6196 cases of rubella and 1936 cases of mumps notified. This can be compared with a decade ago when there were around 9500 reported cases of measles. This type of reduction in the incidence of these diseases can be shown for all the major 'childhood illnesses'.

Obviously, part of the reason for this reduction is the high rate of immunization uptake. On average, 93 per cent of infants complete their primary immunization course against measles, mumps, rubella, polio and meningitis caused by *Haemophilus influenzae*. However, this high uptake rate hides the fact that some regions report significantly lower uptake rates. Some 17 regions within the UK report uptake to be below 90 per cent.

Data of this type are collected for a wide range of diseases and can be used by health staff and policy planners to identify growing health problems, and institute strategies to deal with them. In addition, data of this type can be used to assess the effectiveness of any type of health treatment or intervention, such as a campaign to help prevent an illness.

Platt and Pharoah (1995: 547) stated that a child born in Britain in the 1990s, providing he or she survives the first year of life, can expect to reach the age of 73.9 years for boys and 79.4 years for girls. Infant mortality rates currently stand at 6.2/1000 live births. The perinatal mortality rate for 1994/96 was 8.9, and the neonatal mortality rate was 4.1. Both perinatal and post neonatal mortality rates have decreased for all socioeconomic groups in the years between 1975 and 1990 (*see* Tables 3.1 and 3.2). However, we can also see that the gap between the higher and lower socioeconomic groups remains stubbornly constant.

If we examine the major causes of death for today's children we can see (Table 3.3) that the major causes of death in children under 15 are not the major infections that once caused large mortality rates in children, but are now sudden infant death, injuries and poisonings, closely followed by congenital abnormalities. These causes are amenable to timely interventions, by health professionals working with parents. This screening and preventative work is carried out during the Child Health Promotion Programme (CHP).

Table 3.1 Infant mortality by occupational class: perinatal deaths/1000 total births

	1975	1985	1990
Social classes 1 and 2	15.0	7.6	6.2
Social classes 4 and 5	22.7	11.5	9.5
Rates for social classes 4 and 5 as a % of rates for social classes 1 and 2	151	151	154

Source: Office of Population Censuses and Surveys (1991)

Table 3.2   Infant mortality by occupational class: post neonatal deaths/1000 live births

	1975	1985	1990
Social classes 1 and 2	3.1	2.7	2.0
Social classes 4 and 5	6.4	4.3	9.5
Rates for social classes 4 and 5 as a % of rates for social classes 1 and 2	202	160	202

Source: Office of Population Censuses and Surveys (1991)

Table 3.3   Main causes of death among children in England and Wales, by age group in 1992

28 days–1 year old	1–4 years old	5–14 years old
28% – Sudden infant death syndrome	24% – Injuries/poisons	33% – Injuries/poisons
23% – Congenital abnormalities	19% – Congenital abnormalities	24% – Neoplasm
8% – Respiratory diseases	15% – Other causes	11% – Other causes
8% – Nervous system	12% – Neoplasm	11% – Nervous system
5% – Infections	12% – Nervous system	11% – Congenital abnormalities
5% – Injuries/poisons	7% – Infections	4% – Circulatory system
24% – Other causes	7% – Respiratory system	3% – Respiratory system
	4% – Circulatory system	3% – Infections

Source: Office of Population Censuses and Surveys (1994)

The programme is particularly significant in terms of the assessment of children's health.

INDIVIDUAL HEALTH ASSESSMENT – SCREENING

In terms of contact with the assessment of children, parents will most frequently encounter the measurement of their child when taking him or her to the 'baby clinic' or their GP's surgery. Within community child health, the main focus of intervention has come from the primary health care team through the Child Health Surveillance Programme, and it is to this that we now turn. The CHP outlined below is the backbone of community child health services.

The CHP has a long history. Health professionals have been screening children and providing health education for families for many years. However, resource limitations and a call for a clear and rational approach to resource allocation have meant an increasingly critical approach to the cost and effectiveness of screening. This has meant that it has become essential to evaluate health care activity, and seek the most cost-effective means of delivering a service.

Therefore, questions began to be asked about the screening services for children, and the exact roles of health professionals involved. There seemed to be a lack of consensus on these issues, so that in 1986 a working party was set up with the following terms of reference: 'To review and comment upon the current practice in child health surveillance in the United Kingdom and to make recommendations for future practice' (Hall, 1991: 7).

This review resulted in a report two years later which came to be known as the Hall Report, after the name of the committee's chairman. The Hall Report recommended a set programme of screening tests, but less than had previously been undertaken. The screening tests were to be accompanied by health promotion activities, including health education programmes and immunizations. Despite some criticism, the recommendations were widely accepted and became the basis of child health services in the community.

Two years later in 1990, because of the introduction of many new pieces of legislation and social policy, doctor Colin Wain was asked to review Hall's work and the content of a district programme for child health surveillance. The 1990 review was able to agree on both the content and provision of the programme. In addition, the working party was able to address the issue of which member of the primary health care team should do which part of the programme.

By 1995, there had been much change to the content and organization of the CHP. The main changes were much routine child health screening moving from the traditional baby clinic into the GP's surgery. The screening tests were to be conducted not by community medical officers, but by the child's GP and health visitor. This meant that attendance at community health clinics declined and some closed. However, there remained wide variations in policies and standards between districts. Many health districts failed to specify their aims, procedures, referral criteria or referral routes. Within many districts, arrangements for monitoring and audit of child health surveillance, along with the integration of child health services, remained poor (Hall, 1996).

This resulted in a further review of the service. In order to emphasize that preventative health care for children involves more than detection of defects, the new programme was termed Child Health Promotion Programme. This replaced the term child health surveillance, and it was argued that this change in name marked the recognition of the need for a wider and more holistic approach to improving child health. The programme was to remain within the remit of the primary health care team. However, more flexibility was to be encouraged so that professional judgement should determine what type and level of service were to be given to each child and his or her family. It was argued that the professionals needed to carry out a detailed needs analysis of each family and apply the programme in the light of this analysis.

In order to facilitate this, professionals were encouraged to develop relationships that helped to facilitate better health needs assessments. Health professionals are encouraged to develop their skills in needs assessment and therefore enhance their ability to target interventions more accurately.

Some changes were made to the child health screening programme:

- Checks for congenital dislocation of the hip were now to be carried out as soon as possible following birth, and at 6 to 8 weeks and again at 6 to 9 months.
- Checks for undescended testes to be carried out at 6 to 8 weeks. If the testes have not descended by then, referral to a paediatrician is needed.
- In order to monitor growth, length/height only to be measured at 6 to 8 months and again at 1.5 to 2 years old, and 3.5 and 5 years old.
- Hearing screening: the distraction test should be continued, but two trained professionals are needed to carry out this assessment.

These changes produced a new-look programme for the assessment of child health which also sought to provide health education for parents. In the neonatal period, a neonatal examination is carried out by either hospital staff or the GP, if the child was born at home. By the age of 28 days, the newborn baby will have been examined by midwives and medical staff and will have been subjected to blood tests and injections of vitamin K. By the time the baby is a month old the care of this child will have passed to a health visitor, who will visit the family at home as well as see the child and its parents at their local 'well baby clinic'.

At about 6 to 8 weeks, the child will be examined by a doctor, usually the child's GP. The health visitor will facilitate the sharing of any particular problems, for example infant feeding, and give any help or advice needed. This examination is usually undertaken at the same time as the first immunization is due. Health education topics for this period may include immunization, infant feeding and weaning advice. At 2, 3 and 4 months a child should have received the full primary course of immunizations. There are no specific health checks at this stage, but some districts would choose to re-check a child's hips at the same time as the third immunization.

At 6 to 9 months, the examination can be undertaken by the doctor and health visitor together, but in most health districts, it is the health visitor only. The main assessment at this time is the distraction test to assess hearing. At this time, it is important to enquire about parental concerns regarding the health and development of their child. Height and weight may be checked if indicated. Observations of visual behaviour should be made and any evidence of a squint noted. The topics for health education at this time include accident prevention, anticipated increased mobility, dental prophylaxis and an overview of the child's developmental needs.

At 18–24 months a language assessment review should be carried out. This review should be done as close to the 24 months as possible, as language is more readily assessed in the slightly older child. The assessment is undertaken by the health visitor and is conducted in the child's home. The assessment includes a review of parental concerns regarding vision, hearing and general behaviour. Assessment of language comprehension and range of vocabulary should be carried out in discussion with parents. Assessment of the child's height and gait should also be made. Topics for health education include accident prevention, developmental needs, including language and play, along with the benefits of mixing with other children.

By the age of $3^1/_4$ to $3^1/_2$ years, the aims of this review are to ensure that the child is physically fit and has no medical disorders which might interfere with his or her education. Immunizations should be up to date. This review can be performed by either doctor or health visitor, and primary health care teams are encouraged to be flexible in their judgement as to how much time to devote to this review for each family. The review consists of assessment of vision, hearing, language and general development. Height should also be ascertained and recorded.

Topics for health education are accidents, road safety, preparation for school, nutrition and dental care.

In this section, we have seen that data gathered on the mortality and morbidity rates for children can be used to assess the health of the child population, plan health care services and health promotion strategies. By incorporating health screening, health education and disease prevention, along with the philosophy of working in partnership with parents, professionals have the tools to improve the health of all children.

Education assessment

In the education system, one of the often stated priorities for assessment is that teachers need to know what children understand before they can provide appropriate learning experiences for them. The DES document *From policy to practice* (1989) was published following the Education Reform Act 1988 to explain how National Curriculum requirements would affect schools. It stated that 'national assessment will serve several purposes'. The first two purposes mentioned referred to children; top of the list came formative assessment:

> in providing information which teachers can use in deciding how a pupil's learning should be taken forward, and in giving the pupils themselves clear and understandable targets and feedback about their achievements. It will also provide teachers and others with the means of identifying the need for further, diagnostic assessment for particular pupils where appropriate to help their educational development.
>
> (Department of Education and Science, 1989: 6.2)

Indeed many teachers put 'diagnostic' assessment at the top of their list when asked about the need to assess (Pollard *et al.*, 1994; Broadfoot, 1996). The DES document also mentioned summative assessment, which was said to 'provide overall evidence of the achievement of a pupil and of what he or she knows, understands and can do' (Department of Education and Science, 1989: 6.2).

The balance between formative and summative assessment is crucial. It is probably fair to say that for the wider community summative assessments are seen to be paramount. However, for many teachers they can be seen to be of less worth than formative assessments and, as will be seen, since they are also linked with accountability, teachers might be suspicious of the uses to which they are put.

It is important to note that these two forms of assessment are sometimes seen to be underpinned by different ideas about how children learn. As Pollard and Tann (1993) note, formative assessment is linked with a constructivist view of learning. Teachers engage with the present under-standings of the children and, through a process of assessing their needs while they engage in activities, lead them to further understandings. Gipps et al. (1995), in researching the way that the end of Key Stage One assess-ments had been carried out since their introduction, found that some teachers used intuition associated with their all-round knowledge of the child in making their teacher assessments, rather than refer to criteria from the Statements of Attainment. The teachers claimed to make assessments in an on-going fashion, but did not necessarily keep records, relying on their memory when coming to make summative assessments. They also found that some year 3 teachers were reluctant to look at the assessments of Key Stage One teachers for fear of being influenced by their judgements. They preferred to make their own minds up about children once they got to know them.

Standard assessment tasks can be seen to drive learning, and perhaps lead to a narrowing of learning where teachers 'teach to the test'. In practice, in the early days of the English national assessment process in infant schools it was found that some Standard Assessment Tasks – such as the one for science – which were meant to be summative, were used as formative assessments and helped to widen the curriculum and to inform teachers about good practice (Broadfoot, 1996). Unfortunately, these types of assess-ment were the ones which proved unwieldy and were set aside in favour of more quick and simple tests; the very thing which some teachers feared would narrow the curriculum. Gipps et al. (1995) found that the introduction of National Assessment at Key Stage One in fact had not brought about a narrowing effect on the curriculum. However, since that time, changes in the curriculum and the testing system have produced a much greater focus on reading and numeracy with a consequent lack of emphasis on other areas of the curriculum.

As well as providing information about pupils' understanding, skill and knowledge, assessment can provide teachers with information which helps them to evaluate the effectiveness of their teaching. The DES referred to aggregated information, which could be used to indicate where there is a need for 'further effort, resources, changes in the curriculum etc' (Depart-ment of Education and Science, 1989: 6.2). It also referred to 'professional development' through a process in which teachers could 'evaluate their own work and gain access to new thinking'.

Another important function of assessments is making schools accountable. It is interesting to note what happens when results are published. It is common for parents to look at league tables for GCSE results, among other things, when choosing a secondary school for their children. The focus for attention is the number of pupils gaining the top three grades. The 1997 GCSE results showed an improvement in the number of pupils gaining the top three grades but no overall improvement in the number of pupils gaining GCSE at all grades. Gillborn and Gipps (1996: 43), referring to the 'differential effectiveness' of some schools, pointed to analyses for the Association of Metropolitan Authorities showing that 'some schools which obtain higher than average results for the most able pupils may obtain lower than average results for the less able pupils'. This led to concern that pupils who were not thought likely to gain the highest grades were being neglected.

The function of assessment in upholding standards is an important one. Broadfoot (1996) made the link between the payment by results system of the nineteenth century and the recent developments in the testing of children. She maintained that it was more common for assessment to be used to control educational provision. The need to control educational provision can be traced back to the rapid social change which came about with industrialization. 'Industrialization . . . led to privileged sections of society being more and more forced to resort to schooling as the means of perpetuating the elite status that land and money could no longer ensure' (Broadfoot, 1996: 37).

In industrial societies with rapidly increasing technological advancement, it is important that the workforce is competent to take on specific roles. The assessment of these competencies and the resulting certification give society legitimization for allocating 'unequally desirable social roles' (Broadfoot, 1996: 10). Thus, along with assessment and certification come competition and selection.

Competition for jobs and higher education places makes the gaining of high grades in end of school assessments very important. Rowntree (1987: 17) pointed to the assumption that selection tests for continuing education were needed to ensure that resources are given to those who can best make use of them, but went on to point out that 'comparisons of "A" level results and degree class have rarely shown much of a correlation'. Furthermore, he mentioned that medical students with low grades but with concern and empathy might make better practitioners than academic high flyers. Broadfoot (1996) also pointed to research that suggested that examination results are a fairly weak guide to the quality of future job or higher education performance and cites motivation, effort, introversion, extroversion and confidence as influences. However, selection remains an important function of assessment at GCSE and A Level, as candidates apprehensively awaiting results would readily attest.

It is not so common these days for children to be selected for state secondary education by test, although there are some local education authorities (LEAs) which operate systems similar to the 'eleven plus' and there are always calls from the political right for a return to selection. The eleven plus became controversial, selecting children, as it did, at an early age and determining which sort of education children were to receive from the age of 11 years. It was underpinned by a belief in the inherited nature of intelligence, and the belief that this intelligence was easily assessed. It was said to be free from value judgements and to be a predictor of future attainment. Writing about the demise of intelligence testing, Salter and Tapper (1981) pointed out that at the time when children were selected for secondary education by the eleven plus test, it was found that some pupils who were supposed not to be capable of coping with GCEs, by virtue of failing the eleven plus and thus attending secondary modern school, did better than their grammar school counterparts. It does not take much imagination to guess what being judged a failure at such a young age did for the self-esteem of the children concerned.

THE FAIRNESS OF EDUCATIONAL ASSESSMENT

Broadfoot (1996: 13) claimed 'it is now widely accepted that any kind of educational measurement can be at best only a rough estimate of particular kinds of ability'. She went on to point out that:

> At the individual level, the vagaries of pupil performance and especially of exam stress, of differences between markers and in the difficulty of questions, are only some of the more obvious causes of inaccuracy which would now seem to be largely unavoidable. Research has shown for example that differences between markers, such as speed of reading, fatigue and competence (Lee-Smith, 1990; Broadfoot, 1992), the order and speed of marking or even the marker's personal social situation, may affect the marking process (Braithwaite et al., 1981).
>
> (Broadfoot, 1996: 13)

To add to these problems with reliability, there is the 'halo effect'. Spear (1996: 85) defined this as 'the tendency to allow an estimation of one characteristic of a person to influence the estimation of another characteristic of that person'. Spear described a study where 12 year olds were asked to write an essay about attitudes to science and to write up a science experiment. It was found that markers were influenced when marking the science write-up by the results from the marking of the essay, thus showing a 'halo effect'. Spear also pointed out that markers can be influenced by factors such as race, sex and social class. These are complex areas and need to be considered in some depth.

Gipps and Murphy (1994a), discussing the fairness of testing, noted that in National Assessments for 11 and 14 year olds, girls scored higher than boys, and there were more boys at the extremes. Minority ethnic groups scored lower than other groups, and children whose home language was not

English did less well. Indeed differential achievement of different groups in society has been a concern for many years. Consistently, children in lower socioeconomic groups have been seen to achieve less well (Douglas, 1964, Halsey et al., 1980; Goldthorpe, 1987). Gillborn and Gipps (1996: 16) reported that 'When information on pupils' social class background is collected, there is usually a direct relationship with academic achievement; the higher the social class, the higher the achievement. '

When certain groups consistently do less well in assessments, it is right to look at the assessments themselves to see if they are at fault. Arthur Jensen (1969: 16), working in America, claimed that 'on average, Negroes test about one standard deviation (fifteen IQ points) below the average of the white population in IQ'. His claim that genetic factors explained this difference can be soundly refuted on a number of grounds (Kamin and Eysenck, 1981). One of the most significant deconstructions of the notion of intelligence as an hereditary facet comes from Gould (1996), who deals at length with the recurrent claims about race and intelligence. As far as Jensen's claims are concerned, it is the bias of IQ tests that is the crucial point. Early tests were anglo-centric, that is, based on cultural features of white middle-class society, and underpinned by Western epistemological philosophies.

Gipps and Murphy (1994a) give an example of how the validity of a test can be biased. If a child who is new to the language of the test is tested in arithmetic by a word problem, he or she might fail, not through an inability to do the arithmetic, but through a failure to understand the question due to linguistic difficulties. Gipps and Murphy advocate a variety of assessment techniques as the best way to reduce bias. They also identify the problem of facial bias, referring to Cole and Moss (1989). The test may contain stereo-typic images, which might not necessarily affect its validity but might alienate certain groups. This is illustrated by a study carried out by the Fawcett Society (see Swan, 1992: 103) of 1986 GCE examination papers in a range of subjects. It was revealed that the papers had an 'overpoweringly masculine flavour', maths questions were often abstract and examples tended to be male. Physical science and computing questions were abstract and impersonal – applications were felt to relate to boys' interests and not draw enough on girls' experiences. In English literature, it was rare for texts by female authors to be used, and there were few questions about female characters. Modern languages 'set books' were almost entirely by male authors and there were stereotypic portrayals of adults, with males shown as more active and in control; pictures often showed men 'doing' and women 'watching'.

If education assessment does disadvantage certain groups, what can be done? One of the recommendations from a report from the office of Her Majesty's Chief Inspector of Schools and the Equal Opportunities Commission (1996: 18) is that 'schools can introduce specific initiatives in nursery and Key Stage 1 classes targeting girls who lack experience in constructional activity'. This is a welcome recommendation; however, teachers need to carefully monitor the success of such initiatives. Epstein (1995) showed that, when girls play with constructional apparatus, they do traditionally female things with it such as build a home and play domesticated games in that home. However, Epstein also pointed out that in making the home they do in fact carry out traditionally male tasks such as building.

Trying to bring about equity is a complex matter. Should we, for example, make English tests more favourable to boys by giving multiple choice questions or maths tests more favourable to girls by providing an essay format? This would perhaps be too simplistic a response. Gipps and Murphy (1994a: 273) maintain that there is 'no such thing as a fair test, nor could there be: the situation is too complex and the notion simplistic'. It is perhaps more important to look at the experience that is offered to these groups and identify areas which need to be changed, rather than changing the tests themselves. Gipps and Murphy (1994a) talk of equity rather than equality, and point out that there are problems in trying to make tests have equal outcomes. It is important to be clear about what we want and the best way to bring this about. Even when suggestions are made about bringing greater equity, this can be done in an inequitable fashion. For example, Cohen (1996) points out that, when boys' performance is lacking in a subject, it is suggested that the methods be changed, whereas, when girls' performance is lacking, the deficit is seen in the girls and so they are urged to change.

In the present climate of ever-increasing assessment and decisions about the ways to assess being changed year on year, it is very difficult to determine exactly what effects assessments are having. As Gipps and Murphy (1994a) point out, the speed of test development leaves no time to carry out detailed analysis and trialling to ensure that tests are fair. It is clear that careful monitoring should be applied to both educational provision and assessment. In order to achieve fair outcomes, equality of opportunity is vital. Even if fairer tests were achieved, it is still possible that, if children were not given equal access to educational provision, the outcome would be unfair. As Gipps and Murphy (1994a: 15) state 'the notion of the standard test as a way of offering impartial assessment is . . . a powerful one, though if there is not equality of educational opportunity preceding the test, then the 'fairness' of this approach is called into question'. Assessment of children, particularly educational assessment, is rarely 'fair'. We conclude this chapter with a more detailed examination of some of the effects of educational assessment on children.

THE EFFECTS OF EDUCATIONAL ASSESSMENT

Just as medication produces a planned effect and a side-effect, assessment can serve an overt purpose whilst bringing about desirable and undesirable side-effects. Madaus (1988) talked of 'Measurement driven instruction'. He undertook an extended review of the influence of testing on the curriculum, and maintained that, when tests are used to make social decisions, there is a corrupting influence on the educational system.

The tests can become the ferocious master of the educational process, not the compliant servant they should be. Measurement driven instruction invariably leads to cramming; narrows the curriculum; concentrates attention on those skills most amenable to testing . . . constrains the creativity and spontaneity of teachers and students; and finally demeans the professional judgement of teachers.

(Madaus, 1988: 85)

He maintained that when test scores rise there is not necessarily an improvement in the skill – the teaching is aimed at the test item rather than an all-round skill. There is a narrowing of the curriculum. A high-stakes testing programme can seem to solve a real educational problem; in fact, this is a symbolic solution. Test scores rise because of teaching to the test, but the real problem is not addressed.

Koretz *et al.* (1991) carried out a survey which showed that children who had been prepared for tests did not transfer these results to other tests, and that their test scores had been boosted in a way which did not boost their actual achievement. Teaching to the test is likely when schools are being judged by their test scores – such as the 'league tables' in Britain at present. Airasian (1988) maintained that the popularity of testing programmes as a means to raise standards was due to perceptions that they evoke order, control and traditional moral values rather than any empirical evidence.

Being assessed can inform children of their progress. It encourages them to measure themselves against their peers and to identify their strengths and weaknesses. It can provide a structure and help them set targets. It can give them positive reinforcement and a sense of achievement, help them get a job or proceed to get further qualifications. However, it can also can lead to children being labelled, give them negative reinforcement and a negative self image, make them feel bad, or feel they measure up poorly against their peers. It can exclude them from employment or continuing education. Holt (1964: 92) highlighted the fear of failing: 'Fear destroys intelligence, the way it affects a child's whole way of looking at, thinking about and dealing with life'. He described a child faced with a problem in class: 'Am I going to get this right? What'll happen to me when I get it wrong? Will the teacher get mad? Will the other kids laugh at me? Will my mother and father hear about it?'

Teachers sometimes use children's fear as a way of gaining control in the classroom; at other times, they may try to alleviate fear by playing down the role of assessment. The ways in which teachers respond to their knowledge of this fear has a powerful impact on children. Holt makes the point that children should not fear failing as it is part of the process of gaining success. There is no doubt that notions of success and failure are at the heart of what education has come to be about.

In the late 1960s it was common for children to be streamed, and so there was no doubt in the minds of the lower-stream children where they stood in the academic pecking order. Studies were carried out which seemed to suggest that such children often reacted to their experiences by rejecting school values in order to protect their pride and self-esteem. Hargreaves (1967) talked of 'delinquescent' norms. He described a subculture of pupils in lower streams who reacted to their experience in school. Their low status was aggravated by the behaviour of other pupils and teachers towards them. Lacey (1970) found that pupils who fail exams reject school values and develop an 'anti school culture'. He found that teachers reacted to their bad behaviour and boys lived up to the teachers' expectations.

With the advent of comprehensive schools, it became more common for schools to set children according to attainment in particular subjects rather than stream, and primary schools are very rarely streamed nowadays (although it should be noted that setting for subjects such as mathematics and English is becoming more and more common in primary schools with the implementation of the National Curriculum). However, even in unstreamed classes 'differentiation' (as the practice of organizing the curriculum according to children's abilities became known) is evident, perhaps through ability grouping or by children working through graded reading or mathematics books at different rates, and so on. The classroom differentiation is often mirrored in the formation of friendship groups. Pollard (1985) identified friendship groups among 11 year olds and found that polarization occurred at this age, leading to formation of subcultures based on success and failure. The groups were identified as follows: 'gang' members who were willing to disrupt classes, had low levels of educational achievement and were thought of as a nuisance; 'goodies' who were conformist, fairly able but dull; and 'jokers' who liked to have a laugh, were very able and got on well with the teachers.

More recently, it has been found that children resort to disruptive behaviour when denied the opportunity to succeed. A report from OFSTED, *Exclusions from secondary schools*; stated:

> Children's self esteem is inextricably bound up with success at school; all need to feel that they are learning. All need to be able to read and write, and to master an extensive vocabulary. When topics are presented to them in language they cannot understand, or in a style which fails to engage their attention, they have no basis for acquiring knowledge or for making progress. Repeated failure to understand is demoralising; most children prefer to conceal it rather than to seek help. Some ultimately become resentful and disruptive.
>
> (OFSTED, 1996: 30)

A review of research into the achievement of ethnic minority pupils refers to the informal assumptions that are made, and the ways that schools are sometimes organized, and suggests that this can disadvantage pupils.

> Teachers (in their daily interactions with pupils) and schools (through the adoption of various selection and setting procedures) may play an

active, though unintended, role in the creation of conflict with African Caribbean pupils, thereby reducing black young people's opportunity to achieve.

(Gillborn and Gipps, 1996: 56)

These problems with informal assessments of children have been confirmed recently by another government report (OFSTED, 1999).

Children soon learn that there are some individuals who are more successful academically than others. It has been found that children as young as 8 years old are very good at saying who is the 'best in their class' at certain tasks, even when the teacher does not overtly reveal their own assessments. Crocker and Cheeseman (1991) reported on the ability of children aged 5 to 7 years to rank themselves.

It would appear that the youngest children in our schools acquire a knowledge of those academic criteria that teachers use to evaluate the pupils in their classroom. In this study there was a high degree of agreement between self, peers and teachers as to the rank order of children in any particular classroom.

(Crocker and Cheeseman, 1991: 161)

What are the implications of such a statement? Possibly this depends on the way that the children react to the knowledge. If we take the case of a child who discovers that he or she is not as good as the other children in the class at most academic subjects, this could lead to the child having low self-esteem, and this in turn could lead to the child not doing well in class. The fact that teachers' expectations of children can affect their performance is well known; this was referred to by Rosenthal and Jacobson (1968) as self-fulfilling prophecy.

The increase in public assessment, especially of young children, raises important questions. The results could challenge educators' assumptions or they could narrow their views of children's capabilities. Will this affect expectation and will children live up, or down, to this expectation? What happens when children find out that they have not achieved the required level according to National Assessment targets? Will this affect their self-image and affect future performance?

In order for assessment to be effective, it must inform educators about their future teaching, especially in terms of what action they can take to assist individual pupils to gain the maximum from education. Crooks (1988) addressed the motivational aspects relating to classroom evaluation.

Research has repeatedly demonstrated that the responses of individual students to educational experiences and tasks are complex functions of their abilities and personalities, their past educational experiences, their current attitudes, self perception and motivational states.

(Crooks, 1988: 460)

He maintained that intrinsic motivation is important in bringing about independent learners. The condition necessary for this motivation is when teaching and learning are individualized, and children are given a carefully sequenced series of achievable goals and when competitiveness is minimized. In these circumstances, success and failure are more likely to be attributed to effort rather than ability, and intrinsic motivation is more likely to result.

The different total numbers of children that the health and education systems deal with, and the different aims and objectives, result in quite different priorities and concerns. The individualized nature of the work that health workers do with children has a significant impact on the strategies that are used and the issues that arise. The early historical rationale of international competitiveness as a reason for better health and education has remained and strengthened for education, but lessened for health. In spite of many changes to the systems over the years, assessment remains something that is primarily done *to* children and something they have little influence upon.

The family

Robert Banton, Geoff Fenwick and
Angela Hawtin

The family is a concept with which we are all familiar, and yet one that is the subject of much disagreement. Whether we are born into a family and spend our childhood within it, or as adults we set up other types of family, it may be argued that family relationships and family life are a central feature of most of our lives.

A report commissioned by the European Commission demonstrated that 96 per cent of the population identify family living as the single most valued aspect of life across the European Union (Commission of the European Communities, 1993: 60). Indeed work by Scott and Parren (1994: 263) stated that, in the minds of the vast majority of individuals, family and family life are very important and that 'Family events were by far regarded as the most important aspect of people's lives'.

But why are families held to be so important? Ideas about the family are based on some very deeply held beliefs and assumptions. For example, there is the assumption that there really is such a thing as a traditional family, that such families are good things, that children are best brought up within such families and that children who are not may tend towards antisocial behaviour or at least are disadvantaged. Conventional wisdom seems to state that, when families break down, children do suffer in terms of poorer physical, social and psychological well-being, but is this true, and if so, is the cause the fact of living in a disrupted family *per se*, or the socioeconomic factors that such families live within? This chapter will deal with three main issues: 1) definitions of 'family'; 2) the impact of families on children; and 3) the possible affects on children when they do not live within the 'traditional' family.

Defining the family

When asked to describe a family, most people would probably talk in terms of parents, children and perhaps some extended family members such as grandparents. Bernardes (1997: 3) points to the fact that most individuals still see the family as what sociologists call the 'nuclear family'. Such individuals may also talk in terms of not just who is present in the family, but also what responsibilities and roles family members may have. Clear divisions along gender lines may be described, with the male being the breadwinner, and the female having responsibility for care and nurture of the children and, possibly, older relatives.

In order to survive, it is argued, societies establish institutions that will rear and educate the young. In the majority of societies the main institution for this is the family. In fact, the family may be seen, by many, as the basic unit of society. The family may provide the young with a legitimacy and a status within society, as well as serving as a link between the individual members and the wider society. Human infants require a prolonged time of nurture before they reach independence, and families assume the responsibility for this rearing. Although the structure of the family may change, the overall purpose may be seen to provide for the future and stability of its culture through the rearing and education of the young.

Therefore, sexuality may also be strictly defined in relation to the nuclear family. Young adulthood is often categorized as a period of freedom and choice before 'settling down' to family life. Adults who have reached a certain age and are not yet married or in a stable, functional relationship are often pitied as inadequate, even condemned as deviant. Adults who in other ways fail to conform to the norm also face social and economic sanctions. If we take as an example people who are homosexual, we find that not only does the legal framework prevent them from having the same sexual freedoms as heterosexuals, but it also largely prevents the homosexual couple from becoming parents. Homosexual partners do not enjoy the same legal protection as regards property and other rights as their married or cohabiting heterosexual counterparts. Following on from this, and perhaps fuelled by it, we find that non-heterosexual couples also suffer from social castigation by large sections of society. They are often ridiculed, abused and isolated from mainstream society.

Muncie (1995: 10) argues that the idea of the nuclear family is very powerful and has a remarkable potency such that all other forms of family types are defined with reference to it. Why do so many individuals identify so strongly with this image of the family?

It can be argued that many individuals accept these traditional notions of the family because they are often reinforced by influential institutions within society, such as the media, the church and government. In addition, there appear to be scientific arguments that seem to assert the biological naturalness of the family; children are born to adults and the adults need to care for and nurture the child. The human animal, especially the male, is responsible for ensuring the continuation of his genetic heritage and this can best be done by ensuring his mate is faithful to him, and that there is no competition from the children of other males. The family can thus be seen by some as being biologically necessary and 'natural'. Many writers, like Murdock, also point to what might be seen as the universal fact of nuclear families, that is, nuclear family units featuring in many other societies and cultures.

The nuclear family is a universal social grouping. Either as the sole prevailing form of the family or as the basic unit from which more complex familial forms are compounded, it exits as a distinct and strongly functional group in every known society.

(Murdock, 1965: 2)

However, are these assumptions and ideas really safe and uncontested? Or are there other ways of defining both what the family may be and what function it may serve to the individuals within it and to the wider society?

Family forms exist in a variety of ways, and the word family may have many meanings, depending on culture, race and historical development. The focus of this chapter is mainly on a Western interpretation of family. Although we chose not to investigate the cultural significance of family in detail, the following vignette based on the experience of one of the authors serves as a reminder that the historical and cultural development of societies effects how the concept and practicalities of families and their activities are realized.

These observations are based on a period of employment in East Africa and subsequent visits there. At the time I was influenced by the work of Colin Turnbull (1974), an anthropologist, and Laurens van der Post, a traveller, writer and philosopher.

Van der Post's (1962) description of the Bushmen of the Kalahari emphasized life in an extremely harsh environment where rain is rare, sometimes not falling for over a year. Family groups, inevitably small, consisted of three generations; four in such a climate would have been unthinkable. Co-operation was absolutely vital to survival. There could be no passengers in the Kalahari desert. Life depended upon combining skills and knowledge which enabled the detection of animals, plants and water. Waste was intolerable. Van der Post recalled how one of his colleagues was reprimanded by a Bushwoman when he accidentally spilled a few drops of water.

Turnbull's study described a somewhat kinder environment, the Itari forest in what is now the Democratic Republic of the Congo. Life there for the Bambuti people was by no means as difficult as that in the Kalahari but, nevertheless, demanded close co-operation in small family groups. Hunting in the forest, in particular, was a combined effort.

Many of the Africans that I saw were making a living from the land. To many of them, cities, towns and even villages did not figure greatly in their lives. I became aware that there were a number of family and community groupings and some of the people pursued one of the most ancient occupations, that of hunter-gatherer.

Hunter-gatherers are now few in number, a situation which does not apply to pastoralists, most of whom are semi-nomadic. Although the extended family remains vital, pastoral groups tend to be larger in number. I found that access to education for such groups was an issue, particularly if not seen as directly relevant to their immediate concerns. Lawrence's story illustrates this.

Lawrence belonged to the Karamojong tribe, a pastoral group living in the arid country of northern Uganda. He was unique, being the first of his tribe ever to qualify for secondary education. To take advantage of his scholarship he had to travel several hundred miles south to the capital city and the most prestigious secondary school in the country.

Each vacation Lawrence returned to Karamoja. During one of them he was to receive a visit from two of his teachers who had informed him of the date on which they would be arriving in the district. It was late afternoon and the herdsmen of the community had already started to drive their cattle into the enclosure which was surrounded by a thick thorn fence to keep wild animals out. Everywhere there was dust and noise and stench. In the intense heat, clothing was restricted to short black cloaks and beads. In the midst of all the noise and activity there was one immobile figure. It was Lawrence. He was in his school uniform patiently awaiting his teachers' arrival. Few contrasts could be greater. Here was a boy of two environments. At school he learned Latin, Science and Mathematics. He played tennis and studied Shakespeare. At home in the bush he guarded the cows and tended them.

In order to examine the contemporary patterns of the Western family, two very different sociological perspectives will be used, firstly that of functionalism which presents us with what may be termed a traditional picture of both the family and family life.

Sociological perspectives

FUNCTIONALISM

Functionalism was the dominant school of thought in sociology in the UK and America during the 1940s and 1950s. Prominent theorists included Talcott Parsons and Ronald Fletcher, amongst others. The functionalists saw society in terms of a whole, explaining that it was made up of various interrelated parts which, when taken together, form a complete system; to understand any part of society it must be viewed in relation to society as a whole.

According to the functionalist perspective, if society is to survive, there are certain basic needs which must be met in order for it to remain stable. The smaller constituent systems of society all serve a unique purpose, but are interdependent, and in combination these interrelated sub-systems interact to maintain the order and well-being of society as a whole. This co-operation is supported by a consensual value system based on general agreement about what is to be valued, esteemed and respected. Inequalities in society are acceptable. Functionalists argue that social stratification – a particular form of inequality which is based on an accepted hierarchy of groups – serves the purpose of maintaining social order by ensuring that there is an effective means of allocating social roles and ensuring that society as a whole performs well. Another means of ensuring the maintenance of this social order – which the functionalists regard as crucial to the survival of society – is through the social institutions of a particular society, for example schools, churches, the judiciary, hospitals, and so on. Each of these institutions has evolved with a unique, essential and well defined function to perform.

Parsons (1951) described 'the family' as having 'basic and irreducible' functions which included:

- the rearing and socializing of children in order that they in turn will become productive adults and contribute to the smooth running of society;
- to provide physical and emotional support to the male workforce, thereby ensuring that the material needs of society are met; and
- the stabilizing of adult personalities of the population in order to prevent threat and disruption to the integrity of society as a whole.

Clearly there is an assumption that the main responsibility for ensuring that these societal needs are met should fall at the feet of women – whilst men are expected to fulfil a productive role outside of the family – the home is the work place of women who have the responsibility of nurturing the present and future productive members of society.

The nuclear family emerged from a functionalist perspective. Fletcher (1979) described the modern or nuclear family as:

- founded at a relatively early age of husband and wife and with increasing longevity, therefore of long duration;
- consciously planned to limit the number of children;
- small in size – typically husband, wife and two children;
- separately housed, which satisfies a desire for independence and privacy;
- economically self-responsible, self-providing and therefore relatively independent of wider kin; living at a distance from them, frequently geographically, but also in terms of a diminished degree of intimately shared social life;
- founded and maintained on a completely voluntary basis by partners of equal status; entailing therefore a marital relationship based on mutuality and consideration and sharing of tastes, seeking to be a marriage of true friends;
- democratically managed in that husband and wife (and frequently children) discuss family affairs together during the taking of decisions;
- so centrally concerned with the upbringing of children as to be frequently called 'child-centred'; and
- widely recognized by government and the whole range of social services as being crucially important for the life of individuals and society alike, and helped in its efforts to achieve health, security and stability by a wide ranging network of public provisions.

This picture of family life does seem a little cosy and even rather idealistic given the realities referred to later in this section. However, according to Shorter (1977: 10):

> The nuclear family was a nest. Warm and sheltering, it kept the children secure from the pressure of the outside world and gave the men an evening refuge from the icy blast of competition . . . women liked it too, because it let them pull back from the grinding expectations of work and devote themselves to childcare. So everyone huddled together happily within those secure walls, serene about the dinner table, united in the Sunday outing.

Such a romantic and idealized view of the family is one which is often perceived as the norm in British life, perpetuated by pervasive media images and political ideologies. From such a perspective, the isolated nuclear family is well-suited to the needs of a modern industrial society. It is typically isolated, not being directly part of a wider kinship and therefore mobile and adaptable, thus suiting the needs of the labour market and the specialist functional units of society which have arisen as a result of industrialization.

The feature of social isolation in the modern family is regarded as far from detrimental – instead it strengthens the bonds between marriage partners, and consequently their dependence upon each other serves to help stabilize adult personalities as well as provide an appropriate environment within which children can be nurtured and developed into the kind of adults needed by a stable society. Thus, the family has often come to be seen as a 'haven' for its individual members whilst at the same time fulfilling the requirements of society as a whole.

Some functionalists, including politicians from both the Right and Left, have expressed concern at the 'decline of the family' during the last part of the twentieth century. This is a theme to which we will return later in this chapter. This decline has been seen to threaten the fabric and structure of society. The increase in lone-parent families, the decline of marriage and the increase of divorce, working mothers and the emergence of 'latch key kids', it has been argued, lead to the weakening of parental authority. This situation was exacerbated by the increase in state intervention in health and education. Together these factors had the potential to undermine the socialization of the next generation (Muncie, 1995).

Functionalists such as Shorter (1977) have argued that the family is not, in fact, in decline, and that modern families in industrialized societies have allowed individuals freedom from unceasing work, lack of recreational facilities and poor housing. Thus the modern family has provided the freedom to enable natural emotions and fulfilling relationships to flourish. The nuclear family has provided a kind of 'haven' which acted as a secure emotional base from which relationships can develop so that satisfaction and harmony within the family may translate to the wider institutions of society.

Muncie (1995) points out that parallels have been drawn between these explanations of family functions and the political discourse of the New Right which argues that the properly functioning family instils in children the correct moral values and provides core values which act as the basis for a moral society and that breakdown of the family leads to breakdown in society. Abbott and Wallace (1990) point out that this model of family life is by no means inevitable in reality and that at any one time only 1 in 20 households in Britain consists of the modern nuclear family. This brings us to the point of asking is this traditional picture of the family relevant today, or is the experience of family life becoming much more diverse? Even if the traditional functionalist view represented the dominant form of the contemporary family, would that make it the natural, best or only perspective? Feminist writers have produced a powerful critique of the functionalist perspective on the family and it is to this we now turn.

FEMINISM

Many sociologists work from the assumption that human behaviour is largely directed and determined by culture. Norms, values and roles are culturally determined and socially transmitted. Feminists argue that although women are clearly biologically different from men, gender roles are more a product of culture than of biology and are by no means universal across cultures. Labour has traditionally often been divided in terms of sex and this has frequently been justified as right, normal and proper. Inequalities in power relationships in favour of men have been socially constructed.

Women traditionally have been expected to produce children, take on roles of mother and wife, cook, mend, sew, wash; yet this type of work often goes unrecognized and undervalued. Many women find themselves taking care of men yet subordinate to male authority, both within and outside of the home. Often women find themselves excluded from high-status occupations and positions of power. Radical feminists argue that this is because we live in a patriarchal society – one which has been male dominated since long before modern capitalist society developed. Thus both a cultural subordination of women by men and an economic dependence of women upon men have led to the perpetuation of gender inequalities in our society.

This means that it has been easy for men to dominate and exploit women – these unequal power relationships are built into our society and are often assumed to be natural or inevitable and therefore are accepted and taken for granted. This includes a sexual power relationship. Domestic roles are often regarded as 'natural' so that women who do not take on these roles may be stigmatized or obstructed. Many of the assumptions upon which these inequalities are based are embodied in the 'cereal packet' family: one which is characterized by a husband at the head of the household and children cared for by a smiling wife – an idealized, value-laden image of the family which constantly bombards us through the media. This image of the 'ideal' family has often, despite its limited realism, been exploited by all of the main political parties at different times. Other family forms have been attributed as the causes of social problems such as youth crime. Women have often been implicated in such negative and stereotypical views. Feminists would argue that such misplaced assumptions undermine the potential independence of women.

Another important recent assumption regarding the nature of the family is the idea that the family is becoming progressively more democratic and 'symmetrical'. It is often argued that the roles of husbands and wives are becoming much more similar, with both partners frequently taking equal responsibility for decision making, work inside and outside the home and sharing equally in the family's resources. Feminists argue against this supposition, pointing out that the family continues to be a site of inequality where women are subordinated and the negative aspects of women's roles are perpetuated.

Abbott and Wallace (1990) suggested that, according to feminist perspectives on the family, there are two interlocking structures of subordination of women in the family: first, women's position as wives and mothers, and, secondly, socialization processes in the family during which children internalize male and female attitudes and transmit them to their own children, thus perpetuating male domination and female subordination.

Thorne (1982) provided four themes which are central to the feminist challenge to the conventional sociology of the family:

1. The assumptions concerning the structure and functioning of the family. Feminists challenge an ideology that sees the co-resident nuclear family with a division of labour along gender lines as the only natural and legitimate form of the family. Feminists argue against the view that any specific family form is natural, that is, based on biological imperatives. Rather, they would claim that forms of family organization and ideology are based on social organizations and assumptions about peoples' roles held by the individuals of a given society. For example, there is no inherent reason why men cannot do housework; it is just that people in our society believe that it is not the right thing for them to do and hence they are incapable of it.
2. Feminists have sought to claim the family as an area for analysis; this challenges the gender-based categories of analysis in mainstream sociology.
3. Feminists argue that different members of families experience family life in different ways. They argue that women's experiences of motherhood and family life have demonstrated that families embody power relationships that can and do result in conflict, violence and the inequitable distribution of work and resources.
4. Feminists question the assumption that the family should be a private sphere. While women and children are often cut off from outside contact in the modern nuclear family, this is partly an illusion at the level of public policy. The form that the family takes is heavily influenced by economic and social policies and the family is permeable to outside intervention.

Abbott and Wallace (1990) point out that it is often argued that common-sense beliefs about the nature of the family deny women the opportunity to participate in the wider society and gain equality with men in areas such as the labour market, political life, cultural and social life.

Not all feminists view the family in entirely negative terms, and there are many feminist authors who share different views within the tradition, yet most would recognize a struggle to combine love and commitment, caring and freedom in ways which might prove less oppressive to women than they have in the past. Writers such as Oakley (1974) and Elliot (1986) challenge the view that the industrialized family has always provided an emotional haven and source of growth and fulfilment. The family has been seen as a source of oppression by regulating women's labour through the role of housewife; giving men more power and control over women's sexuality and fertility; and by reproducing and reinforcing inequality through different and sepa-rate gender roles. Women's work within the home has been unrecognized, of low status and unpaid as well as isolating and monotonous; thus women have often been more alienated than male industrial workers. Where they have worked outside the home, they have usually been in part-time, insecure jobs which they have had to juggle alongside the demands of the family.

The family is regarded as a means of reproducing and supporting an ideology which places women in the private and men in the public domain. Inequality and dependence are perpetuated through the idea that men should be breadwinners and women domestic and maternal. Women coerced into a dependent role have also been historically regarded as the property of their husbands. Feminists argue that families are key agents in women's oppression as they actively deny women the same opportunities as men.

The pattern of family life today

Ferri and Smith (1996: 8) argued that family life in the 1990s is characterized by change, diversity and uncertainty. Families have got smaller and the average number of children per woman has declined to 1.8. Mothers are getting older and the average age at childbirth has gone up to 28 in England and Wales (Woodroff, 1993).

It also seems that as many people will be living alone as sharing a home within marriage by the year 2016. The trend for solitary living stems partly from a wish for independence by young people, who stay single longer after leaving home and setting up on their own. This is reinforced by increases in the number of elderly widows living alone and boosted by increasing levels of divorce, leading couples to seek two homes in place of one, as well as the growth of single-parent families. The result is that the proportion of one-person homes, only 18 per cent of total households in 1971, is now 29 per cent, and will be up to 36 per cent by 2016. At the same time, married couple households, 71 per cent 25 years ago and already down to half of all homes, are set to drop to just 42 per cent. The average size of households has almost halved since the beginning of the century. It currently stands at 2.4 people per household and is set to fall further. As a result, the number of homes is forecast to rise from the present total of 20 million to 23.5 million by 2020.

Looking even further ahead, the number of retired people will increase by 50 per cent by 2034, but the number of children will fall by 15 per cent. Life expectancy rose to 73.7 years for men and 79.2 years for women in 1992 – an increase of more than 3 years – but statistics show no comparable increase in recent years in the length of healthy life. Statistics for 'healthy life expectancy' – the average age at which illness and disability start to affect life – show that men can expect to live healthily until the age of nearly 60 and women to nearly 62. This suggests that the extra years of life gained by elderly people are likely to be spent with an illness or disability rather than in enjoyment of a healthy retirement.

The popularity of living in rural areas at the expense of inner city and industrial areas was due partly to what has been called the 'Laura Ashley' factor; a desire for chintzy, rustic cottage styles and decor. A total of 10.4 million people now live in rural areas, a fifth of the population, compared with less than 9 million in 1971. Despite the move to the countryside, people are walking less. Average distances walked per person fell by a fifth over 20 years, to 321 kilometres a year in 1995.

The divorce rate has increased markedly. Divorce is now dropping slightly, although it is still at high levels, with more people divorced each year in Britain than in any other country in Europe except Belgium. Contrary to expectations, it is the youngest married couples who experience the highest rate of divorce. The number of marriages within the UK in 1971 totalled 208 000, two-fifths fewer than in 1971. Between 1971 and 1996 divorce rates for couples under 25 more than quadrupled, and the divorce rate was highest for those in the group aged 25–9 years. Marriage itself continues to decline in popularity, with only 192 000 first marriages in 1995, down 16 000 on the previous year and for the first time in decades the number has dropped below 200 000. By comparison, the number was just under 400 000 in 1970. There has been a large rise in the proportion of children whose parents are living together but are not married. The proportion of single women cohabiting increased from 9 per cent in 1981 to 27 per cent in 1996–7, while the rise in divorced women cohabiting has been small in comparison – from 20 per cent to 32 per cent over the same period.

Today, more than one in three babies are born outside marriage, more than four times the proportion in 1971. Four-fifths of these births are registered by two parents, three-quarters of them giving the same address, implying that most are brought up by parents who prefer to live together without marrying. The number of babies born outside marriage rose from 5 per cent of all births in the early 1960s to 33 per cent in 1995. The latest increase followed the first year for more than 30 years, 1994, when there was no rise. Therefore it might seem that it is not the arrangement of two adults bringing up children which is in such a decline, but rather the institution of marriage that many adults do no feel able to commit themselves to.

There has been a large rise in the proportion of children being brought up in a family headed by a lone parent. More babies are being born to unmarried mothers. The number of families headed by a single parent has fallen after more than 30 years of steady increases, according to government statistics. The drop coincides with a slight fall in the number of divorces, suggesting that more couples with children may be staying together. However, the figures provide little comfort for supporters of the traditional family because cohabitation continues to increase and fewer marriages take place now than at any time since the Second World War.

The Office for National Statistics in the 28th annual issue of Social Trends (Department of Health, 1997) shows that lone-parent families have fallen to 21 per cent of all families compared with 23 per cent the previous year. It is the first fall in a picture which has risen every year since the 1960s and which has seen the proportion of lone-parent families triple since 1971. The consequence is that about 2 million children live with about 1.3 million lone parents, although the composition of these families is constantly changing. The report estimates that one in seven lone parents finds a new partner each year – suggesting that the average time spent alone is about 4 years.

Many children in lone-parent families lose contact with their absent parent. Lone parents report that after two years of lone parenthood about 40 per cent of absent parents are out of contact with their children. A significant number of children now live in stepfamilies. The General Household Survey of 1991 (Office of Population Censuses and Surveys, 1994) reported that 8 per cent of families with dependent children contain one or more stepchildren.

So we can see that the model of the traditional family seems to be failing in terms of the number of families that can be said to be traditional or nuclear. Has the traditional family really broken down? How many families still hold to the nuclear family pattern? Is the nuclear family really becoming a thing of the past? Some writers have suggested that in fact the nuclear family may never have existed as the dominant form of family in our society. Bernardes (1997: 9) cites a number of studies that show this (*see* Table 4.1).

Bernardes states that many authors would rather acknowledge that the nuclear family is in decline than the fact that it never really existed. Peter Laslett's argument that there is in fact no single British family (Laslett, 1982: 12) seems to hold water. Families may exist in one of many ways.

Evidence from the 1991 UK Census published in 1994 showed that there were 21 879 322 households in the UK. Some 1 503 888 contained one adult male and one adult female with between one and three dependent children where only one of the adults was in employment. This suggests that 14.6 per cent of households contained this particular household form. Again Bernardes states that:

This proportion will include, however, unmarried adults, unrelated adults and children, chronically sick persons (some 8% of all age groups) and all other variations that can be thought of. It seems likely

Table 4.1   Studies on composition of families

Authors	Date	% of conventional families
Bowley and Hogg	1925	5% of families in the northern counties of the UK
R. and R.N. Rapoport	1978	20% of UK households contained single breadwinners
Rimmer and Wicks	1981	15% of households in the UK
Westwood	1984	5% of households in the UK

indeed that the proportion of households matching a stricter definition of the nuclear family will be a small fraction of 1%. Putting the point most simply, even the roughest analysis suggests that the nuclear family is so rare as to render the whole idea of the nuclear family entirely redundant.

(Bernardes, 1997: 10)

It would seem then that the nuclear family is not the dominant form of British family, and perhaps has not been so for a very long time.

Political discourse on the family

Changes to family life have prompted cries that the family is in crisis from both politicians and academics in certain quarters. Because of the concern about the rise of non-traditional families, especially single-parent families, Peter Lilley, the Health Minister in 1995, stated that Britain was experiencing 'widespread collapse of the traditional family', and Tony Blair, leader of the Labour Party, talked of a 'cycle of family disintegration, truancy, drug abuse and crime' (Utting, 1995: 6). Many commentators believed that the family was in a state of crisis: numbers of marriages were falling, divorce was on the increase and there was a large increase of unmarried mothers and parents who ignored marriage and chose to live together. These trends were seen to be undermining the traditional family and causing many of the social problems referred to by Tony Blair. This seems to be a central issue: when policy makers talk of the family, it is nearly always in relation to children, and how they should be cared for, who should teach them the values and morals of our society, who should have responsibility for their welfare. In addition, concerns are raised about the nature of the role of the state in providing help and services for families, especially lone-parent families. Politicians from the New Right and ethical Left argue that when non-traditional family patterns emerge, such families rely on state benefits for survival. This gives rise to families who, instead of being able to stand on their own, need the welfare state, thereby increasing public spending. This also creates a culture of dependency.

The relationship between the family and the state is a complex one. Goldson (1997: 23) states that a relationship is negotiated between parents and the state which provides parents with obligations towards children and a right to exercise authority and control over them. This negotiation is formalized by social policy which is interpreted by the legal system and those whose professional work is with children and families. The nature of this relationship is inherently mobile. The family may be the preferred place to raise children, but the form and practice shift both in time and space.

These shifts are, according to Shamgar-Handleman (1994: 253), always a subject for 'overt, organised and legitimate, or covert and indirect negotiation'. This negotiation may be open public discourse or, as has been suggested, the product of a hidden agenda. Such a case may be reflected by the early years of Margaret Thatcher's first term as prime minister. New Right politicians in the early 1980s were appalled by the 'permissiveness' of the 1960s and 1970s and this, coupled with the belief that the welfare state had become too big, invasive and expensive, meant that many felt that action was needed to safeguard the family. This was, in part, to be achieved by rolling back the frontiers of the welfare state. Political debate centred around the themes of failing morality and a general decline in traditional family values. The rise of feminism, children's rights, liberal welfarism and policies aimed at making divorce quicker and easier were all blamed for this moral decline. In order to address these issues, Vicki Coppock (1997: 64) argued that clandestine activity by the Family Policy Group resulted in the publication of a series of radical proposals for strengthening the family via policy reforms.

Policy makers felt happy to talk about the family, its structure, purpose and role in child rearing. John Redwood, former Conservative Party cabinet minister and later challenger for the party leadership, stated that:

> It is still the case that two parents bringing up children in a loving, married relationship is the best ideal to aim for . . . it may not always be possible, but tax, benefits and welfare policy should help to reinforce the traditional family not undermine it.
>
> (Fletcher and Johnson, 1996: online)

The successor to Margaret Thatcher, John Major, promised that he would ensure that the welfare benefit system did not discriminate against traditional families in favour of non-married couples and single parents.

Politicians from all sides of the political divide feel able to talk freely about the family. Prior to and since the general election of May 1997, New Labour have talked of the value of family life. Tony Blair, in a speech launching part of his manifesto in October 1996, stated that a central theme of his party's policy would be to 'strengthen family and community life' and to act against what he saw as 'a tide of lawlessness and the undermining of family life . . . Parents have a responsibility to know where their children are and what they are doing'. His comments clearly state that parents are responsible for their children, and that 'the family is an important moral unity in which children learn the difference between right and wrong, good manners and respect'.

Jack Straw, as Home Secretary in a speech to the Parliamentary Family and Child protection Group (Travis, 1998), observed that strengthening the institution of marriage as a basis for bringing up children was the cornerstone of Labour's modern family policy, although he did go on to say that 'couples who choose not to marry do provide a loving and stable environment for their children'. However, he also emphasized that there was a presumption that the stability needed was most readily provided by two participating parents, 'whilst not stigmatising other family groupings'.

Again the strength of the government's commitment to the traditional notion of the family can be found in the £2 million given to fund a National Family and Parenting Institute which will provide support for the growing movement of local parenting groups which advise on bringing up children and run support schemes aimed at preventing the breakdown of relationships. The tone may be a little more liberal, but the message is the same: families are vital to a stable and just society, and, if families need help to fulfil their obligations, it is up to the state to provide the means for this. Again it is interesting to note that much policy is aimed at keeping families together and providing a mixture of financial incentives and child care services that will help with child care.

The 'Child Care Challenge' recognizes three key problems: firstly that quality of childcare can be variable, standards vary considerably and many child care workers lack formal qualifications. This is to be addressed by better integration of early education and childcare, with the development of 25 new 'early excellence centres' up and down the country and a more consistent regulatory system with new standards for childcare and early education. There will be new training and qualification frameworks for childcare workers as well as more opportunities to train as childcare workers, including up to 50 000 places through the 'New Deal' scheme. Secondly, the cost of care is high and is out of the reach of many parents. A family on average earnings with two children could pay as much as a third of their income on childcare. In response to this, a new childcare tax credit and 'Working Families Tax Credit' will replace Family Credit in 1999. This may mean up to £70 per week for one child and £105 per week for two children to help with the cost of childcare. Lastly, in some areas, there are not enough places for children, and parents' access to them is hampered by poor information. Three hundred million pounds is going to be made available for increasing childcare places, of which £170 million will come from the National Lottery. Plans were introduced to secure a place for every 4 year old in an educational nursery. The above, as an example, shows that although the presentation is different, and some of the exact measures are very different from plans by the previous government, the underling philosophy is very much the same.

We can see, then, that the notion of the traditional family is very strongly held by policy makers, lay people and often by professionals who work with children and their families. However, how valid are such notions? As already mentioned, many individuals, when asked to describe a family, will talk in terms of the nuclear or extended family structure. But as is illustrated, the family has changed and is continuing to change. This change is so pronounced that new labels are needed to describe the structures within which people are living. Labels such as single-parent family, reconstituted family, and bi-nuclear family are used to try to describe the diversity of contemporary living arrangements.

To conclude the chapter, we now turn to the question of just what happens when families do break down, and some of the implications for children raised in non-traditional family structures.

What happens when family breakdown occurs?

These days, one in four British children will experience the break-up of their parents' marriage before they are 16 years old. For many, it will be the most traumatic event of their lives. The legal system has a significant impact on families and children when the family separates. Although the upward trend in the divorce rate may have levelled out, this is perhaps because more people are choosing to live together rather than marry. Statistically, such parents are more likely to split up than husbands and wives. A quarter of all children born today are to cohabiting couples, so it is likely that even more young people will at some point have to deal with the break-up of their families. When such family breakdowns occur, the legal system is usually part of the process. There are a number of areas where the law unsatisfactorily deals with people involved in family breakdown.

Single parents are often treated more harshly in order to ensure that they do not become a burden on the tax payer or the state. An example of this can be found in the implementation of the Child Support Act 1991 which states that a single parent who is claiming state benefits must by law co-operate with the Child Support Agency (CSA) to help trace the absent parent and recover money from him or her, ostensibly for the benefit of the child. Whether this approach does in fact benefit the child appears to be of little concern to the CSA as long as the single parent stops claiming state benefits. Violent and abusive partners can be helped through the work of the CSA to contact mothers and children who have attempted to make a break from them. It should be noted that only single parents who are claiming state benefits are compelled to co-operate in this manner; single parents who do not rely on state benefits have the option of whether to involve the CSA or not with the collection of child maintenance. This highlights the more informal ways in which single parents are viewed as 'abnormal' and of less social value than the traditional family. There is a view that single parents are 'scroungers' from the state, that their children are more likely to fare badly at school and eventually turn into juvenile delinquents. Single mothers are often depicted as those who decide to become pregnant and start a family in order to get state benefits or state housing. The media are fond of portraying single parents in this way and cases can always be found on which the condemnation of all single parents is based.

There is a corresponding popular assumption that all married or even cohabiting couples engage in meticulous family planning, that two parents are always better than one, and that the existence of a permanent relationship is fulfilling for all concerned. This view is reflected in approaches to divorce law in this country. The Family Law Act of 1996 has been widely condemned as making divorce 'too easy'. This, together with the outcry from some quarters at the removal of a 'fault' basis in the divorce process, demonstrates the view that there should be some 'sanction' against those who wish to break up a family, that one partner should be shown to have committed some fault against the other before the marriage is allowed to be dissolved, and the process and procedures involved with obtaining a divorce should not be made too easy so as to dissuade people from following this route. In fact, the changes made to the law on divorce do not make the process any 'easier' and we suggest that the removal of emphasis from 'fault' should ensure that any divorce process is less adversarial and therefore less traumatic for all concerned, including any children.

Many experts argue that when parents divorce, the children may well suffer. One such study by Crockett and Tripp (1994) examined the behaviour of children who were living in reordered families, that is, their parents were separated or divorced and some had remarried and taken on a stepfamily. The authors found that the children from reordered families were more likely to have health problems, need extra help at school, experience friendship difficulties and to suffer from low self-esteem. Those who had experienced multiple changes were worse off than those with a one-parent or stepfamily. Children living in households where there was marital discord did less well than children in the control group, but better than children in the reordered families. It seems from this research that marital breakdown causes more problems for children than discord alone, and that the more disruption a child suffers, the worse the adjustment.

Much has been written about the negative effects of divorce on children in the family. However, it is worth considering whether it is the *outcome* of divorce or the *process* of divorce which is more unsettling. The value attached to traditional marriage and family groupings by the state and society, and the stigma and sanctions which operate against those who do not conform, indicate that the family is a highly prized institution which should be fought for at all costs. Why might this be so? Some argue that the social function served by the family is mainly one of control, where everyone, including the children, has his or her allotted place and role. The family grouping allows gender and age-related roles to be perpetuated through generations by the actions of family members themselves, as well as by society as a whole.

If we consider the development of roles within a family, it is possible to suggest that women are generally more economically independent, that men generally have a more active role in child care and that children generally enjoy more freedom and right of expression than was the case, say, 50 years ago. However, gender and age-related roles within the family unit to a large extent remain and are perpetuated through law, social policy and societal attitude. Examination of the legal framework shows that the law is careful to avoid anything which may appear to be discriminatory or biased in favour of one gender. The Sex Discrimination Act 1975, the Equal Treatment Directives, the Matrimonial Causes Act 1973, the Family Law Act 1996, the Children Act 1989 and the Child Support Act 1991 are worded in such a way as to imply that each partner in a marriage or cohabiting relationship is equal as regards the right to work, the right to have main responsibility for the rearing of any children, the duty to maintain any children, and so on. However, closer inspection reveals some inherent beliefs in gender roles within the family. For example, the Children Act 1989 describes 'parental responsibility' as lying automatically with the mother but only with the father where the parties are married at the time the child was born. Case law on Residence Orders under the Children Act reveals a bias in favour of mothers, although Contact Orders are almost universally granted to the father.

Alternatives to family care are seen as a 'last resort'. The provisions in the Children Act 1989 (S31) in relation to Care Proceedings are strict. The children themselves cannot apply to be taken into the care of the local authority, and the processes by which this occurs almost imply that once a decision has been made that a child can no longer live with his or her family then a 'societal failure' has occurred. The local authority, in applying for a Care Order, must submit a Care Plan to the court and it is on the basis of this Care Plan and other factors that a decision on the child's future will be made. However, once the Care Order is made there is no mechanism for the courts to police the implementation of the Care Plan, and therefore no guarantee of the standard of care the child will receive once in care.

What is the impact on children when family life changes? In general, it has been felt that family breakdown is a traumatic and potentially harmful time for the child. The child may be party to the preceding period of parental arguments, and, in some cases, violence. When parents do split up, the child will have to come to terms with limited, little, or even no access to one parent, often the father. As highlighted earlier, within 2 years, as many as 40 per cent of these children will have no contact with the absent parent. At some stage, it seems likely that they will have to adjust to a new family member, a step-parent.

Parents may be able to reduce children's post-divorce distress through simple actions: the need to present a united front and give the children proper explanations, tell them when and where they will see the other parent again, and never expect the children to act as go-betweens. The temptation may be to keep the knowledge of the break-up from the child, but parents need to understand the likely effects of the way they handle the divorce process so that conflict can be avoided for the children's sake. It is possible that the new Family Law Bill, with its emphasis on promoting mediation rather than allocating blame, could help.

The importance of such efforts cannot be overestimated. Dr Mavis Hetherington of the University of Virginia maintains that for 2 years after a marriage break-up, all children are disturbed. After that, 70 per cent emerge largely unscathed. But the other 30 per cent suffer complex and long-term effects. These include disruptive behaviour, low self-esteem, lower levels of educational attainment and poorer economic performance in later life. If the split happened during adolescence, they are also more likely to drop out of school, become unemployed, become sexually active at a younger age, have children out of wedlock and use drugs.

Why some children come through relatively easily while others 'go off the rails' defies simple explanations. Adolescent boys with divorced parents, for instance, tend to do better if there is a stepfather in the house, but girls are more likely to flourish if their mothers do not remarry. Young children often feel guilty about their parents' divorce, but teenagers can also react badly, feeling their adolescence has been hijacked. Some of the worst off are the children whose parents' new relationships break down, as they often lose touch with their extended family.

Socioeconomic factors as well as personal characteristics can affect the family formation as well as family breakdown. Haskey (1994) described stress associated with low income and debt, unemployment and poor health as factors which may lead to family breakdown. A relationship can also be demonstrated between higher rates of breakdown among women who were young at the time of marriage, and among those who have had a relatively long period of employment prior to the birth of the first child. The most significant risk factor associated with having a baby outside marriage or cohabitation seems to be lower educational attainment; however, unemployment and higher welfare benefits were also found to be significant factors.

Lone parenthood following separation is commonly accompanied by a reduction in income for the lone parent and the children, and poverty is associated with poor outcomes for children. A crucial question in the interpretation of the research results and the consideration of policy responses is how far adverse outcomes for children of lone parents are due to lone parenthood (or the separation of parents) as such, and how far they are caused by the poverty in which many lone parents live.

Ferri's work (1993) offers a glimpse of this issue. Ferri analysed the data for children aged 11 years old from the National Child Development Study and allowed for the current income level of the children's families by taking the receipt of free school meals as a proxy, and their current housing conditions, as well as their social class origin. Ferri compared performance in reading and maths, and found that achievement was generally lower in children from disrupted families, but when differences of socioeconomic status were taken into account these differences were reduced or in some cases eliminated. Joshie *et al.* (1998: 2) stated that:

> Differences are not great for age-adjusted reading and maths, though in the expected direction. They are larger for behavioural adjustment (though not significantly different from zero) for reconstituted step families and lone mothers since birth.

So, although children from disrupted families may suffer slightly in ter[ms of] academic achievement and behavioural indicators, can these differences [be] attributed to factors within the family other than it not being a nuclear family? Again Joshie *et al.* (1998) point to the fact that such families are at a disadvantage as far as parental education, housing tenure and parental employment are concerned. Family break-up may bring about poor out-comes through an effect on material circumstances, but there are probably more complex processes at work. It may be argued that it is often better for the children of a couple to divorce rather than to stay in an unhappy marriage.

Much conventional thinking is still dominated by the notion that the best place for children is within the 'normal' family unit. In spite of recent moves towards ascertaining the wishes and feelings of children, UK society still applies pressure on children to conform to its norms and to accept that the nuclear family underpinned by functionalist philosophies is the 'right' one for them. Yet if we consider the historical and continuing changes to family organization, it is not beyond the bounds of possibility to imagine a society where 'family' might positively mean a group of people who live together in order to nurture and protect each other.

hildren at risk

ela Hawtin, Robert Banton
and Dominic Wyse

In Chapter 1, one of the constructions that we referred to was that of the 'welfare child'. We described how society in the early part of the twentieth century had realized that the abuse and neglect of children were a particularly worrying problem. The 'welfare child' resulted from attempts to protect children from abuse and neglect through the Children Act 1908 and the setting up of school medical inspections and health visiting services. In this chapter we take the notion of the welfare child as a starting point and develop a number of related themes. Contemporary society offers many inherent risks for children, but it is the deliberate harm of children that raises some of the strongest emotions. The development of the Children Act 1908 perhaps set a precedent for the pivotal role that the legal system plays in the protection of children from risk. For this reason, and in the light of the recent national and international legislation, we look in some detail at aspects of law. (A legal emphasis is developed and critiqued in Chapter 6 on children's rights.)

Defining 'risk' is a difficult task: it concerns potential or actual harm to children. It is fair to say that all children are at risk at some times in their lives. Some children have greater degrees of risk than others, and significant numbers of children are actually harmed. The risk of harm comes from a wide range of sources: poor health, violence, discrimination, drugs, the environment, homes, abuse, recreation, and so on. This chapter touches on all of these, but we have chosen to focus mainly on risks caused by violence and the abuse of children.

This chapter is divided into two parts. The first part looks at the powerful influence of the law in relation to children at risk. The theoretical strand of this part looks at theories that have suggested causes for violence. These theories are followed by examination of the legal implications of violence, and health and safety risks. The first part of this chapter puts forward the notion that, in many ways, children's protection from risk by the legal system is compromised by the different ways that the law recognizes children and adults. The second part of this chapter is concerned with child abuse and child protection. In modern times, these two issues have become central to many discussions about children. An examination of the child protection system is concluded with an in-depth review of the teacher's role. The reflections on the teacher's role also make reference to the role of other professionals in the child protection process.

Empowerment and the law

Historically, the development of legislation and societal attitudes in relation to children has done little to empower children; rather, it has replaced one set of constraints with another. 'Saving' children from the factory or mine, where at least they had some economic power, led inevitably to children with nothing to do and no means of income. This led to the 'delinquent' child who required a different sort of protection, protection from immorality, irreligion and corruption, as evidenced by the growth of the 'child rescue movement' mobilized by the Society for Investigating the Causes of the Alarming Increase of Juvenile Delinquency in the Metropolis of 1815 (Goldson, 1997: 5). The answers appeared in the guise of formal structures to control children, whether this was the reformatory institutions or industrial schools of the mid-1800s or the compulsory schooling required by the 1870 Education Act.

Legislation alone will not prevent an adult being attacked in the street or in his or her home, though it may be a deterrent. The reason it may be a deterrent is that the perpetrator of the violence or abuse knows that the adult victim has the right to complain to the law and have his or her evidence heard against the perpetrator; however, this will not always be the case. For example, there are complicating factors in certain types of violence, such as domestic violence, which may prevent the victim from even making a complaint. When we consider how society attempts to deal with risks of violence, abuse, death and disease in the adult population, we will find that one of the main ways in which these risks are addressed or minimized is through empowerment of the individual. Unlike children, the adult has the inalienable right to take the protection offered by the legal system or to reject it.

When considering their health, adults have the absolute right to make decisions affecting their treatment and, with minimal exceptions (such as traffic laws, illegal drug use and so on), they also have the right to indulge in behaviour which carries risk to personal safety and well-being, such as smoking, drinking alcohol and other dangerous activities. The reason why society is reluctant to legislate or intervene in these rights is that adults are deemed to know the risks associated with these behaviours and make an informed choice as to whether or not to take these risks. 'They have no one to blame but themselves' is the comment often heard when an adult is injured or suffers harm as a result of risk-taking behaviour.

Within the confines of the criminal law which aims to protect person and property, the adult, regardless of his or her mental capacity, level of actual knowledge or ability, has autonomy of action and the right to self-determination. When we seek to protect *children* from the risks associated with daily living, we do so by a method of exclusion and removal of the right to self-determination. This approach is founded on particular constructions of childhood within society: the rationale for such an approach seems questionable.

The idea that we need to have a 'children's rights movement' can be viewed in some ways in the same context as other anti-discrimination legislation such as the Sex Discrimination Act 1975 and the Race Relations Act 1976. By acknowledging the fact that there was a need for such legislation, society recognized that women (usually) and people from different ethnic and cultural backgrounds would not automatically attain the rights which the rest of the population took for granted. The difference between this type of legislation and, for example, the UN Convention on the Rights of the Child (CRC) is that it seeks to ensure that all *people* get equal rights whereas the CRC tends to highlight the difference between children and adults.

[It] serves to reinforce the adult/child distinction, while at the same time defining children not only as vulnerable, but also as privileged citizens. It is the very inequality and continuation of this inequality between children and adults which gives children, so to speak, a right to rights. Children have rights because they do not have, and cannot be expected to have, *full citizens' rights*. [emphasis in original]

(King, 1997: 170)

The legislation informed by adult values which aims to protect children from risk in our society is founded on a view of children and childhood with which we, as adults, are often comfortable. It is difficult to envisage a world where children are fully empowered rather than protected because to do so would perhaps threaten adult status and adult roles in society, 'the child is the source of the last remaining, irrevocable, unchangeable primary relationship' (Beck, 1992: 118).

The theory is that children need protection from the various risks in our society. These risks include the health risks associated with drugs, tobacco and alcohol; social risks from violence, abuse and exploitation; and risks associated with infringement of basic human rights such as lack of legal capacity. Most, if not all, of these risk factors are associated with the way we organize our society, our (adult) views of what is right and wrong, our view of children and the ease with which the organization of our society allows us to harm children. We seem to be failing to make radical changes to society to address these underlying problems. Instead, we organize society in such a way as to increase the vulnerability and dependency of children and we expose them to more risks by making them dependent for far longer than they need be. Most acts of 'rebellion' in children and young people are quickly quashed 'for the child's own good'. As Scraton stated in relation to children:

Deviation from the charted path leads to condemnation, punishment and even expulsion (from school, from church, from home). Within this context of discipline, regulation and correctionalism, passive or active

resistance by children and young people is always defined as negative, as a challenge to legitimate authority.

(Scraton, 1997: 163)

The 'good of the child' is also the 'good of the adult', whether that is a parent who needs to fulfil a role defined for him or her by society or a professional whose existence relies on the vulnerability and need of children. We cannot, and perhaps do not want to, imagine a world where children do not need protection and tutoring from adults any more than any other member of society. It is suggested that maybe such a world is beyond our imaginings in the same way as space travel, computer technology, contraception, micro-surgery and so on were beyond the imaginings of our ancestors.

The tale of Nema (Stainton Rogers and Stainton Rogers, 1992) is a short science-fiction story that gives us a glimpse of a future society where tech-nology and attitudes have advanced to such an extent that there is no minimum age limit for driving or working; 'clever' cars which can sense hazards mean that children of 3 and 4 years old can drive safely; advances in the technology of teaching and learning mean that, by about 7 years old, most young people can run their lives more or less independently and have a wide network of friends who move about as a gang. Loyalty is to the gang rather than to 'olders', and the gang is the place to experiment with sexual and interpersonal relationships. Most young people choose to have their children in their early teens. Anyone 'competent' has the right to control over their body, including sexual relations. 'Olders' have little to do with the young, and little power over them – one result is that physical and sexual abuse across the ages is virtually unknown. It is interesting to consider whether this story fills the adult reader with intrigue or fear; where are the risks from which children need to be protected? What might this mean for the role of the adult? If this scenario were real, what might happen to marriage, monogamy and stability?

If we move away from science fiction and focus on the present day, we find that the current concerns about the crisis facing childhood are under-pinned by the belief that children who are not controlled and protected by adult society will run amok, harming themselves and others. 'What an incredible irony this represents given the apparently insatiable appetite that much of the adult, patriarchal world has for violence, brutality, war and destruction' (Scraton, 1997).

Causation of violence theories

It could be said that there are three predominant theories of aggression and violence: that man is aggressive by nature; that man possesses an aggressive drive engendered mainly by frustration; and that man is born with the cognitive and morphological potential to act aggressively but whether or not he learns to do so depends on his environment. These theories are to a large extent mirrored in the writings of early social philosophers such as

Hobbes, Locke and Rousseau. Hobbes' writings in the seventeenth century reflected the belief that man was born aggressive because of his impulse to self-preservation (Lefkowitz, 1976) and it was due to this nature that totalitarianism was not only desirable but essential. Locke, on the other hand, believed that man was born essentially good and that the government of man should be concerned with ensuring the good of everyone. As we described in the Chapter 1, the writings of Rousseau put forward the proposition that man is born good and that aggression is environmentally determined.

Instinct theory holds that man is by nature aggressive, that the instincts of anger and violence are present from birth in all of us, ready to erupt at any moment. This belief in innate aggression was a common feature of those in the psychoanalytic school of psychology. An example of this is the belief held by Freud that cruelty and the desire to hurt others are a prominent feature of the human psyche. He attributed this desire to the death instinct, or Thanatos, one of the two fundamental human drives. This drive towards death, which Freud believed begins from the moment of inception, is not limited to the individual, but affects societies and is the main cause of societal conflicts such as war. He believed that it would never be possible to rid man of his aggressive tendencies and that the best we could hope for was to channel them in less destructive ways.

Ethology is the science of animal behaviour and the science of character formation in human behaviour. This school of thought also holds that man is innately aggressive. A proponent of this school, Lorenz (1966) argued that *Homo sapiens* are even more aggressive than other animals because of their tendency to intra-specific (within species) aggression. Lorenz argued that man is basically a harmless omnivore who lacks the physical structure to kill big prey and at the same time lacks the innate safety mechanisms that prevent carnivores from abusing their lethal powers to kill conspecifics (same species). Genetically based, these instincts rapidly programme the animal and serve natural selection, providing the best mate, the best offspring and then the protection of that offspring.

A slightly less radical view from the ethological school is that of Tinbergen (1968). He agreed with Lorenz that most species other than man usually manage to settle disputes without resort to killing or even bloodshed, and that aggression in these species is limited to disputes about territory, mates, food gathering and protection of young. Man is the only mass murderer; whereas violence in other species seems to be about survival, in man it appears to be the opposite. The explanation offered by Tinbergen is that cultural evolution is responsible for man's uninhibited intra-specific aggression and he cites the following factors as directly attributable: population density through overcrowding due to advances in medicine, long-distance communication, the upsetting of the balance between aggression and personal fear and man's ability to make and use long-distance weapons. Tinbergen reinterpreted Lorenz's view that aggression is spontaneous, and suggested that both instinct and external variables produce violence. Both Lorenz and Tinbergen thought that education cannot eliminate these internal aggressive drives and that the best way to address this was by manipulation of external variables. They argued that redirection of the aggressive drive is the only way to save man from destruction and that man has already begun to realize this and unite together in conquests of space, the sea and other forces of nature.

There are many critics of the theory of innate aggression. The concept of instinct applied to man is unhelpful scientifically because it offers limited explanation. Montagu (1976) likened the description of innate aggression to that of original sin and innate depravity. Hinde (1966) criticized Lorenz for the notion of spontaneous aggression and argued that the main determinant for aggression is contextual. Lorenz is also criticized for ignoring the role of learning in the shaping of aggression (Bandura, 1973). Behavioural scientists would argue that man's behaviour is influenced by his experience and even if there are genetically determined responses, these can be modified by manipulating the environment. Ethological theory is also criticized for failing to take into account man's cultural evolution.

There are theories of aggression which focus on the physiological aspects of the organism. Studies of neural factors suggest that areas of the brain principally in control of aggression lie deep in the temporal lobes and sub-cortical structures known as the limbic system. In humans, disturbances in the cerebral cortex disinhibit the sub-cortical structures such as the limbic system from higher control. Damage to the cortex from anoxia may result in abortion and prenatal death, but sub-lethal damage can be shown in such disorders as cerebral palsy and learning and behaviour disorders. Manifestations in children of hyperactivity, temper tantrums and rage behaviour are considered to be a sub-lethal part of this continuum (alcohol, which is believed to suppress the cortical control functions, has also been shown to have a strong link with violence). Head injuries can damage the cortex, as can acute drug intoxication, and these can lead to a wide range of violent behaviours. Lesions such as tumours in the sub-cortical structures of the limbic system can result in violent behaviours. There is also documented evidence that a frequent behavioural result of tumours in the limbic system is an increase in irritability, temper outbursts and even homicidal attacks of rage. Tumours elsewhere in the limbic system have also been shown to cause patients to demonstrate these kinds of symptoms. The behavioural changes that occur could result from an irritative focus of the tumour which activates some of the mechanisms for aggression, or it could result from the destruction of inhibitory mechanisms.

Hormones secreted by the endocrine system can produce an effect on behaviour. Males are generally more aggressive than females and there are data to support the hypothesis that male aggressiveness is associated with male hormones. It has been suggested that four factors support this theory: the cross-cultural universality of sex differences; the fact that male hormones are found as early in life as the behaviour can be observed; the similarity of these differences in man and primates; and the fact that females can be made more aggressive by the administration of male hormones. Of the male hormones, the most important in relationship to aggression is testosterone.

The presence or absence of sex hormones during development of the foetus is of critical importance in the development of the genital tract and the neuro-mechanisms that mediate sexual behaviour. Studies of rhesus monkeys showed that not only sexual behaviour, but also social behaviour, could be influenced by testosterone. Castration has been shown to reduce fighting behaviour in animals, and in the past this has been used to control violent male sex crimes, though anti-androgenic substances have been developed which can have the same effect. It is not only in the male that hormones have been thought to play a part in aggression; in a number of early studies 62 per cent of crimes and 49 per cent of crimes of violence were found to be committed by women during the pre-menstrual period. Low blood sugar has also been linked to an increase in aggressive tendencies and crime.

Social learning theory seeks to find the external rather than internal focus of aggression. Bandura (1973: 92) stated that 'in predicting the occurrence of aggression, one should be concerned with predisposing conditions rather than predisposed individuals'. The social learning model of aggressive behaviour has three main components: the first is concerned with the origins of aggression, specifically how our aggressive behaviour patterns are acquired or developed; the second is concerned with instigators of aggression and how aggressive behaviour is provoked; and the third deals with reinforcers of aggression and attempts to answer the question of how aggressive behaviour is maintained once it is started. Most behaviours are acquired through imitation or observational learning. This learning can be deliberate or unintentional based on the influence of example. In the case of aggression, there are three main sources of observational learning: family, subculture influences and symbolic modelling.

There was certainly early evidence to suggest that violent or aggressive children came from homes where the family either indulged in violence within the home or parents tended to favour aggressive solutions to problems. Subcultural influences include situations where status is gained primarily through fighting or other physically aggressive means. Thus the individuals who are successful by aggression are the role models who are copied. Symbolic modelling occurs largely through mass media. A substantial body of research has supported the idea that children acquire patterns of aggressive behaviour through symbolic modelling, though this must be read in the light of conflicting evidence.

Another way in which aggressive behaviour is acquired is thought to be through direct experience in which certain behaviour is followed by rewarding or punishing contingencies. In relation to maintenance of aggression or reinforcers of aggression, Bandura (1973) described three main categories: external, vicarious and self-reinforcement. External factors can include tangible and non-tangible rewards, release from pain, and social and status rewards. Vicarious factors include, for example, when the aggressive behaviour is observed and 'rewarded' through praise or emulation. In relation to self-reinforcement, we must remember that humans tend to behave in a way that produces self-satisfaction and feelings of self-worth. In some, therefore, aggressive behaviour is a source of personal pride and self-esteem, in others the self-punishment, which can mitigate aggressive behaviour, can be circumvented by blame apportioned to the victim and dehumanizing of the victim.

Some theories of the causes of aggression and violence seem more credible than others. The theory of innate aggression has been seriously undermined and physiological causes of aggression account for only a minority of cases. Social learning theory seems to offer the most logical explanation of why children act in violent and aggressive ways. However, neither the innate aggression theory nor the social learning theory really accounts for the fact that some children can be subject to a violent and abusive upbringing and yet show no signs of violent behaviour themselves, while children who are brought up in 'stable' and loving environments can be capable of extreme violence themselves. Research has suggested that the roots of adult violence can be traced back to disturbances in normal development or a combination of genetics and nurture, but these causes or 'risk factors' are somewhat nebulous at best and at worst lay the blame for child violence at the feet of the parents or adult role models. There is a need to search for reasons why children behave in ways which are in direct contrast to the image of the 'innocent', not least because this type of behaviour often causes as much harm to the child as to their victim.

Children and violence

Children are at risk from violence in the home, the playground, the streets and parks and, in some areas of the world, on the battlefield. It could be argued that children are not alone in being subject to this risk; many adults fear for their safety when walking home alone at night. Society makes a conscious effort to protect children from exposure to and involvement in violence, but what is the thinking behind this and how effective is it? The freedom of very young children to go outside the house without an adult is curtailed, not by legislation but by societal views and adult beliefs (usually well founded) that the world can be a very dangerous place. Not all parents conform to this view of course, and on many streets it is possible to find children as young as 2 or 3 years old alone or in the 'care' of other young children. However, much of the violence to which children are exposed occurs not in the streets or parks but in their own home, either through witnessing domestic violence or through watching dramatized violence on television or video. How may they be protected from such violence?

Domestic violence legislation prior to the 1996 Family Law Act permitted the court to exclude a partner from the matrimonial home only if he or she had committed violence against the other partner or relevant child and were likely to do so again. In this sense, it could hardly be called protective legislation, except in the sense that it might protect a child/spouse from *prolonged* violence. The 1996 Family Law Act also includes provision for protection of children from domestic violence through exclusion of the violent partner from the family home, whether he or she has a legal right of occupancy or not and through non-molestation injunctions. A power of arrest can be attached to a non-molestation order, which may be exercised immediately upon breach of the order. Prior to the 1996 Act, case law demonstrated that courts were very reluctant to exercise their power of exclusion from the family home and stressed that this was to be taken as a 'last resort'. Unfortunately the wording of the 1996 Act seems to imply that a similar view would still be taken. The 1996 Act also states that a child under the age of 16 years of age may not apply for a non-molestation order or occupancy order without the leave of the court. Once again, children do not have inherent rights, but are at the mercy of the adults in the case unless they can prove to the satisfaction of the court that they are competent to apply for such an order, when they may be given leave. This legislation, like the previous domestic violence legislation, does not and cannot provide for the spouse or partner who will not or cannot make an application for an order due to fear of reprisals or ignorance of his or her rights.

Much has been made in recent years of the effects of violence in television and video on young children. The Jamie Bulger case, perhaps more than any other, provoked a definite change in attitude from the concept of a 'bad child' being the product of bad parenting to one of the inherently bad child. In spite of this, society in general prefers not to comprehend that children can be inherently evil or malicious and so still seeks someone or something to blame for this state of affairs; the increase of violence in television programmes and videos which are available to children is often seen as a factor.

Censorship in the UK is among the strictest in Western society, with tight controls over what can be shown in various categories of television or film and warnings to parents via classification of films and videos. The access which children may have to this type of material, along with violent and/or pornographic literature, cannot be legislated against as much of the exposure to such material takes place within the privacy of the child's home, or at least not in public. Cursory inquiries as to the age of children before admitting them to a cinema or renting them a video will usually result in the children (or even the accompanying parents) lying about their age. Perhaps this lax attitude by the gatekeepers of such materials is due to the fact that adolescents constitute a large part of the market and as such represent profits for all concerned. Another possibility is that the majority of children, young people and their parents do not share the views of some self-styled 'experts' who would have us believe that exposure to a film involving violence puts the child at risk of becoming a violent offender in the near future.

One such expert is Elizabeth Newson, who is credited with being influential in securing the amendment to the 1994 Criminal Justice Bill which increased the powers of the British Board of Film Classification to decide what was allowed on video. Professor Newson's paper, written at the invitation of MP David Alton, gave rise to many headlines and purported to show the links between violence in children and the viewing of so-called 'video nasties'. It called for the protection of our children from this risk and cited much 'evidence' in support of this argument. This paper has been heavily criticized by many, including Martin Barker, who takes each of the claims made by Newson and demonstrates the lack of evidence to support it. He also attacks the central argument made by Newson (and many others) that television must have an effect on us, otherwise why would advertisers spend billions of pounds persuading us to buy through the medium of television? Barker cites research which suggested that negative presentations are the least likely to be 'copied' by viewers, which is why the only advertisements which contain negative messages are those against drink driving or drug taking (Barker and Petley, 1997).

Health and safety risks

There are many ways in which society seeks to protect children from a variety of risks to their health, safety and well-being. Many of these are grounded in legislation, some in traditional 'unwritten' rules and norms passed from generation to generation, and some are based on practical considerations linked with biological, physiological and psychological immaturity. In some ways children are much less at risk in modern society, for example the risks of mortality and morbidity associated with illness are much reduced due to improved living conditions and medical care. Conversely, modern society can present many more risks to the child, for example in terms of accidents in the home and on the roads, substance abuse (alcohol, tobacco, drugs and solvents), armed conflicts, terrorism, sexual exploitation and abuse on the internet. We can and do legislate that children under a certain age should not be left alone in the home but we do not legislate that children cannot be left alone in the street or shopping precinct, we leave that to the common sense or caring instincts of the parent or carer.

A professional carer or an adult *in loco parentis* has a much higher duty of care in relation to the general safety and well-being of a child in his or her care than a parent. While parents may be criminally liable for non-accidental injuries to a child they will not be liable for an accident. If a child suffers an injury through an accident at school, in hospital or at nursery, it is likely that the parents would bring a civil action for damages. This is an interesting state of affairs which suggests that the concept of 'ownership' by parents of children has not been diminished by the concept of parental responsibility outlined in the Children Act 1989. There is legislative protection from risk of injury from household appliances, children's clothes, toys and so on through the Sale and Supply of Goods Act which ensures that products conform to minimum standards and even offer advice on use. Again, however, there is little protection for children whose parents give them an inappropriate toy to play with which results in injury or who are put into a night-gown which is not flame resistant and sat in front of an open fire. The protection of the child in these instances is put entirely into the hands of the parent or carer, with little or no sanction against the parent who, through carelessness or thoughtlessness, allows a child to become injured or worse through inappropriate use of products.

We need to ask the question as to why children may be protected in law from the 'mistakes' of professional carers but not from the mistakes of their main care givers. Society's approach to the protection of children in this area would seem to be focused on the right of parents to bring an action against another adult who mistakenly harms their child but not on the right of the child to seek any kind of sanction against those whose actions or omissions cause accidents in which the child is injured. As children under 18 years of age have no legal capacity, any legal actions must be brought through a 'next friend' who will usually be the parent or guardian. It is therefore unlikely that a parent who has caused injury to a child through an accident in the home will pursue such an action on behalf of the child.

The increase in recent years of the type, amount and availability of illegal drugs has brought with it an increased risk of harm to certain sections of our society, mainly young adults, but, increasingly, children are being exposed to this risk. The criminalization of certain drugs has not had any noticeable effect on their availability. It could be argued that the criminal justice system seeks to protect vulnerable groups such as children from the dangers of drugs by making the sanctions harsher for possession with intent to supply drugs than for simple possession. Research has shown the health risks associated with legal drugs such as alcohol and tobacco and so society attempts to protect children from these risks by making it illegal for a child under 16 years of age to buy cigarettes or under 18 years of age to buy alcohol. However, it is not illegal for a child of any age to smoke cigarettes or to drink alcohol, merely to buy these products. The thinking here would seem to suggest that as it is illegal for minors to purchase these products, the only way they could get hold of them would be through adults, who are far too sensible and caring to allow children in their care to smoke or drink alcohol.

Apart from the obvious problems in policing the implementation of this legislation, there is also the fact that children and young people make up a large section of the market for these products. In fact there have recently been criticisms that the marketing of some alcoholic products is specifically targeting the younger age groups. Under-age drinking and smoking are tolerated by society much more than illegal drug use, perhaps because drinking alcohol is a socially accepted adult activity, as is smoking, though the latter is becoming less so. In terms of protecting children from health risks associated with drugs, alcohol and tobacco, adult value systems appear to influence the extent to which existing protection systems will be enforced by society.

One of the health risks to children which has diminished over the years is that of death or morbidity resulting from disease and injury. Many of the potentially fatal infectious diseases of childhood have been eradicated or substantially reduced. This is largely due to efforts by the state to ensure that children are immunized against these diseases. Resources have been made available to ensure that immunization is available to every child in this country; education programmes abound on the benefits of immunization and the potential threats to the health of children who are not immunized. Do children have the right, then, to be protected from these potentially fatal diseases? The answer would appear to be 'yes', as long as the parents or guardians agree that this should be the case. Doctors and other health professionals can advise and suggest, but the parent will have the ultimate say.

Information based on research is available on possible contra-indications for immunization and advice will be given accordingly; however, parents can choose not to follow medical advice or may simply not take their child to the clinic or hospital. There is no protection provided by the state for the children of such parents. In the case of general medical treatment, the law does give some protection to children whose lives may be at risk due to the fact that their parents refuse to consent to medical treatment. A parent may not unreasonably deny all medical treatment to a child whose life is capable of being saved by such treatment. This could amount to a criminal offence and be punishable as such. However, parents may refuse palliative treatment on behalf of their child or even life-saving treatment if the child has a serious mental or physical handicap. Conversely, a parent may overrule the wishes of a child not to have treatment and put the child through potentially distressing medical intervention which he or she has no wish to have, such as a transplant or radiotherapy/chemotherapy.

The basic tenet in issues of consent with adult patients of sound mind is that they have the absolute right to say what will happen to their bodies; no adult can give or withhold consent on behalf of another and any health professional who carries out medical treatment without any or informed consent by the patient is likely to have an action brought against them for trespass to the person and/or negligence. This absolute right allows us, as adults, to make decisions which others may not agree with, and maintains the idea that in one area of our lives (perhaps the most important area) we have autonomy and the right to self-determination. While children have some protection in this area, either from the criminal law or from the Gillick ruling (Gillick v. West Norfolk and Wisbech AHA 1986), generally we class all children below the age of 16 years of age as being unable to make such decisions. This approach could be interpreted as saying that a child's body belongs to the adults who have the care of the child. This message is often in direct conflict to the one which we attempt to give children in relation to child abuse.

Child abuse and child protection

RISKS FROM CHILD ABUSE

Of all the ways in which children are put at risk in our society, the one which appears to cause the least contention is that of injury and death due to child abuse. While there may be some disagreements as to what actually constitutes 'abuse', the extremes of abusive behaviour perpetrated by adults against children come in for universal condemnation. In the UK, the bulk of the legislation pertaining to child protection relates to protection from abuse at the hands of parents or carers. In developing countries where children are at risk from many forms of exploitation such as child labour, denial of access to education and so on, the overriding concern for reformers is usually focused on deliberate injury and abuse caused by parents and carers. Perhaps this is due to the fact that in some ways this is easier to tackle, or maybe because deliberate harm to children attacks the very roots of how a society views itself. Whatever the reason, it cannot be denied that, in terms of reducing risks to children, protection from child abuse has the highest profile.

The types of abuse to which children fall prey have only relatively recently been 'rediscovered', that is, brought fully into the public domain. The risks associated with abuse for the child are many and include not just the physical and/or psychological injuries which they may suffer but also the damage to their health and well-being which can arise out of the protection process itself. The Children Act 1989 resulted in agreed definitions of child abuse for all people concerned in the child protection process:

- Neglect: persistent or severe neglect of a child, or failure to protect from exposure to any kind of danger, including cold and starvation, extreme failure to carry out important aspects of care resulting in significant impairment of the child's health or development.
- Physical abuse: actual or likely physical injury to a child, or failure to prevent physical injury or suffering to a child, including poisoning, suffocation and Munchhausen's syndrome by proxy.
- Sexual abuse: actual or likely sexual exploitation of a child or adolescent.
- Emotional abuse: actual or likely severe adverse effects on the emotional and behavioural development of a child caused by persistent or severe emotional treatment or rejection.

(Department of Health, 1991a)

Many lessons have been learned from such cases as those involving Jasmine Beckford, Tyra Henry, Kimberly Carlilse and others, and also from incidents involving actual or alleged child abuse such as in Cleveland and the Orkney Islands. The Children Act 1989 attempts to overcome the problems highlighted in these earlier cases and balance the rights of the child to be protected from the risks of child abuse with the civil rights of the parents not to be falsely accused. There is no doubt that the Children Act 1989 represents a major improvement in the way child abuse is detected and managed, not least in the way that it advocates and in some areas legislates for a multi-professional approach so as to ensure all of the needs of the child are met. However, as Hendrick states, '. . . the much vaunted Children Act, 1989, though providing provision for "listening" to children's viewpoint has, it seems, done little to enhance their rights' (Hendrick, 1997: 57).

It would seem that children have been intentionally hurt and killed by adults for a very long time. Lloyd deMause in his book *Childhood in history* stated that:

The history of childhood is a nightmare from which we have only just recently begun to awaken. The further back in history one goes, the more likely children are to be killed, abandoned, beaten, terrorised and sexually abused.

(deMause, 1974: 1)

Everyone might acknowledge that children are harmed by adults, but beyond that questions arise that cause heated debate. Some of the questions which are constantly being asked by both policy makers and individual professionals dealing with children and families are: what behaviour towards a child can be considered abusive? How many children are the victims of such abuse? Why are children abused? What can society do about the problem?

Child abuse itself may also be seen as a construction, that is, its definition is governed by the time, society and culture within which it is discussed. Taylor (1989) stated that:

> no behaviour is necessarily child abuse . . . some sets of facts come to be labelled as cases of child abuse because they go beyond the limits of what is now considered to be acceptable conduct towards a child. These standards change over time, and not only between cultures, but also between different members of the same culture. Child abuse is thus a social construction whose meaning arises from the value structure of a social group and the ways in which these values are interpreted and negotiated in real situations.
>
> (Taylor, 1989: 46)

Parton (1985) and others have argued that it was not until the 1960s that child abuse was rediscovered. An American doctor called for and commenced a systematic study of children who were hurt by their carers or parents. Dr Kempe coined one of the first definitions of child abuse. 'Child Abuse is the difference between a hand on the bottom and a fist in the face' (Kempe et al., 1962). Kempe talked in terms not of child abuse, but of 'child or baby battering'; his definition poses some interesting issues. Kempe seemed to suggest that abuse is excessive use of physical violence towards the child. He asks the reader to compare the picture of the 'hand on the bottom' symbolizing the 'normal', even harmless, physical punishment of the child by a parent, with the violent image of a child being punched in the face. Today this conception can be attacked on a number of fronts. Abuse is much more than physical violence and encompasses other harmful actions. Also, child abuse does not just happen to babies or small children, but to children of all ages and from across the whole of society. Kempe suggested that there was an acceptable level of physical punishment but that smacking was an unproblematic issue; today, many would have a problem with this assumption. It must be remembered that Kempe was writing in the 1960s and at the time the issue of whether to smack a child or not was less contentious.

Kempe believed that child abuse was a disease whose carrier was the parent and whose victim was the child. In 1970 the Department of Health and Social Services issued a circular called *The battered baby*. The publication outlined the incidence, aetiology (causes/origins of disease), clinical picture and the management that this 'disease' needed. This medico-scientific approach to child abuse has been very influential both in how legislation and how individual professionals have reacted to allegations of child abuse. There was an assumption that child abuse was in fact a medical reality which needed a clear diagnosis, treatment and if possible some form of preventative strategy.

Child abuse was seen as a problem of individuals: an individual adult, for whatever reason, would harm an individual child. However, writers such as Gill (1975) offer a very different perspective on the issue. Gill argued that any definition of abuse which does not incorporate such social factors as poverty is inadequate. Gill suggested that in terms of numbers, factors such as poverty cause far more damage to children than individual harm to a single child. He also pointed to the fact that such abuse can be perpetrated by individuals, communities and even society as a whole.

> Every child, despite his or her individual differences and uniqueness, is to be considered of equal intrinsic worth, and hence should be entitled to equal social, economic, civil and political rights, so that he/she may fully realize his inherent potential and share equally in life, liberty and happiness . . . therefore any act of commission or omission by individuals, institutions or society as a whole . . . which deprives children of equal rights or liberties and/or interferes with their optimal development constitutes by definition abusive or neglectful acts or conditions.
>
> (Gill, 1975: 346)

Here Gill places the concept of child abuse alongside the notion that children are entitled to rights equal to those enjoyed by adults. Abuse can therefore be defined as anything which infringes these rights and prevents a child reaching his or her optimum potential. This prevention can be perpetrated by individuals, adults or even other children, institutions or a whole society. In the light of Gill's views, we might reflect on the current spate of investigations into allegations of children having been abused whilst in the care of the local authority children's homes. Individuals may have abused the children, but what of the local authority; did they fail to protect the children by not monitoring their care more closely and was there any attempt to deal with allegations made by the children at the time, or were they dismissed?

THE CHILD PROTECTION SYSTEM

Figure 5.1 illustrates the stages in the child protection process which the Children Act 1989 made a statutory responsibility of local authorities.

There are two important principles to bear in mind when thinking about the process. There is a separation between criminal investigations of

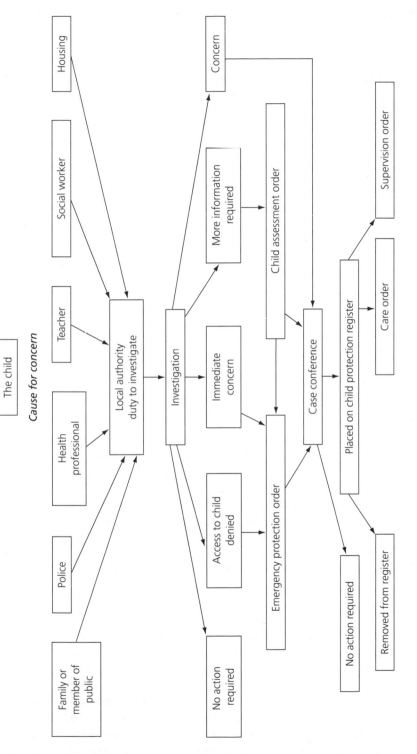

Figure 5.1 Stages in the child protection process

suspected abusers (where a crime may have been committed, particularly in cases of sexual and physical abuse) and the protection process. In other words, action can be taken to protect children irrespective of whether criminal prosecutions are secured. The other important point is that the purpose of the case conference – which is quite a long way along the process – is not to decide on guilt, but to decide whether a child is at risk and what action should be taken.

So how have the Children Act 1989 and the subsequent changes in approach to child abuse helped to protect children from the risks associated with abuse? The local authorities now have a statutory duty to investigate reports of suspected child abuse where there is 'reasonable cause' to do so. The various agencies involved such as social services departments, local education authorities, local housing authorities and health authorities have a statutory duty to communicate and collaborate with each other in the investigation of abuse. The state can remove a child from his or her home without the consent of the parents where the child is thought to be in immediate danger. The state can perform physical and mental examinations and assessments of the child without the parents' consent where there is a requirement for further information. The state can order the child to be permanently removed from his or her home where the parents are not providing an accepted level of care and the child is suffering as a result.

The child can report abuse by talking to a teacher, neighbour, nurse or health visitor; however, the child will be dependent on the adult in whom he or she confides to follow correct procedures and ensure that the child is not put at further risk. The child can report abuse through the National Society for the Prevention of Cruelty to Children (NSPCC) or through such agencies as Childline. The heightened awareness of abuse supported by media cover- age and education programmes has done as much to protect children as the legislation. There is no doubt that these provisions have saved children from abuse or from further abuse; however, the words of Butler Schloss LJ at the end of the Cleveland Inquiry that 'the child is a person and not an object of concern' are hard to reconcile with some of the provisions of the Children Act 1989. For example, it is stated in the Act that the child will be removed from the home if he or she is in danger from an adult, not that the adult will be forced to vacate the home until the matter is investigated.

Domestic violence legislation includes provision for exclusion orders or ouster orders where a spouse or cohabitee has committed violence and is likely to do so again. However, case law in this area stresses what a draco- nian measure it is to exclude someone from their home and that it should only be used as a last resort: this is where adults are involved. Where children are involved, who we are told have the right to be brought up in a secure family home, they are the first ones to be removed from this environment when their safety is threatened. One of the reasons why this is the approach taken may be that convictions of adults for offences against children are notoriously difficult to achieve and, without such convictions, it would be difficult to permanently exclude an alleged abuser from the home.

Examination of the criminal justice system shows why this situation often prevails.

There are a number of hurdles for the child to overcome before his or her alleged abuser may even be brought to trial. The first of these is whether the child is deemed competent to give evidence at all. There is a presumption in law that all adults are competent to give evidence unless proved to be otherwise. This presumption is reversed in the case of children, who have to 'prove' their competence by being verbally examined in open court by the judge. The nature of the questioning by the judge will be to determine whether the child understands the difference between truth and lies, right and wrong, the importance of telling the truth in this particular setting, and so on. The judge will then make a decision as to whether the child is competent. It is interesting to note that the same 'test' is used by the courts for mentally ill or mentally handicapped persons. Having been judged competent to give evidence, the child may then have to overcome attitudes and values commonly held by adults that children have unreliable memories, are egocentric, are highly suggestible, have difficulty distinguishing fact from fiction, tend to make false allegations and do not fully understand the duty to tell the truth (Spencer and Flyn, 1993). These attitudes towards children obviously have an effect on the weight and credibility of any evidence which they do give, despite the fact that research has shown that many of the allegations made above in relation to children may be equally true of adults.

This collective view of children as different, innocent, malleable and unreliable could be likened to the views held of prostitutes who give evidence in a rape action. The very fact that this witness has worked as a prostitute or has engaged in extramarital sex in the past would diminish her evidence in the eyes of a jury and so the court is not allowed to hear about her past without leave of the judge This option to 'hide' potentially prejudicial information from a jury, whatever one might think of those prejudices, is not available to the child. For the court, it is usually obvious when a child is present, this fact cannot be withheld from the jury and so the court will always be subject to the possibility of perpetuating societal views regarding the ability of the child to give credible evidence.

In some cases involving adults and children, the courts have permitted a screen to be used in order to shield prosecution witnesses from defendants who may intimidate witnesses by their very presence in the same room. The Criminal Justice Act 1988 as amended by the Criminal Justice Act 1991 allows for live television links to be used when children under 14 years of age (when the case involves personal violence) or under 17 years of age (when the case involves sexual assault) give their evidence and for them to be cross-examined while they are in a separate room. The judge must give leave to use this type of link and the onus is on the prosecution to prove that it is required. It may of course be the case that some prosecutors do not request this facility because they believe that the impact of a traumatized child in the witness box will have a positive (from their point of view) effect on the jury.

The fact that juries need to be 'convinced' of a child's story by tears and distress says little for us as a society. There are calls for the criminalization of child harm to be reviewed and questions raised as to whether it is in the best interest of the child to have to go through the trauma and distress which a criminal trial can bring. The answer may not lie in legal reform but in a more deep-rooted examination of the way that children are categorized and responded to in society.

> Most would agree that cruelty, neglect and sexual abuse to children are in principle (and practice) criminal, the process of judgement . . . to which such criminal acts are subject is one which is inherently prejudicial to children; it is unlikely to produce a result, potentially and actually traumatic for the complainant and unlikely to produce the result the complainant would want, that is compensation or adequate retribution.
>
> (Parton *et al.*, 1997: 106)

The protection offered to children at risk from abuse and the consequences of abuse could be summarized as being well intentioned but let down by the fact that children are once again excluded from most of the decision making, subject to assumptions which prejudice the ability to prosecute child abusers effectively, and dependent once again on adult intervention and interpretation to ensure what rights they have are recognized.

DEVELOPMENT OF THE SYSTEM

Since the 1960s, a number of legislative initiatives, developments in professional practice and a rapidly growing body of professional knowledge have led to many changes in the way child abuse has been dealt with. The 1970s and 1980s saw a number of publications all of which widened the scope of the problem and saw the genesis of terms such as 'non-accidental injury' and eventually to 'child abuse'. The basis of our current child protection system with case conferences, 'at-risk' registers and area review committees came into being following the 1974 report into the death of Maria Colwell (Department of Health and Social Security, 1974). The report also emphasized the need for professionals from different agencies to work together in the identification and management of child abuse cases. Arguably the most all-encompassing changes occurred following the publication of the Children Act 1989 and its attendant document *Working together under the Children Act 1989* (Department of Health, 1991). These documents have been the focus for much change in the practice of all professionals involved in child protection.

In 1991, the UK government signed and agreed to the United Nations Convention on the Rights of the Child. This convention is discussed in more depth in the next chapter; however, a number of the articles deal with protection from violence and harmful behaviour. Article 19 sets out the right to be protected from all forms of violence. Children must be kept from harm and be given proper care by those looking after them. Children also have the right not to be punished cruelly or in any way that would belittle them (Article 37).

Smith and Grock (1995) estimated that as many as 350 000 children live in environments which may be classified as low warmth and high criticism. Such children are in need because their families are unable or unwilling to meet the basic needs of the child, and without intervention from professionals or services, the child's health and physical development will become significantly impaired. Many of these children may be helped by professional intervention under section 47 of the Children Act 1989.

Research by the Dartington Social Research Unit (Department of Health, 1995) estimated that every year 160 000 referrals are made to social services because of concern for a child's welfare and result in an initial investigation by a social worker. How the investigation proceeds is often determined by social and administrative factors. Cleaver and Freeman (1995) stated that the first enquiry is frequently undertaken without the knowledge of the parents. The child protection records are checked and contact is made with workers in other child-care or welfare agencies. At this stage of the child protection process, good multi-agency co-operation is usually achieved. However, even at this stage, of the 160 000 investigations which are initiated, approximately 40 000 stop and are deemed to require no further action.

A small number of children will be removed from the care of the parents or carers under an Emergency Protection Order due to serious immediate concerns. This means that 120 000 children will proceed on to the next step which will mean a visit to the family to further the investigation. It is at this stage that the concerns become public, and it is generally a very stressful time for all concerned, especially the family. Again, at this stage, a further 80 000 children will be lost from the process and the suspicions will not be taken any further; very few children will be removed from the home at this stage. The 40 000 children who are now left in the system will be subject to an initial child protection conference. It can therefore be seen that only one quarter of the entire initial referrals make it to the case conference.

The child protection conference is a forum for all professionals to share and discuss any information about the child and family that may have a bearing on the child's safety. Since the advent of *Working together under the Children Act 1989* it is common practice that parents and, where they are old enough, children are invited to the conference. Thorburn et al.'s (1995) study showed that parents are invited to the conference about 87 per cent of the time. However, parents attended all or part of the meeting in about 69 per cent of cases. In nearly one in five cases, the parents do not attend at all, even though they are invited. This should not be seen as especially surprising as it will be difficult for a parent to enter a meeting and sit around a table with imposing professionals, many of whom will be complete strangers, who are questioning their parenting ability.

The function of the conference is to make an assessment of the risk to the child, and to decide how best to protect him or her, if protection is needed. *Child protection messages from research* gives a review of what is discussed at such a conference:

> There will certainly be discussion of the child's health and develop-
> ment, the parents' past history, and the relationships within the family,
> especially the quality of parenting including what has worked in the
> past . . . a parent's inability to cope is frequently linked to other diffi-
> culties so the conference discussions extend to housing, social support
> and finances.
>
> (Department of Health, 1995: 29)

When examining the content of the average case conference it might also be pertinent to consider what is not included in the wider discussion. It would seem that the type of maltreatment does not feature as highly as one might think and that the severity of abuse, except in cases of serious sexual abuse, is not the major factor in determining the outcome of the conference. Indeed one might be tempted to ask why the parents, their past and the social circumstances seem to have a higher priority than that of the particulars of the abuse itself.

Once the meeting has discussed such issues it must reach a decision about how best to proceed. Again a number of possible options are open to the conference. Of the approximately 40 000 children who enter the conference, about 11 000 have no further action taken; 3 000 are retained within the system for further investigation. About 25 000 children's names are placed on the child protection register and of these 3000 children are accommodated on a voluntarily basis and 3000 will be taken into care.

It can be seen, therefore, that of the original 160 000 children referred to the social service professionals, 24 500 children were added to the child protection register in 1992. These figures are, of course, only estimates, as many factors serve to render them less than precise. One major factor is that children may leave the system due to no further action being taken, only to be re-admitted at a later date, therefore being counted more than once. In 1993 a total of 32 500 children were on local authorities' child protection registers. By 1994, this had risen to 34 900 children who had been considered to be suffering, or likely to suffer, significant harm (Children Act 1989 s47).

Despite widespread changes to the child protection system, the advent of multi-agency training and casework, tighter procedures for case conferences and the child protection register, there are still many concerns. Writers are critical of the child protection process; work by Falmer and Owen (1995) found that in only 30 per cent of cases were the needs of the main carer met; that it was common for the needs of the main carer to be given little priority; important areas of difficulty went unrecognized such as drug and alcohol use and family violence; and neglect of parents' needs often had an adverse effect on the child's progress.

Despite the work to include parents in partnership, concerns are still expressed about its true nature. Parents may have mixed motives for working with professionals. Jordan (1988) argues that parents co-operate with the child protection services not from partnership but in order to ensure that children are returned, or not removed, or to secure the help of professionals in accessing other services such as financial support and rehousing applications.

The term partnership might be a little meaningless to parents who feel that unless they enter such a relationship they stand to lose out to the powerful professionals:

> Child protection is the area where family participation leads to most anxiety and where the term partnership is most stretched. When an agency takes a decision to intervene through court proceedings, partnership may seem a meaningless concept. Power is very much concentrated on one side.
>
> (Family Rights Group, 1991: 18)

The authors also found that children are often not protected. Nearly one third of their sample of registered children had not been protected by the work carried out during the investigation and registration process. *Child protection messages from research* (Department of Health, 1995) concluded that between 25 and 30 per cent of children are re-abused after coming to the attention of the child protection agencies. The vast majority (over 70 per cent) of children who were protected had been separated from the family. This may show how difficult it is to adequately protect children who still do live at home with an abusing parent. In addition to concerns regarding the protection of children, Cleaver and Freeman (1995) found that, in their study, 39 per cent of families broke up within 2 years of the allegations being made. This points to the stress and anxiety attendant with the child protection process, and to possible lack of support for families during and following the process.

The professional group which has perhaps the most potential in helping to protect children from abuse is, ironically, probably the most under-used although there is recent evidence that schools and teachers are making increasing numbers of referrals. Teachers are in a unique position, because of their daily contact with children over long periods of time and their potential to build relationships with children, to play an enormously useful role in the protection process. In the final section of this chapter we will examine the role of the teacher in relation to protection of children from abuse and highlight the fact that effective protection of children is best achieved by a combination of protection and empowerment. Although we have chosen to focus on the work of teachers, many of the underlying principles are applicable to other groups of people who work with children.

THE TEACHER'S ROLE IN CHILD PROTECTION

It is recognized that not all agencies involved with children have investigative or interventionist roles, and this is certainly true of the teaching profession. The unique position of teachers in relation to children in their care allows them to play a significant role in recognition and referral of abused children, in support of children who have disclosed abuse, and, in some cases, in prevention of abuse.

In terms of recognition and referral, a number of inquiry reports have highlighted the teacher's role.

There are two separate aspects to the role of the school in relation to management of the child abuse system. The first . . . is to act as a watchdog . . . in spotting children who show signs of abuse. The second is as a monitor over children who are in care . . . and/or on the Child Abuse Register.

(Blom-Cooper, 1985: 73)

In relation to recognition of abuse, first of all, teachers need to be able to examine their own feelings and attitudes to the subject. Child abuse is an issue which in most people gives rise to feelings of horror and repugnance. It is sometimes all too easy to allow these negative emotions to influence responses to indicators of abuse; to allow ourselves to think 'that can't possibly be happening'. It is acknowledged that it is a fine line to tread between seeing potential abuse in every bruise or change in a child's behaviour and refusing to see what is glaringly obvious.

Teachers need to be able to acknowledge that abuse can possibly be happening to a child in their class and use their skill and judgement to decide whether a situation requires further investigation. In order to do this, teachers need to have knowledge about possible indicators of abuse as described above, knowledge of referral mechanisms and procedures and also be able to cope effectively with disclosures of abuse which may be made to them.

It is possible that the teacher may be the only adult in a child's life that the child feels he or she can trust with a disclosure; such disclosures should always be treated seriously and with respect. It is tempting to feel so protective towards a child who discloses abuse that the need to give reassurances outweighs practicalities. The teacher should not promise anything to the child which cannot be guaranteed, such as 'Don't worry, I'll sort this all out'. Similarly, in relation to confidentiality, secrecy cannot be maintained and the child should be made aware of this, if possible, before disclosures are made. The teacher has a responsibility to report any disclosures to the named person in the school and any promise of secrecy would only damage the teacher–child relationship.

The teacher should keep a careful record of any disclosures made, as soon as possible after the event, and ensure that the child is kept informed at all stages of the process. In addition to being alert to indicators of abuse and aware of referral procedures, the teacher's role can also encompass prevention through teaching children about their rights and also in recognizing and respecting those rights. Just as water safety and accident prevention are taught in schools, personal safety can be taught to children. Teachers are used to teaching children about discipline; schemes such as 'assertive discipline' have made this process more explicit. Children can be shown through discussion and visual resources that physical contact is appropriate in certain contexts but not in others. Circle discussions, perhaps in the carpet area, can be a useful time for teachers to discuss dangerous situations and the notion of acceptable secrets and unacceptable secrets.

Schools can set up personal safety programmes; these often rely on the motivation of the special needs co-ordinator (SENCO). Parents may need to be consulted and given the option of withdrawing their child from the sessions if they wish. This kind of consultation is typical of the preparation for sex education programmes, and work on personal safety could usefully be included with such programmes. Before beginning such a scheme teachers would need education and training in the area. There are a number of organizations that run sessions for professionals. Often the SENCO will attend and this information is then disseminated through in-service training meetings for the benefit of all teachers in the school. Other agencies that can offer help include the NSPCC and the National Children's Bureau.

There are a number of ways to approach personal safety programmes and obviously teachers will adapt strategies to suit their own teaching style and the context they are working in. One approach is described in *Beyond the scare* (Buchanan, 1989). This scheme involves seven half-day sessions spread over 7 weeks and covers the following:

- memory work: training in observational skills, conveying to children that people are not necessarily what they seem;
- children's rights: exploration of what our rights are, who decides who touches us and in what manner, the concept of taking advantage and being taken advantage of;
- identifying dangerous situations, discussion of feelings of comfort and discomfort with situations, strangers and non-strangers;
- strategies for coping with dangerous situations, assertion training, what to say and how to say it, standing up for yourself, tactics for a range of situations; and
- telling someone, the difference between good and bad secrets, how to choose who to tell if you have a problem, that telling someone is always the right thing to do.

Whatever strategies teachers adopt they need the confidence to open discussion on abuse and the training and support to deal with situations which may arise out of such programmes.

It is unrealistic to imagine that learning about personal safety will always prevent abuse; it certainly will not prevent potential abusers approaching children. However, it is often the powerlessness and vulnerability of children that can make them prey to abusing adults. Learning self-protection techniques can make children more confident in themselves and their rights, and therefore less vulnerable. As Elliot (1986) suggested, 'all children have the right to be safe. It is the responsibility of adults to protect this right. '

The recognition that society presents a number of possible risks to children has resulted in a strong focus on the protection of children. Although it is necessary to safeguard children there is always the possibility that some forms of protection can have negative consequences themselves. There needs to be a shared realization that empowerment through the communication of full and appropriate information, coupled with active strategies for self-protection may help society to empower its youngest citizens.

Children's rights

6

Dominic Wyse and Angela Hawtin

Children represent the most disadvantaged group of people in society. In modern times, we have seen women assert their rights through the struggle for the vote accompanied by the development of feminist thinking. We have also seen minority ethnic groups struggle to ensure that their voice is recognized in society and state. People with special needs have made significant advances in terms of society's recognition of their particular circumstances. But children, to a large extent, have been unable to achieve the kind of recognition for their rights that have been achieved by other oppressed groups. Part of the reason for this is perhaps that most adults have not paused to think about the very concept that children should have rights just like any other member of society. This conceptual difficulty has resulted in only limited thought being given by many people in society to the nature of children's rights.

The significance of children and their rights has relatively only recently received international and national attention, particularly in terms of the law. This has coincided with the work in the emerging discipline of the study of childhood. As we illustrated at the beginning of the book, there is much debate about some fundamental questions in relation to children and childhood. What is a child? What is childhood and when does it end? We would argue that, as the link between years of age and the definition of the child has been questioned, even the term 'childhood' needs careful thought: 'childhood' can carry with it connotations of passivity and the past which sit uneasily with the more recent conceptualizations of children's rights as immediate and current.

The difficulties in providing answers for these fundamental questions include the problems that exist when trying to document histories of childhood. In part, this is because, as Stainton Rogers and Stainton Rogers (1992) point out, the wide range of attempts to describe the history of children and childhood have been weakened by a lack of reflexivity. It is not our intention to look in-depth at the history of children's rights. However, although the short following account of the history of children's rights will deal mainly with the twentieth century and particularly legal developments, we argue that children have been fighting to assert their rights since the beginning of humanity. Just as history can be seen as a construction rather than an absolute truth resulting in, for example, histories from the perspective of women (Miles, 1989) and black people (Fryer, 1984), we must assume that if it were possible, historical accounts written from the child's point of view by children themselves might reveal radically different perspectives. However, as was pointed out in Chapter 1, it is the *writing* that has presented part of the problem for children.

Accepting that most of the accounts concerning children's struggle are mediated by adults, it is worth looking at two examples that reflect a child-centred concern. Ian Hislop narrated a programme for television that looked at the history of education in the UK. It depicted a strike by school children complaining about the use of the cane. Newspapers reported that children in Hull, Manchester, Liverpool and London walked out of their classrooms as a protest. One of the interviewees who was at school in London during the strike recollected some of the events:

> In the middle of a lesson suddenly we heard a noise which grew louder and louder. We realized it was children shouting. As they got nearer we realized they were in the playground. We all stood – very daring – we all stood on our seats and these boys were shouting louder and louder, 'Come out, come out!'

There was a double irony in the outcome to this remarkable piece of struggle, as the mothers who had previously resisted the imposition of long hours of education came and forced the children to return to school. This also causes us to reflect on the problems that can exist when women's rights are automatically assumed to be synonymous with children's rights. It is arguable that, in this incident, the women denied the children their freedom to protest.

This kind of direct action is not unique; Searle (1998) documented a lifetime of work that resulted in his involvement with groups of children actively reclaiming their school curriculum and taking action to protest about injustice.

> Their own 'cultural action' was confirmed on the green outside the school, next to the churchyard where many of them had composed their poems. Eight-hundred students – virtually the entire school, came out on strike and rallied against the sacking of a teacher who had published their poems. Even as they boycotted class they sang and proclaimed poems. They held aloft a banner with their own poem in support of their sacked teacher and sang an old music-hall song, 'Roll out the Barrel' punning on the name of the headteacher, Geoffrey Barrell.
>
> (Searle, 1998: 23)

The UN Convention on the Rights of the Child

The legal position of children's rights in the twentieth century has received a considerable boost by the important United Nations (UN) Convention on the Rights of the Child (CRC). These words stand as an important testament to the pioneering work of Eglantyne Jebb, founder of Save the Children: 'I believe we should claim certain rights for children and labour for their universal recognition'. In 1923 she summarized some of the essential rights of children in five points. These five points became the Declaration of the Rights of the Child and were agreed by the General Assembly of the International Save the Children Union in 1923. One year later, the declaration was adopted by the League of Nations and the five points subsequently became known as the Declaration of Geneva.

Following the Second World War, the UN concentrated on the production of the Universal Declaration of Human Rights which was adopted in 1948. In the declaration, the rights of the child were only implicitly included and it was felt to be insufficient to safeguard their specific rights. Much work was done to persuade the UN that a separate document was needed. On 20 November 1959, the UN General Assembly adopted the Declaration of the Rights of the Child. This comprised 10 articles and incorporated the guiding principle of 'working in the best interests of the child'.

To further strengthen children's statutory rights, it was necessary to work on a treaty. The government of Poland submitted a draft convention on the rights of the child to the UN Commission on Human Rights in 1978, hoping to see it adopted during the International Year of the Child. The response to their proposal was not enthusiastic, and there began a decade of debate about the nature of children's rights. The involvement of non-government organizations (NGOs) in this process was significant and their impact was one of the forces that helped the drafting of the Convention on the Rights of the Child.

The convention was submitted to the General Assembly of the UN in 1989. It was adopted, without modifications, on 20 November 1989, exactly 30 years after the 1959 declaration. It achieved a record first day response with 61 countries signing up on 26 January 1990. On 2 September 1990 the Convention on the Rights of the Child entered into force as international law. At the time of writing it had been signed by all nation states of the world apart from Somalia, and ratified by all states apart from Somalia and the USA.

The convention is a comprehensive instrument that addresses children's rights in a wide range of situations including emergency and non-emergency contexts. In order to give an indication of the style of the convention it is useful to comment on some of the articles.

Article 3

1. In all actions concerning children, whether undertaken by public or private social welfare institutions, courts of law, administrative authorities or legislative bodies, the best interests of the child shall be a primary consideration.

This article is important because it means that statutory bodies have an obligation to consider the best interests of the child. This has been replicated in the UK Children Act 1989 where, for example, the ascertainable wishes and feelings of the child have to be taken into account in cases related to the care and upbringing of the child. However, it is also important to consider the means that are used to determine the child's best interests and the extent to which children have true involvement in that process. An important example of this is the lack of consideration given to the wishes of the child in contact cases.

Article 12

1. State parties shall assure to the child who is capable of forming his or her own views the right to express those views freely in all matters affecting the child, the views of the child being given due weight in accordance with the age and maturity of the child.

Here the significant wording is 'all matters affecting the child'. At an institutional level, there have been some instances of good practice but too often, even if children's views are sought, there is little obligation to ensure that those views are acted upon. There are also difficulties in the potential assumption that the older children are, the better they are able to express their views. Some people who interact daily with children have found that they are constantly forced to challenge their own age-related expectations in terms of the capabilities that children have to understand issues and express their opinions.

Article 19

1. State parties shall take all appropriate legislative, administrative, social and educational measures to protect the child from all forms of physical or mental violence, injury or abuse, neglect or negligent treatment, maltreatment or exploitation, including sexual abuse, while in the care of parent(s), legal guardian(s) or any other person who has the care of the child.

In the UK, physical punishment of children by parents remains a legal act. This is often justified on the grounds of reasonable force and, ironically, in the best interests of the child. The most common example is the one where a child has run into the road and the parent smacks the child to make sure he or she never does it again. Smacking remains a substantial denial of children's rights in the UK.

Article 31

1. State Parties recognize the right of the child to rest and leisure, to engage in play and recreational activities appropriate to the age of the child and to participate freely in cultural life and the arts.

In many nation states, including the more complacent richer states, there is a danger that the arts can be marginalized. Often financial reasons are put forward for such lack of attention to the cultural life and the arts. However, children's own enthusiasms are often captured by involvement in drama, music, art and play, and for this reason these areas should perhaps be given a higher priority. The financial argument is difficult to counter (although later in the chapter this issue is examined in more detail) as Article 27 states that 'State Parties, in accordance with national conditions and *within their means*, shall take appropriate measures to assist parents' in maintaining an appropriate standard of living.

The second part of the convention (Articles 42 to 45) deals with the technicalities of implementation. Included within these articles are the requirements that state parties make sure that the convention is widely known about – including by children – and that they report on the progress that they have made 2 years after initial adoption and every 5 years after that.

One of the benefits of the convention is that it serves to remind us that children's rights are an international and inter-disciplinary concern. The notion of multi-professional or multi-worker practice must include the constant development and evaluation of links at local, national and international levels. A period of work in Jordan for the British Council brought this home to us. During 1997, we were invited to carry out some work for the British Council in the areas of child protection, child representation and the development of an action research proposal.

Children's rights and multi-professionalism: an international example

As a 'developing' country, some people might assume that Jordan would be inferior to richer states such as the UK in *all* matters regarding children's rights. It was certainly the case that poverty resulted in some very difficult conditions for adults and children alike. However, while the statistics indicated that, for example, there were severe problems related to extreme poverty for large sections of the community, particularly in the *badia* (desert/rural) areas, there were also initiatives where creative thinking had resulted in a higher level of participation by children in matters that might be regarded in other states as only appropriate for adults.

Our arrival on our first visit coincided with much media discussion concerning the plight of a group of orphans to whom the late king had decided to donate one of his palaces. The influence of the monarchy was a factor that we soon realized was of profound importance. The 'Jordan River for development projects' included a series of workshops that we were invited to run that looked at child protection. The workshops were opened by one of the king's daughters whose presence also contributed to the media interest that had been sparked initially by the plight of the orphans.

Our early concern was to ensure that a multi-professional perspective was maintained and that this would be reflected in all the aspects of the work we carried out. For that reason, the participants included representatives from the Ministry for Education, NGOs, lawyers, school-based counsellors, health workers, researchers and so on. Our initial interviews with a number of key figures who worked in the area of child protection began to reveal the complexities of the Jordanian context. A member of the police force emerged as a brilliant advocate for children and their rights. His tireless enthusiasm for tackling the issues was remarkable and had resulted in him pursuing some extremely valuable research, initially in his own time. He made us aware of the concept of the 'dark numbers': these were the cases of child abuse that had not been reported. He also felt that one of the problems with the Jordanian system was the difficulties in communicating with children about their rights.

The workshops during our first visit were characterized by great commitment and enthusiasm by all the participants. It was difficult to work out whether this enthusiasm was partly because of the early stage in the development of child protection systems or whether it represented a substantive difference from some of the experiences we had had in the UK. One of the workshop participants included a member of the secretariat from the National Taskforce for Children. The establishment of the National Taskforce for Children was a very interesting development by any international standard and this high level of political recognition for children had also been mirrored by the establishment of a children's parliament to contribute to the emerging democratic process. Our contact with the National Taskforce for Children subsequently resulted in work on our second visit which contributed to the development of a National Coalition for Children. The coalition represents a structure for bringing together the wide range of groups and individuals in Jordan who have involvement with children. Once again, this represented a bold vision supported by direct political action to enhance the lives of Jordanian children. The vision of the British Council staff encouraged by the influence of the CRC resulted in significant initiatives to support the in-country work on children's rights. This short example of work in another country enabled us to reflect further on the state of children's rights in the UK.

Progress in the UK

The UK, like other countries, was required to submit a report to the UN Committee on the Rights of the Child on the progress of implementation of the CRC after 2 years. It is interesting to examine some of the recommendations of the UN committee. The concluding observations of the committee were initiated with some positive comments. For example, there was praise for the 'working together' initiative. This came from the Children Act 1989 and, as we have seen, the initiative encourages multi-professional and interdisciplinary approaches to child welfare (this is a theme that we return to later in this chapter). The committee also took note of the government's intention to extend the provision of pre-school education.

The committee had 15 areas of concern in relation to the report submitted by the UK. First on this list was their worry that the UK registered six reservations about the convention. The committee considered that the most serious of these was the reservation that the UK may not apply the convention in the case of refugees. The committee felt that this breached Articles 2, 3, 9 and 10 on non-discrimination, the best interests of the child, separation from parents and family reunification. The second concern registered by the committee was the lack of an independent means to co-ordinate and monitor the implementation of children's rights. It was in the light of this problem that the Children's Rights Development Unit (CRDU) produced their *UK agenda for children* (Children's Rights Development Unit, 1994) which was an analysis of the extent to which law, policy and practice in the UK complied with the principles and standards contained in the convention. The CRDU consulted more than 180 voluntary, statutory and/or professional organizations that worked with children and held 40 consultation sessions with children and young people throughout the UK.

The introduction to the *UK agenda for children* provides a stark contrast to the rosy picture portrayed by the UK report to the UN Committee on the Rights of the Child.

> The UK's initial report to the UN Committee illustrates not progress but complacency. It is dishonest by omission, highlighting particular laws and statistics that indicate compliance, without adequate recognition of gaps, inconsistencies and blatant breaches.
>
> (Children's Rights Development Unit, 1994: xi)

This situation underlines the importance of pushing for meaningful involvement of children in political processes. The UK government felt a political necessity to present a report that showed the UK progress in a positive light. However, if British society was structured to give children greater political rights, this would include a contribution to such reports perhaps resulting in a less biased picture.

The *UK agenda for children* is divided into 14 reports covering personal freedoms, care of children, physical and personal integrity, an adequate standard of living, health and health care services, environment, education, play and leisure, youth justice, child labour, immigration and nationality, children and violent conflict, Northern Ireland, abduction, and international obligations to promote children's rights. As an illustration of one of these sections we have chosen to look in more detail at the report *An adequate standard of living*.

The first question that *An adequate standard of living* deals with is 'does poverty exist?' The answer to the question is not so obviously self-evident, as most governments tend to downplay the existence of poverty. Questions of finance get to the nub of the political agenda and as such are fought strongly by governments. For example, whereas to many the payment of very high wages to significant segments of society is obscene and represents an indication of inequality, governments tend to argue that a lack of incentive to earn large sums of money would have a number of negative consequences. In the context of strong resistance by government it is difficult to argue that a) poverty does exist and b) children are suffering. Statistical claims and counter claims are often used to frustrate positive action. CRDU suggested that the two best definitions of poverty include the level of income support, or to define the poverty line as 50 per cent of average full-time income after housing costs, which is widely used in many European countries. In the European Community between 1957 and 1985, the UK had the largest increase in the incidence of poverty where the percentage of children living in poverty had increased from 9 per cent in 1980 to 18 per cent in 1985. Government figures published in July 1993 revealed that there were 13.5 million people including 3.9 million children living in poverty – one in three of all children.

As was seen above, Article 31 of the convention safeguards children's rights to play and leisure. However, *An adequate standard of living* indicates that poverty interferes with that basic right. In modern British society, the expectations of parents go far beyond the basics necessary for survival (although this is not to minimize the importance of the fact that thousands of children do not have these basics): parents are expected to provide a range of toys, outings, holidays and so on. Poverty restricts the parents' ability to provide the increasing range of experiences that are deemed necessary. One aspect of play and leisure is the provision, or lack of provision, of free outdoor play facilities. An indication that these facilities are perhaps inadequate in the UK has been provided by the business community's recognition that outdoor and indoor play facilities adjoining pubs can make money.

The following quote from the report gives some idea of the seriousness of poverty and its implication for children's rights:

A survey of poor families in the North East of England concludes: 'The picture that emerges . . . is one of constant restriction in almost every aspect of people's activities . . . The lives of these families and perhaps most seriously the lives of children within them, are marked by the unrelieved struggle to manage with dreary diets and drab clothing. They also suffer what amounts to cultural imprisonment in their homes in our society in which getting out with money to spend on recreation and leisure is normal at every other income level'.

(Children's Rights Development Unit, 1994: 87)

Clearly, there are conflicting views on the status of children's rights in the UK and in comparison with other nation states. In order to look further at the issues raised by the response to the CRC, it is useful to examine the picture in relation to one particular area of children's lives. Many children in the UK use the health service, which can have a significant impact on their lives. The people who work with children in this setting have a duty to uphold children's rights. So, before we turn to some cautionary notes about the positioning of children's rights within the discipline of law, we refer to some of our own previous work (Hawtin and Wyse, 1997) to examine aspects of the UK legal position in relation to health care and children's rights.

Legal rights and health care

One of the most basic and fundamental rights in health care is the right to say what can and cannot be done to your person; the right to consent to treatment. This right, for the mentally competent adult, is firmly protected by law so that medical treatment given without consent can give rise to an action in civil law of trespass to the person or even in criminal law of assault and battery. Consent which is not 'informed' consent, that is, the patient is not given all the information required to make an informed decision as to treatment, can give rise to an action in negligence, though this right has been diluted somewhat by the notion of 'therapeutic privilege'. Therapeutic privilege is the term applied to situations where the health care professional (usually a doctor) can make a professional decision to withhold certain information from the patient if it is deemed to be in the patient's best interests. This concept has given rise to much debate in terms of the notion of patient autonomy and yet it is applied almost universally to child patients by doctors, nurses and parents alike.

The Family Law Reform Act 1969 at section 8 states that competent young persons over the age of 16 years old can give consent to medical treatment without regard to the wishes of their parents or those with parental responsibility. However, this does not give young people total autonomy, as the ability appears to relate only to the giving of consent and not to the withholding of consent. When the treatment which is being refused is life-saving treatment, the courts may intervene and override the wishes of the young person, as shown by the case of Re W (a minor) (medical treatment) (1992) 3 WLR 758. This case gave the principle that a young person's views, regardless of their competency, could be overriden under the 'best interests' principle. This seems to be an attack on the right to autonomy and self-determination which would probably not be tolerated or sanctioned by the adult patient.

The right of children under 16 years old to make their own decision about medical treatment was until relatively recently non-existent. However, following the case of Gillick v. West Norfolk and Wisbech AHA 1986, the principle was put forward that children under this age could consent to treatment without parental authority if they were deemed to be of sufficient maturity and understanding to do so. Although this case dealt specifically with contraceptive treatment, the principle of 'Gillick competence' has been applied to other areas of treatment.

Whether or not a child is 'Gillick competent' is dependent on each individual case. There is not a predetermined age at which a child will become competent and the variables to be taken into account include the complexity of the issue to be considered: some issues require a higher level of understanding than others. Competence also needs to be assessed on a long-term basis rather than as a 'snap shot' in time. The decision as to whether a child is 'Gillick competent' will usually be taken by the health care workers involved in the child's care, sometimes with direct input from clinical psychologists, teachers and so on.

It is sometimes suggested that there can be a problem due to the potential conflict of priorities between the child and the health professional. The 'medical model' upon which most doctors base their practice does not readily allow for individual decision making by children. Although changing, the training of doctors encourages a disease/cure-orientated approach rather than an holistic approach to total patient care. Although some doctors will involve children in decision making in relation to their treatment, too often communication with the child is confined to what will be done rather than whether it will be done and the parents are seen as having total authority in relation to the child's treatment.

This leads to another major problem with respect to children's rights and medical treatment; too often staff caring for children – and the children themselves – are unaware of children's rights in this area. Rights are meaningless without the knowledge that one possesses them. Children are often uninformed in this area, and although literature has been produced to inform children of their rights, it is rarely available in the health care setting. One of the main functions of the paediatric nurse is to act as the child's advocate, and yet many nurses, both students and qualified staff, are unaware of the concept of 'Gillick competence'. Children do not have automatic rights in relation to medical treatment as adults do: children may have to fight for their rights in this area and prove that they are competent to make such decisions. This is difficult enough with the assistance of health workers who are aware of and recognize children's rights; however, when these same professionals ignore or are ignorant themselves of these rights, children may as well have no rights at all.

The law also recognizes a duty of confidence between a doctor – or other health professional – and his or her patient in relation to information obtained in a professional capacity. In terms of children as patients, the question as to whether they can expect the right to confidentiality appears once again to turn on their capacity to form a confidential relationship with the doctor. The implication of this approach is that when children are unable to form such a relationship, doctors are obliged to disclose to the parents what they have learnt. In relation to the child with complete incapacity to enter into a confidential relationship, there is what almost amounts to a legal duty on the doctor in favour of disclosure. Breach of this duty could give rise to an action in negligence if the doctor failed to disclose and harm resulted to the child. The disclosure would need to be to the person most capable of protecting the child, which would normally be the local authority. If the doctor does disclose information to a third party, again evidence of resulting damage to the child would have to be found before an action could be brought.

If the child is deemed to be capable of forming a confidential relationship, the obligation of confidentiality applies as it would to an adult patient; however, even here, the right is not absolute. A doctor may disclose confidential information where it is in the public interest to do so (among other justifications). This may allow a doctor to disclose information about a competent child if he/she can show it is in the child's best interest, *Re C (a minor) (evidence: confidential information)* (1991) 7 BMRL 138, CA.

The first section of this chapter has looked at some of the national and international legal aspects of children's rights. It can be seen that the rights of the individual child in relation to health care and medical treatment are not so much given to the child as owned by adults in positions of responsibility whether parent or health worker. This is a position that characterizes many of the societal contexts that children find themselves in, as we have seen throughout this book. The next section suggests some problems with the CRC and goes on to examine some of the difficulties associated with children's rights being contextualized mainly in the discipline of law.

Problems with legal structures

The early success of the CRC represented by the high numbers of signatories was inevitably preceded by some areas of compromise. The convention extends the rights of the child in many ways but it is not politically radical, for example none of the articles pushes for the right for children to vote. This is perhaps a reflection of the difficulties that might be faced in securing this right in a range of different political settings, although the same might have been said about the process of securing votes for women. While there can be problems with assuming that children's rights are synonymous with women's rights, many of the arguments used to try to deny women their rights have been used to deny children their rights.

The adoption of the convention has given nation states some considerable tasks to overcome. The differences in progress between different countries are in part a reflection of the difficulties of enforcement. As was described earlier, one of the requirements of the convention is that countries submit a report in order to communicate the progress that is being made in implementation; however, national governments are under no obligation to provide this information. The enforcement of the convention is still a significant issue and, to a large extent, this is secured through a mixture of positive or punitive media exposure and through diplomatic influence. The convention is sometimes described as 'soft' law and is more effective when it is integrated into national law.

As an example of the problems with enforcement, we can consider physical punishment. The convention states that:

Article 19

1. State Parties shall take all appropriate legislative, administrative, social and educational measures to protect the child from all forms of physical or mental violence, injury or abuse, neglect or negligent treatment, maltreatment or exploitation, including sexual abuse, while in the care of parent(s), legal guardian(s) or any other person who has the care of the child.

In spite of this requirement, it is disturbing to note that in many countries the number of children who receive regular physical punishment exceeds 70 per cent (Newell, 1995). This was the case in countries as diverse as Australia, Barbados, India, Korea, New Zealand, Romania and the USA. In the UK, it is still not an offence for a parent to physically discipline a child. This clearly contravenes Article 19 because legislative measures have not been taken to protect children from 'all' forms of physical violence. However, it is insufficient to reflect on this issue solely in relation to the law.

In the UK, there is general agreement that at times children may need the occasional smack to ensure good behaviour. While we strongly disagree that this is true, we recognize that this cultural attitude needs to be changed if a new law were to be effective. In 1979, Sweden was the first country to prohibit physical punishment. A major implication of their legislation was the need to persuade and educate parents and guardians about the importance of abandoning physical punishment. In the UK, not only does physical punishment continue, but we note with great alarm that the Education Act 1997 extends the rights of teachers to physically restrain pupils. The Times Educational Supplement reported a summary of the new proposals:

> Reasonable force can be used to prevent pupils: . . . 4. Engaging in behaviour prejudicial to maintaining good order and discipline. Teachers can: physically interpose between pupils or block a pupil's path and can touch, hold, push, pull, lead a pupil by the arm or shepherd a pupil away by placing a hand in the centre of the back. Force is only regarded as reasonable if the situation warrants it. The degree of force employed must be in proportion to the circumstance of the incident and the seriousness of the behaviour or the consequences it is intended to prevent.
>
> (Carlton, 1997: 14)

Ironically, but not surprisingly, the article title positioned teachers as the victims. The notion of 'reasonable force' is a dangerous one. Issues to do with the protection of children are once again to be dealt with by courts. This seems a worrying development in the light of the difficulties that the judicial system has had in protecting, for example, abused children. In spite of what appears to be a direct contravention of the UN Convention on the Rights of the Child, the answer to the question of whether a particular child was assaulted or was the victim of 'reasonable force' is to be dependent partly on the merits of a particular lawyer. One of the children interviewed by the children's news agency 'Children's Express' responded to the new proposals: 'I'm shocked these things could happen in school. You're young and you're learning, you shouldn't get hit. It will lead to anger. Anger will build up inside and pupils will retaliate.' While this comment might represent an exaggerated response, it is a response that may well be a common one. The establishment of legislation cannot determine how particular laws will be interpreted by society.

Changes in the law have had significant positive effects on children and their rights. However, the strong association between children's rights and the discipline of law is not without problems. The very conceptualization of this book is built on the importance we assign to multi-professional and interdisciplinary approaches to children and childhood. Because of this, we see that the predominant ownership of children's rights in the discipline of law has the potential to marginalize the contribution of a wide range of other disciplines. The background in education of one of the editors has sometimes prompted the comment or thought during children's rights events 'well, why are you here?' We would not wish to argue that the law does not have a significant role to play, but developments in the law must be supported by an emphasis on empowerment of children and communities, direct work with practitioners, continuing recognition of the role of NGOs, interdisciplinary strategies, and research followed by reflective action.

Boyden (1997) makes some very important points in relation to the nature of human and child rights discourse. The CRC tends to emphasize special protection rights. Clearly the baseline for children must be their right to life and protection from physical harm; however, a focus on emergency situations alone can lead to ignorance of endemic and daily denial of children's rights for much greater numbers of children. This focus also has the danger of encouraging complacency in richer countries that may not have child soldiers, large numbers of street children, infanticide and so on but that do have serious problems in relation to children and their rights. As Boyden (1997: 220) points out: 'human rights discourse tends to detract from careful ethnography, as often as not calling forth simplistic explanations and solutions, many of which are inappropriate or ineffectual'.

In the UK, the practice of law has traditionally been dominated by elites and this continues to the present day. The diversity of society is not yet fully recognized in the judicial system and those who work in the system still often come from rather stereotypic backgrounds. For this reason, the emphasis on the legal aspects of children's rights and the control of such rights by the legal system should be viewed with caution. It is important that this is balanced by an equal concentration of activity carried out by people who possibly have the ability to empathize better with children and who work regularly with a range of children. The suggestion that the developments in law have not always been satisfactorily democratic and consultative is supported by Boyden, who makes the crucial point that:

the global construction of childhood is one that children have played no part in whatsoever: children definitely did not participate in the drafting of the convention; nor have they been consulted as to the most effective manner of implementation.

(Boyden, 1997: 222)

This notion of exclusivity, and the problem that it can have for multi-worker approaches, has been alluded to by Smith (1997). She convincingly argued that, in the field of social work, the recent moves towards an emphasis on children's rights diminished the importance of an understanding and concentration on values and needs. Legal frameworks are accompanied by externally measurable outcomes, but these outcomes rarely focus on the qualitative aspects of relationships which are one of many crucial aspects in relation to children's lives. Smith argued that one of the significant differences between rights and values is that the current rights discourse revolves around the formally codified nature of the legal rights. She goes on to say:

A child's right to a warm and accepting relationship carries some formal weight, but will be void of feeling unless it is informed by the value which we attribute to this particular child and the value which we place on meeting his/her needs . . . King and Piper (1995: 78) set out to elucidate children's rights in a particularly legal context but their comments reflect my own concern when they suggest that: 'To see social relations in terms of "rights" is also to structure and understand the world in a very different way than to evaluate them, for example, according to the level of love or trust they contain. The value of "rights" for the law is in its reductionist nature.'

(Smith, 1997: 12)

It is precisely the 'reductionist nature' of legal structures which means that they can never be the only, or even necessarily the primary, solution to improving children's rights, rather that legal measures should be seen as one of a range of inter-connected contemporaneous and longitudinal strategies.

Children's rights in the English education system

Our emphasis on inter-disciplinary work has so far resulted in a number of foci in this final chapter: the effects of poverty; health and the law; physical punishment; leisure activities; social welfare and so on. The next section will look at children's rights in relation to the English education system. As part of our work on children's rights, we have been carrying out a research project that has started by examining children's rights in primary and secondary schools. The aims of the research were to develop theory in relation to children's rights by examining their experiences in schools and discussing their opinions with them. We chose to focus on education initially as the education service works with the largest numbers of children and we also had questions about the current profile of children's rights in primary and secondary schools. Prior to starting the research, we examined the current position by looking at some areas of interest: education law, curriculum reform and discipline.

If we examine education law in England we can see that children's rights issues appear to be subsumed within the rights of parents and the state. The Education Act 1944 set up the system for the organization and management of education in England, and though there have been a number of additions and amendments since then, that system remains largely unchanged. The central authority in relation to education is held by the Secretary of State for Education and administered through the Department for Education and Employment (DfEE). The DfEE allocates funds to local education authorities (LEAs) which are under a statutory duty to ensure that children in their area receive a satisfactory education. There is no statutory right held by the child (directly or indirectly through parents) to an education. The right to education is achieved through various legislative measures which confer responsibilities on parents and LEAs as follows:

- There is a duty on LEAs to provide sufficient schools for children in their area (Education Act 1944 s8(1)).
- There is a duty on parents to ensure that their children receive an education (Education Act 1944 s36 as amended by Education Act 1981 s17).
- There is a duty on LEAs to take legal action against parents who fail to ensure that their child is educated (Education Act 1944 s37).

It can be seen, therefore, that the right of the individual child to an education is necessarily dependent on adults.

The power to allocate funds and pupils to schools within an area lies with the LEA. However, the Education Reform Act 1988, in line with the 'market forces' construction operating at the time, was enacted to ensure that decisions in relation to allocation of resources were based on 'consumer choice'. The 'consumer' in this context is not the child but the parent. There is a presumption that the wishes of a parent in choice of school will correspond with the wishes of the child. This presumption allows the child to be virtually excluded from all stages of the process, including any appeals procedure. For an example see S (a minor) v. Special Educational Needs Tribunal [1995] 1 WLR 1627 (QBD), in which it was held that only parents can appeal to the High Court against a decision of the Special Educational Needs Tribunal, not the child.

The area of special educational needs provides a worrying example of the ways that all children – including those who arguably most need protection – find that the state does little to support their rights. The Education Act 1993 sections 165 and 167 provides that the LEA is required to identify and make an assessment of any pupil for whom they are responsible and who they consider has special educational needs. Examination of some of the aspects of this statutory provision gives an indication of the place of the child in the process.

Before proposing a statement of special educational needs, the LEA is required to issue *parents* with a copy of the proposed statement and also issue a notice which sets out parents' rights to make representations and to express a choice about the school the child should attend (Education Act 1993, schedule 10 paragraph 2; Education [Special Educational Needs] Regulations 1994, 12 and 13). Parents have a right to express a preference as to the school they want their child to attend (Education Act 1993, schedule 10 paragraph 3). The LEA must explain these rights to parents (Education [Special Educational Needs] Regulations 1994, 12). Before ceasing a statement, the LEA must notify parents of its decision and advise parents of their right to appeal to the tribunal (Education Act 1993, schedule 10 paragraph 11). In deciding whether to carry out an assessment of special educational needs, the LEA should consult with parents and *the child's school* to gain the necessary information to decide whether to make an assessment (Education [Special Educational Needs] Regulations 1994, 11).

The above are all statutory requirements; the law gives rights to parents to take an active part in this important process. The right of children to have a voice in making decisions which will have a major impact on their lives is confined to the weaker 'Code of Practice' and is couched in terms which allow a child's wishes and feelings to be ignored, if they are ascertained at all:

> Every school should *make every effort* to ascertain the child's wishes and feelings . . . and to involve the child in the process. This should be as a matter of principle and for the practical benefit that the child's support will be crucial to the implementation of the education programme.
> (Department for Education, 1994a: 2.34–2.37)

The question arises that if the child's support is acknowledged as crucial to the implementation of the education programme, why is the child not given any statutory rights in relation to decision making in this process? The result in practice is that while the minority of schools whose philosophies place an emphasis on the wishes of children uphold the letter of the Code of Practice, many others can ignore those sections of the documentation that specifically encourage them to act on the wishes and feelings of the child.

In relation to exclusion from school, not only does the law give children no individual rights, but in some cases the behaviour of the parent can affect a decision to exclude a child from school, see *R v. Neale Ex p S* [1995] ELR 198 (QBD) in which it was held that a headteacher was entitled to have regard to a mother's failure to co-operate or sign a behaviour contract when deciding to exclude her son from school indefinitely for behaviour problems. 'Behaviour problems' are regularly cited as reasons for exclusion from school and excluded pupils are often defined as culprits rather than victims; even the government publication *'Pupils with problems* (Department for Education,

1994b) is written in such a way as to locate the problems with the individual children. As Parsons suggested:

> The political and administrative environment in which exclusion is understood and managed is condemnatory rather than caring. The law, regulations and circulars are constructed to clarify disputes and ensure 'justice' not to protect rights. There is a sense in which these pupils are outcasts and are allowed to be.
>
> (Parsons, 1996: 184)

As was suggested in Chapter 2, another important area that affects children in school is the curriculum. It is the curriculum that determines the kinds of activities that children are engaged in while they are at school. The continuing emphasis on reform of the primary curriculum provides a useful focus. It is instructive to examine curriculum organization and reform in primary education since the Education Reform Act 1988 and to reflect on the nature of children's rights in this context.

As was seen earlier, the CRC strengthens the rights of children as autonomous members of society but recognizes the important role that parents and guardians can play in upholding those rights. Similarly, as teachers are *in loco parentis* there is a complex relationship between the rights of teachers and children. This relationship has meant that reforms that affect teachers have a significant bearing on children and their rights.

Since 1988, the reforms of primary education have been characterized by an autocratic style that has resulted in the denial of teachers' rights to proper consultation and ownership. However, whereas teachers have had limited channels for comment through professional bodies, the voices and opinions of children concerning curriculum reform have been completely absent. The introduction of the National Curriculum following the Education Reform Act 1988 set the tone for the style of curriculum reform that shows little sign of abating in spite of a government with a declared commitment to human rights.

In 1987, Kenneth Baker published the 'consultation' papers for the original National Curriculum; however, he chose not to publish the responses. In spite of the timing of the consultation – during the summer holidays – 20 000 responses were received. Haviland (1988) collected some of these responses and he highlighted the response given by *The Campaign for the Advancement of State Education* which he says was representative.

> None of the documents makes any mention of the effects the proposed changes will have on present pupils of our schools, their teachers or on the role and responsibilities of headteachers. None draws on either experience or research to inform the ideas contained in them. There is a fundamental inconsistency in the proposals which is so blatant that we must look to the political philosophy which has generated them to find an explanation.
>
> (Haviland, 1988: 5)

Such political arrogance has resulted in an appalling waste of money, with the original National Curriculum documentation having to be rewritten: a third rewrite is due in September 2000. The rewrites of the curriculum have mainly come about because of the inadequate consultation. This lack of proper consultation has resulted in the curriculum being characterized by too much content and a poor understanding of the links between discrete subjects and cross-curricular work in primary schools. The imposition of an unrealistic curriculum has resulted in many teachers trying unsuccessfully to fit National Curriculum activities into the limited time available. This has had a negative impact on children, as what little choice and control over the curriculum and activities that they might have had in the past has been, and continues to be, eroded.

The other area we looked at prior to the research was school discipline. There appears to be a fear that lack of strict control over children in school will lead inevitably to anarchy and that loss of 'authority' in the classroom is to be avoided at all costs. The renewed national emphasis on traditional discipline in recent years in the UK is one aspect that has contributed to schools being blamed by society for poor discipline among young people and this in turn has led to continued emphasis on the development of whole school policies in the area of discipline, although the term 'whole school' rarely genuinely involves the pupils. Many school-based policies have as their basis the proposition that adults must have organizational control over children's activities, and that the level of powerlessness of children varies according to how the adults in a specific social setting conceptualize children and childhood.

> The independence that teachers say they aim for in children turns out to be a conformity with school norms, both academic and social. Adult knowledge and moral codes are not regarded by the adults at school as negotiable by children.
>
> (Mayall, 1994: 122)

Typically, rules and sanctions receive more attention than rewards. Whereas it could be argued that some rules, mainly relating to safety, are found in adult organizational settings, the same could not be said for actions taken against children for breaches of these rules. Although physical punishment is unlawful in state schools, there are many ways in which children are sanctioned which involve psychological and emotional punishment as well as restrictions on their freedom. The detaining of whole classes of children in primary schools and formal detention sessions in secondary schools are widely used. This sanction of detention for breaches of certain rules would certainly not be tolerated in the adult world and would, in effect, amount to the offence of false imprisonment.

Children are often punished as a group for the alleged or actual misbehaviour of one child. In a case reported to the Ombudsman for Children in Norway (and it is significant that Norway's strong record on human rights resulted in the establishment of an Ombudsman for Children), a class of children had been made to stand outside without coats in minus 20°C temperatures until one of them 'confessed' to moving a teacher's keys. The issue of group punishment itself was debated, but the important question was asked 'would all the teachers have been punished for a misdemeanour by one of them?' (Flekkoy, 1991).

The three areas of interest that we have touched upon represented our thoughts prior to carrying out the research; however, the process of research made us think again about these and many other issues. This final section of the book reports some of our early findings and reflections.

CHILDREN'S RIGHTS IN FOUR ENGLISH SCHOOLS

The research was carried out in two primary and two secondary schools. The schools were chosen following an invitation to most of the schools in a local authority. It was a concern to us that many schools cited OFSTED inspections as a reason for not taking part in the research. It may have been that this simply represented a convenient reason for not taking part in a research project, but assuming these responses were genuine, we are not the first to raise questions about the negative influence of OFSTED. A meeting was held with the headteacher of each school that had expressed interest and the schools were then chosen on the basis of those that we felt would be best able to support the research. They represented a mix of inner-city and suburban areas with predominantly monolingual white children and small numbers of black and bilingual children; none of the schools was single sex and they included one church school and three local authority schools.

We spent a total of 24 days in the four schools and the data were gathered from interviews with children, classroom observations and interviews with school council members, prefects and headteachers. For each school, two groups of six children were chosen to be interviewed on each of the three visits. For the primary schools, the teachers of year 5 and 6 children chose one child who was then encouraged to select the other five children. We felt that the option to choose participants would result in better group dynamics, facilitating more discussion, and that this would outweigh the potential risk of peer pressure influencing the children's views. For the secondary schools, two children from year 8 were asked to select five other year 8 children to be involved. All the interviews took place during lesson times. In total, we interviewed 48 children in groups of six.

One of the major themes to emerge from the research related to the nature of children's participation in their education. Although, as we have seen earlier, the CRC establishes children's rights to be consulted in all matters that affect them, we found a contrast with the ideals represented by the convention. Participation rights were not the only contrast with the convention: for example, the requirement to inform children and adults about the CRC itself was poorly reflected by the fact that, on completion of the data collection, the headteacher from one of the primary schools was the only person from all the children and teachers who we met who was aware of the convention. This, perhaps, is an indication of the work to be done, particularly in light of the fact that nation states are under an obligation to widely publicize the convention as part of its implementation.

There seemed to be agreement from all the children to whom we spoke that the opportunity to discuss their rights and to participate genuinely in their education was severely limited. Our early realization that the opportunity simply to engage in an equal dialogue – and/or to air views – was so restricted resulted in us encouraging the children to think about the changes that they felt were needed in their schools. This was used as a strategy to explore the nature of their participation or lack of it. To some extent, the views of the children were influenced by the particular characteristics of their own community and school. For example, the recent building of a new school entrance and the fact that children were only allowed to use it at certain times caused controversy in one of the schools. Also, as we attempted to ensure that all the children in the groups had a voice in the discussion, it became clear that a wide range of independent and differing views were held.

When asked about the changes they would like to make, the children at Illingworth Primary School (in the following account, all names of schools, teachers and children are fictional) had particularly strong views about how they were treated by the teachers and particularly how they spoke to them. Such strength of feeling was not evident to the same extent in the other schools, although the issue was raised by most of the children we interviewed. We linked this issue with how the children saw the overall quality of their teaching, a matter on which some children had sophisticated views.

The quality of teaching remains a nationally controversial issue. At a national and a local level, it is one that requires sensitivity. However, if children are to participate fully in their education, then their opinions on the effectiveness of their teachers and their education are, perhaps, fundamental. There was no evidence that children were consulted in any way in relation to their views about the quality of their teaching. During individual lessons, we saw no attempts by teachers to encourage students to evaluate the quality of the activities. If schools had student councils, this kind of issue was one of a number that the children felt was not open for discussion. They, perhaps also pragmatically, recognized the social complexities of commenting on the quality of their teachers.

At Illingworth Primary School, the children related quality of teaching to the way they were spoken to by the staff. One of the group described a situation where he had been in trouble and the Head had phoned his mother. When talking to his mother on the phone, the Head had used a 'nice voice' but as soon as she had finished on the phone she started shouting. To many adults this would simply be explained by saying that the Head was annoyed with the child not the adult, hence the harsh tone for the child. At another level it could be argued that the political implications for headteachers of sustaining relationships with parents and the general acceptance that it is acceptable to shout at children give a sense of legitimacy to such an exchange. Yet the child clearly felt particularly aggrieved by the tone of the voice more than the disapproval of wrongdoing.

During our classroom observations, we witnessed very few admonish-ments with voices raised in anger and we saw much teaching that would be deemed to be of a high quality under the current educational climate. However, there was some evidence that the teachers quickly equated the subject of our visits with conceptions of how they should act in the class-room when we were observing. Following a very recent successful OFSTED inspection at Illingworth Primary School, there seemed to be a tendency and natural desire to 'put on a good show'. For example, one of the only incidences in all the schools of children having choice over their activities involved one of the classes being asked to vote for the game that they would prefer in a physical education lesson. It emerged in the subsequent discussion with the children that this was only done 'because [we] were there'. The differences between observed and unobserved teach-ing perhaps suggest that, although we heard few angry voices during our observations, this did not necessarily contradict the children's perceptions about their treatment. At first we conjectured that many adults shout at children and to a certain extent this is a 'normal' aspect of society. How-ever, the strength of feeling that the children expressed forced us to readdress our assumptions about this 'normality'.

There was some direct evidence that supported the children's claims about the way they were spoken to. During one dinner time, the children were all in the hall eating their lunch. One of the teachers exploded with anger directed at one of the children in the hall. The outburst was so dramatic that most of the children in the hall were silenced and momentarily stopped eating their dinner. When, during afternoon break, we asked the teacher about the incident, she struggled to remember what the problem was but finally remembered that the girl had not brought in the friend who it had been agreed could accompany her.

Throughout the research, we felt a tension between wanting to take the views of the children seriously while being appropriately cautious about their claims. Given an opportunity to offer views in a group situation, many people will express negative feelings which obviously offer a one-sided picture. Direct evidence of classrooms revealed a range of positive inter-action that at times contradicted the views of the children. Direct evidence to support the children's claims about their treatment tended to arise outside of formally observed teaching sessions. The fact that the strength of feeling expressed at Illingworth Primary School was not expressed by children in the other schools that we worked in, brought us to the conclusion that the way that the teachers spoke to the pupils was only one part of a wider issue to do with quality of teaching and that this was related to children's lack of participation within that context.

Railton Secondary School offered another perspective on the children's views on the quality of teaching. In order to examine this issue further the following scene draws heavily on the observation and field notes from a particular lesson.

Dominic (one of the researchers) is walking with Jane (a child) who has been assigned to escort him throughout the day. A number of the children in the different schools have identified and defined the issue of quality of teaching. Dominic is concerned not to be too much of a burden to the child or to make her feel uncomfortable while with her peers, but realizes that the fact of his presence will probably do this to a certain extent.

R: So what's your next lesson?

J: English . . . Mr Carter is a good teacher.

R: Oh yes, what makes him a good teacher?

J: One of the things is that he is frightening . . . he keeps control.

R: Are the lessons interesting?

J: Fairly . . . he's been away for quite a long time . . . someone in his family died.

We enter the classroom. There is a particular calmness and quietness. The children seem attentive and ready to start the lesson. This may be a result of knowing about the personal situation of Mr Carter, but Dominic suspects it is a combination of this and a sense of respect that they have for his abilities as a teacher.

T: I am sorry that I have been absent for so long . . . from now on there will be a bit of continuity.

The lesson is to do with simile and metaphor. The teacher poses a series of questions and offers information. The children suggest some answers. At this point Dominic's attention is drawn to the kinds of phrases the teacher is saying to the children.

T: Listen! Learn! (forceful) . . . . You steal an object you rob a person . . . someone robbed my pencil case . . . . The clouds floated across the blue summer sky like? Complete these as fully as you can . . . . (written examples). We seem to have forgotten that if you have something to say you raise your hand . . . . Baby vowel /a/ grown up vowel 'A'. That believe it or not is a capital J . . . what's your name? . . . . Yes I remember . . . excellent . . . good, smashing (referring to child's examples).

After the lesson Dominic walks with the teacher.

R: It's a long time since I have studied similes and metaphors.

T: I have been away for quite a while . . . to be honest I was quite nervous.

(This surprised Dominic as this was a teacher with many years of experience who was well regarded by the children that we spoke to.)

Later in the day the opportunity arose during the group interview to discuss further the issues connected with the qualities of the English teacher and teaching in general.

R: OK, I want to ask you about, you said something to me about the English teacher, it was really interesting actually to see that lesson. You said something like, he's a good teacher.

C1: It was good this morning, the way he explained.

R: So he's a good teacher, I asked why is he a good teacher and you said something like, well, he keeps good discipline, he's frightening you said. Is he frightening?

C1: Yes, when he shouts.

R: You don't have the same one, or do you? (directed at a child from a different class).

C2: We used to, but then we changed.

R: What's his name?

C2: Mr Hamilton.

C3: He used to tell us good stories, that's why we liked him so much, the teacher we have now he just makes us copy out everything.

C1: He reads you stories and the other teachers write and we just copy.

R: So he does what, he reads you stories?

C1: No he makes them up.

C4: Not with Miss Byron we don't.

C5: Miss Byron sent some of the pupils who mess about to a lower set and that's not fair is it?

C4: She doesn't.

C5: She did, she sent Ben down, just because there was too many.

R: I noticed in that lesson everybody was quiet.

C1: He's a good teacher, he can keep control.

C3: He's interested as well.

R: So it's not just that he's good at discipline, he also does interesting things with you.

C4: Miss Byron's a good teacher.

R: So you think you have a right to have good teachers?

All: Yes.

R: What makes a good teacher for you is good discipline? Interesting activities? And it's also more than that isn't it, isn't it also the way that they talk about things.

C1: You know you said we should have good teachers, well they say we should be good, we must be good pupils because we want good teachers.

R: Yes, I agree . . . . I think it's not easy to be a good teacher, it's a very skilled job isn't it?

C1: You know when the teachers say treat us like we treat you, sometimes, you know when you give them backchat back, it's like . . .

Interruption:

T: Sorry to disturb you, have you got any of the people from that end room?

R: No there was a group in . . .

T: I know, but I've just had to shout at them and I've spoken to some of these as well for hanging out the window.

R: OK.

T: They're disturbing the lesson . . .

R: Well if they can do that they can go back to the lessons.

T: Well if they do it again I'll be up . . .

Teacher leaves.

C1: Is that recorded?

R: Yes.

C5: Oh, I'm gonna get [inaudible] for that.

R: You think so? It's quite interesting actually, we're talking about children's rights and a teacher comes in and says, if you don't do this you're in trouble (laughter). Anyway, you were saying something.

C1: When they treat you as they like to be treated back, when they treat you like rubbish and you treat them like rubbish and you get done for it.

C5: It's not fair because they can say what they want to us and if you say something back you get done for it.

Prior to the moment when the physical education teacher (who was aware of the reasons for our interviewing) interrupted, the exchange illustrated a number of issues. The researcher attempted to ask if the children thought that their expectations of teachers were reasonable by asking them to empathize with the teacher's job. At other times in the interviews, the children were often able to empathize and subsequently offer a modified opinion while maintaining their original point. In this instance, neither the researcher's remark or the subsequent interruption distracted the children from what they felt was a particularly important point concerning equal treatment. The point was significant in that it revealed what they saw as the unequal distribution of power. The teachers expected particular types of behaviour and felt that this was necessary to maintain discipline, but the children saw this as unfair. The children felt that they had a right to good teaching irrespective of conditions made about behaviour.

C1: You know you said we should have good teachers, well they say we should be good, we must be good pupils because we want good teachers.

R: Yes, I agree . . . . I think it's not easy to be a good teacher, it's a very skilled job isn't it?

C1: You know when the teachers, say, treat us like we treat you (i.e. speak openly about opinions)*, sometimes, you know when you give them backchat back, it's like . . .* (interruption)*.*

C1: When they treat you as they like to be treated back, when they treat you like rubbish and you treat them like rubbish and you get done for it.

C5: It's not fair because they can say what they want to us and if you say something back you get done for it.

Railton and Graysham Secondary Schools both had school councils, unlike the primary schools which lacked any formal mechanism for finding out the children's views. The councils were designed as formal opportunities for the children to offer their views on a variety of issues that they were concerned about. At first we thought that these councils might offer the opportunity to deal with important issues such as the quality of teaching and learning, but their status as merely a good idea in the light of the impending OFSTED inspections resulted in dissatisfaction with the way they operated. At Graysham Secondary School, it was agreed that a school council was a good idea 'if it worked, but it wouldn't always work'. The head girl articulated with great clarity some of the reasons for the school council not being effective. She felt that although it had not been deliberately disbanded, it had been neglected. One of the main obstacles to the effective working was that 'they [the teachers] need to listen to what people say. They have our views but they don't listen to them. ' It was agreed that the fact that the council secured some lockers was a good thing, but that the locker issue was relatively unimportant. There was a perception that most issues raised by the school council members resulted in a lack of action combined with a lack of communication over the reasons for this lack of action.

Both secondary schools also had a prefect system and Railton Secondary School had a head boy and girl. As it became clear that the schools councils were not working, we wondered if the head boy and girl might offer a useful means of communicating the children's wishes.

R: Do you think the head boy and girl, because they're pupils the same as you, do you think they could be useful for you in helping to express your views, is that how it might work?

C: We used to . . . when we used to go to him every week, he used to write everything down and give it to Mr Norden and Mr Norden passed it on to Mr Coole but he never does anything like that, the only thing he's done is lockers, which everyone knew we were getting anyway.

R: So if you don't feel that the head boy and girl can help you, what's the answer then, because they're like the head boy and girl aren't they, if they can't be advocates for you – do you know what an advocate is? Someone who speaks on your behalf, somebody that takes your side of the argument and puts it forward to someone else.

C: I don't think it's really their fault, I think it's Mr Norden, he doesn't do anything about it.

C: We were asking about our class . . . we wanted to change it but he hasn't got back to us.

Our concerns about the bleak picture of children's participation were reinforced by the views of the headteachers. At Graysham Secondary School any notion that the boundaries between child and adult might be problematic was clinically dispatched: 'Children are children: adults are adults. Children are different . . . . We "love" the children in a way but we are in control. As they get older they get more responsibility. They have rights and responsibilities.' The Head at Railton Secondary School also conceptualized rights with their corresponding responsibilities and emphasized the responsibilities. He felt that rights on their own could cause confrontation and felt that, in the recent past, the pendulum had swung too far in favour of rights: 'A right is an idea which has to be balanced; counterweights – I am in the middle ground.' A bold vision of the future was not on the agenda of this Head (although fortunately the new century is almost upon us):

Ideally there should be an audit of what happens but schools have been asked to do colossal amounts – almost like everything the church used to do schools now have to do. We are not as cohesive as we used to be. This rights thing does not bring about citizenship. Nobody should use the term 'right' until the next millennium.

Our concern for valid findings resulted in us carefully searching for evidence of meaningful participation in order to evaluate the children's claims. One of our strategies in the interviews was occasionally to play 'devil's advocate' to the children's views. Their robust disagreement with some of our suggestions and moments of shared laughter were an indication that they were comfortable with this strategy. The children's views, evidence from lessons and the views of headteachers all served to reinforce our conclusions that the children's rights to participate in their education – and specifically over matters related to the quality of teaching and learning – were worryingly neglected.

Internationally, there has been much attention to the issue of children's rights and for some it has perhaps become a 'fashionable agenda' item. Yet our analysis of the legal situation in the UK leads us to conclude that we are only at the beginning of a long fight. Similarly, by listening to children's views in schools, it is clear that radical improvement is required if society is genuine about the contribution that children and young people might make.

This book has looked at children and childhood from the perspective of a group of professionals with a shared interest. We hope that these different voices have made a contribution to the conceptualization of childhood, particularly by drawing on practical and academic experience in a range of settings, and by starting to confront some of the challenges posed by inter-disciplinary and multi-professional practices that are so significant to society as a whole, and in particular to children.

References and bibliography

Abbott, A. and Wallace, C. (1990) *An introduction to sociology.* London: Routledge.

Abbott, L. (1994) Play is fun but it's hard work too! The search for quality play in the early years. In Abbott, L. and Rodger, R. (eds) *Quality education in the early years.* Buckingham: Open University Press.

Ahlberg, J. and Ahlberg, A. (1978a) *Each peach pear plum.* London: Penguin.

Ahlberg, J. and Ahlberg, A. (1978b) *The jolly postman or other people's letters.* London: Heinemann.

Airasian, P. (1988) Measurement driven instruction: a closer look. *Educational Measurement: Issues and Practice,* Winter: 6–11.

Alanen, L. (1988) Rethinking childhood. *Acta Sociologica,* 31 (1): 53–67.

Alcott, L. M. (1868) *Little women.* (reprinted 1974) London: Dent.

Andersen, H. C. (1974) *The complete fairy tales.* London: Gollanz.

Aries, P. (1962) *Centuries of childhood.* London: Jonathan Cape.

Ashton, J. and Seymour, H. (1988) *The new public health: the Liverpool experience.* Milton Keynes: Open University Press.

Bagley, C., Mallick, K. and Verma, G. K. (1979) Pupil self-esteem: a study of black and white teenagers in British Schools. In Verma, G. K. and Bagley, C. (eds) *Race, education and identity.* London: Macmillan.

Baistow K. (1995) From sickly survival to the realisation of potential: child health as a social project in twentieth century England. *Children and Society,* 9 (1): 20–35.

Baldwin J. (1998) *Young people in 1997: the health related behaviour questionnaire results for 37,538 pupils between the ages of 9 and 16.* Exeter: Schools Health Education Unit.

Bandura, A. (1965) Influence of model's reinforcement contingencies on the acquisition of imitative responses. *Journal of Personality and Social Psychology,* 1: 589–95.

Bandura, A. (1973) *Aggression: a social learning analysis.* London: Prentice Hall.

Barker, M. and Petley, J. (1997) *Ill effects: the media/violence debate.* London: Routledge.

Barnes, D., Britton, J. and Rosen, H. (1986) *Language, the learner and the school.* London: Penguin.

Barthes, R. (1957) *Mythologies.* London: Vintage.

Bates, H. E. (1939) *My Uncle Silas.* London: Jonathan Cape.

Bawden, N. (1973) *Carrie's war.* London: Gollanz.

Beck, U. (1992) *Risk society.* London: Sage.

Bennett, N., Wood, L. and Rogers, S. (1997) *Teaching through play – teachers' thinking and classroom practice.* Buckingham: Open University Press.

Benton, M. (1978) Children's response to stories. *Children's Literature in Education,* 10 (2): 68–85.

Bernardes, J. (1997) *Family studies: an introduction.* London: Routledge.

Blom-Cooper, L. (1985) *A child in trust: report of the panel of inquiry into the circumstances surrounding the death of Jasmine Beckford.* London: Borough of Brent.

Blyton, E. (1942) *The Famous Five find a treasure island.* London: Hodder and Stoughton.

Bonel, P. and Lindon, J. (1996) *Good practice in playwork.* Cheltenham: Stanley Thornes.

Bowlby, J. (1982) *Attachment and loss (Volume 1). Attachment* (2nd edn). New York: Basic Books.

Boyden, J. (1997) Childhood and the policy makers: a comparative perspective on the globalization of childhood. In James, A. and Prout, A. (eds) *Constructing and reconstructing childhood* (2nd edn). London: Falmer Press.

Boyes, G. (1995) The legacy of the work of Iona and Peter Opie: the lore and language of today's children. In Beard, R. (ed.) *Rhyme reading and writing.* London: Hodder and Stoughton.

Briggs, R. (1978) *The Snowman.* London: Hamish Hamilton.

Broadfoot, P.M. (1996) *Education, assessment and society.* Buckingham: Open University Press.

Browne, A. (1977) *A walk in the park.* London: Macmillan.

Browne, A. (1983) *Gorilla.* London: Random Century.

Browne, A. (1989) *Piggybook.* London: Reed Consumer Books.

Browne, A. (1990) *Willy the Champ.* London: Mandarin Paperbacks.

Browne, A. (1992) *The tunnel.* London: Walker Books.

Bruce, T. (1991) *Time to play in early childhood education.* London: Hodder and Stoughton.

Bruner, J. S. (1976) *Play, its role in development and evolution.* London: Penguin.

Buchanan, M. (1989) *Beyond the scare.* Brighton: Class Productions.

Bukatko, D. and Daehler, M. V. (1995) *Child development – a thematic approach* (2nd edn). Boston: Houghton Mifflin.

Burningham, J. (1987) *John Patrick Norman MacHennessy: the boy who was always late.* London: Cape.

Carle, E. (1970) *The very hungry caterpillar.* London: Penguin.

Carlton, E. (1997) Victims dispute violence advice. *Times Educational Supplement,* 20 February.

Carrington, B. and Short, G. (1989) *'Race' and the primary school: theory into practice.* Windsor: NFER-Nelson.

Carroll, L. (1863) *Alice's adventures in Wonderland.* (reprinted 1984) London: Gollanz.

Childline (1996) *Children and racism.* London: Childline.

Children's Literature Research Centre (1996) *Young people's reading at the end of the century.* London: Roehampton Institute.

Children's Rights Development Unit (1994) *UK agenda for children.* London: CRDU.

Cleaver, H. and Freeman, P. (1995) *Parental perspectives in cases of suspected child abuse.* London: HMSO.

Clegg, A. (1964) *The excitement of writing.* London: Chatto and Windus.

Cohen, D. (1987) *The development of play.* London: Croom Helm.

Cohen, M. (1996) Is there a space for the achieving girl? In Gipps, C. V. and Murphy, P. F. (1994b) *Equity in the classroom.* London: Falmer Press.

Cole, B. (1986) *Princess Smartypants.* London: Hamilton.

Cole, B. (1991) *Tarzana.* London: Hamilton.

Cole, N. and Moss, P. (1989) Bias in test use. In Linn, R. (ed.) *Educational measurement* (3rd edn). New York: AERA/NCME and Macmillan. Quoted in Gipps, C. and Murphy, P. (1994a) *A fair test? Assessment, achievement and equity* (Buckingham: Open University Press): 25.

Commission of the European Communities (1993) *Eurobarometer 39.0/ The Europeans and the family; results of an opinion survey.* Brussels: Commission of the European Communities.

Commission For Racial Equality (1989) *CRE code of practice for the elimination of racial discrimination in education.* London: CRE.

Cooke, T. (1994) *So much!* London: Walker Books.

Coolidge, S. (1872) *What Katy did.* (reprinted 1968) London: Dent.

Coppock, V. (1997) Families in crisis. In Scraton, P. (ed.) *Childhood in crisis.* London: UCL Press.

Corby, B. (1993) *Child abuse: towards a knowledge base.* Buckingham: Open University Press.

Cox, R. (1996) *Shaping childhood: themes of uncertainty in the history of adult–child relations.* London: Routledge.

Crain, W. (1992) *Theories of development. Concepts and applications.* Englewood Cliffs, NJ: Prentice Hall.

Crocker, T. and Cheeseman, R. (1991) The ability of young children to rank themselves for academic ability. In Woodhead, M., Light, P. and Carr, R. (eds) *Growing up in a changing society.* London: Routledge.

Crockett, M. and Tripp, J. (1994) *Children living in disordered families. Social policy research findings. No. 45.* York: Joseph Rowntree Foundation.

Crompton, R. (1922) *Just William.* (Reprinted 1983.) London: Macmillan.

Crooks, T. J. (1988) The impact of classroom evaluation practices on students. *Review of Educational Research,* 58 (4): 438–81.

Dahl, R. (1969) *Matilda.* London: Penguin.

Dahl, R. (1982) *Revolting rhymes.* London: Jonathan Cape.

Damon, W. and Hart, D. (1988) The development of self understanding from infancy through adolescence. *Child Development,* 53: 841–6.

deMause, L. (1974) *The history of childhood.* New York: Atcom.

Department for Education (1994a) *Code of Practice on the identification and assessment of special educational needs.* London: HMSO.

Department for Education (1994b) *Pupils with problems.* London: HMSO.

Department for Education and Employment (1996) Personal correspondence.

Department for Education and Employment (1998) *Meeting the childcare challenge: a framework and consultation document.* London: HMSO.

Department of Education and Science (1967) *Children and their primary schools (The Plowden Report).* London: HMSO.

Department of Education and Science (1975) *A language for life (The Bullock Report).* London: HMSO.

Department of Education and Science (1981) *West Indian children in our schools (The Rampton Report).* London: HMSO.

Department of Education and Science (1985) *Education for all (The Swann Report).* London: HMSO.

Department of Education and Science (1988) *National Curriculum science for ages 5 to 16.* London: HMSO.

Department of Education and Science (1989) *From policy to practice.* London: HMSO.

Department of Education and Science (1990) *Starting with quality: report of the Committee of Enquiry into the quality of educational experiences offered to 3 and 4 year olds (The Rumbold Report).* London: HMSO.

Department of Health (1991a) *Child abuse; a study of inquiry reports 1980–89.* London: HMSO.

Department of Health (1991b) *Laboratory confirmed rubella infection.* London: HMSO.

Department of Health (1991c) *On the state of public health.* London: HMSO.

Department of Health (1995) *Child protection messages from research.* London: HMSO.

Department of Health (1997) *Better value for money in social services: a review of performance trends in social services in England*. London: HMSO.

Department of Health and Social Security (1974) *Report of the committee of inquiry into the care and supervision provided in relation to Maria Colwell*. London: HMSO.

Department of Health and Social Security (1982a) *Report of the panel of inquiry into the death of Lucy Gates, to the London Borough of Bexley and Bexley Health Authority*. London: HMSO.

Department of Health and Social Security (1982b) *Report of the panel of inquiry into the death of Richard Fraser to the London Borough of Lambeth, Inner London Education Authority, Lambeth, Southwark and Lewisham Area Health Authority*. London: HMSO.

Departments of Health, Education and Science, Home Office and Welsh Office (1991) *Working together under the Children Act 1989*. London: HMSO.

Dickens, C. (1965) *Great expectations*. London: Macmillan.

Dixon, B. (1990) *Playing them false: a study of children's toys, games and puzzles*. Stoke on Trent: Trentham Books.

Dodge, K. A. (1983) Behavioural antecedents of peer social status. *Child Development*, 54: 1386–99.

Doll, B. and Doll, C. (1996) *Bibliotherapy with young people: librarians and mental health professionals working together*. Englewood: Colorado.

Donaldson, M. (1978) *Children's minds*. Glasgow: Fontana.

Dorn, A. (1985) Education and the Race Relations Act. In Arnot, M. (ed.) *Race and gender: equal opportunities in education*. Oxford: Pergamon Press.

Douglas, J. W. B. (1964) *The home and the school*. London: MacGibbon and Key.

Elliot, F. R. (1986) *The family: change or continuity?* London: Macmillan.

Elliott, M. (1986) *Keeping safe*. London: Bedford Square Press.

Epstein, D. (1995) Girls don't do bricks: gender and sexuality in the primary classroom. In Siraj-Blatchford, J. and Siraj-Blatchford, I. (eds) *Educating the whole child. Cross-curricular skills, themes and dimensions*. Buckingham: Open University Press.

Erikson, E. H. (1963) *Childhood and society* (2nd edn). New York: W. W. Norton.

Exley, R. and Exley, H. (1973) *To Dad*. Walford: Exley Publications.

Falmer, E. and Owen, M. (1995) *Child protection practice: private risks and public remedies*. London: HMSO.

Family Rights Group (1991) The Children Act 1989: working in partnership with families: a reader. London: HMSO. Quoted in Thorburn, J., Lewis, A. and Shemmings, D. (1995) *Paternalism or partnership? Family involvement in the child protection process*. (London: HMSO): 8.

Ferri, E. (1993) *Life at 33: the fifth followup of the National Child Development Study*. London: National Children's Bureau and City University.

Ferri, E. and Smith, K. (1996) *Parenting in the 1990s. Family and parenthood policy and practice*. London: Family Policy Studies Centre.

Flekkoy, M. G. (1991) *A voice for children speaking out as their ombudsman*. London: Jessica Kingsley.

Flekkoy, M. G. and Kaufman, N. H. (1997) *Rights and responsibilities in family and society*. London: Jessica Kingsley.

Fletcher, B. (1979) *The family and marriage in Britian: an analysis and moral assessment*. Harmondsworth. Penguin.

Fletcher, D. and Johnson, P. (1996) Traditional family dwindles as population heads for decline. *Daily Telegraph*. September 27.

Forrester, H. (1974) *Twopence to cross the Mersey*. Oxford: Bodley Head.

Frank, A. (1954) *The diary of Anne Frank*. London: Penguin.

Frodi, A. and Smetana, J. (1984) Abused, neglected and non-maltreated pre-schoolers' ability to discriminate emotion in others: the effects of IQ. *Child Abuse and Neglect,* 8: 459–65.

Fryer, P. (1984) *Staying power: the history of black people in Britain.* London: Pluto Press.

Gaine, C. (1988) *No problem here.* London: Hutchinson.

Gaine, C. (1995) *Still no problem here.* Stoke on Trent: Trentham Books.

Gill, D. (1975) Unravelling child abuse. *American Journal of Orthopsychiatry,* 45: 346–56.

Gill, T. (1996) (ed.) *Electronic children: how children are responding to the information revolution.* London: National Children's Bureau.

Gillborn, D. and Gipps, C. (1996) *Recent research on the achievements of ethnic minority pupils.* London: HMSO.

Gipps, C. V. (1994) *Beyond testing – towards a theory of educational assessment.* London: Falmer Press.

Gipps, C. V. and Murphy, P. F. (1994a) *A fair test? Assessment, achievement and equity.* Buckingham: Open University Press.

Gipps C. V., and Murphy, P. F. (1994b) *Equity in the classroom.* London: Falmer Press.

Gipps C. V., Brown, M., McCullum, B. and McAlister, S. (1995) *Intuition or evidence.* Buckingham: Open University Press.

Gittins, D. (1998) *The child in question.* London: Macmillan.

Goldson B. (1997) Childhood: an introduction to historical and theoretical analysis. In Scraton, P. (ed.) *Childhood in crisis.* London: UCL Press.

Goldthorpe, J. H. (1987) *Social mobility and class structure in modern Britain.* Oxford: Oxford University Press

Gould, S. J. (1996) *The mismeasure of man.* (revised and expanded edn) London: Penguin Books.

Gollnick, D. (1992) Multicultural education: policies and practices in teacher education. In Grant, C. A. (ed.) *Teacher education in research and multicultural education.* London: Falmer Press.

Graves, D.H. (1983) *Writing: teachers and children at work.* Portsmouth, NH: Heinemann Educational.

Graziano, R. and Barber, R. (1956) *Somebody up there likes me.* New York: Hammond and Hammond.

Groos, K. (1898) The play of animals. London: Chapman and Hall. Quoted in Bruner, J. S. (1976) *Play, its role in development and evolution.* (London: Penguin): 68.

Gunter, B. and McAleer, J. (1997) *Children and television.* London: Routledge.

Hall, M. B. D. (ed.) (1991) *Health for all children.* Oxford: Oxford University Press.

Hall, M. B. D. (ed.) (1996) *Health for all children* (3rd edn). Oxford: Oxford University Press.

Hall, N. (1989) *Writing with reason: the emergence of authorship.* London: Hodder and Stoughton.

Halsey, A. H. , Heathe, A. F. and Ridge, J. M. (1980) *Origins and destinations.* Oxford: Oxford University Press.

Hargreaves, D. H. (1967) *Social relations in a secondary school.* London: Routledge and Kegan Paul.

Hart, C. H. , De Wolf, D. M. , Wozniak, P. and Burts, D. (1992) Maternal and paternal disciplinary styles: relations with pre-schoolers' playground behaviour orientations and peer status. *Child Development,* 63: 879–92.

Hart, N. (1985) *The sociology of health and medicine.* Ormskirk: Causway Press.

Haskey, J. (1994) Estimated numbers of one parent families and their prevalence in Great Britain in 1991. In *Population Trends,* 78. London: OPCS/HMSO.

Haviland, J. (1988) *Take care, Mr Baker!* London: Fourth Estate.

Hawtin, A. and Wyse, D. (1997) *Children's rights: a national and international perspective.* London: British Council.

Hayes, M. and Williams, C. (1995) *Family law; principles, policy and practice.* London: Butterworths.

Hendrick, H. (1997) Constructions and reconstructions of British childhood: an interpretative survey, 1800 to the present. In James, A. and Prout, A. (eds) *Constructing and reconstructing childhood* (2nd edn). London: Falmer Press.

Hendrick, J. (1997) *Child care law for health professionals.* Oxford: Radcliffe Medical Press.

Her Majesty's Chief Inspector of Schools and the Equal Opportunities Commission (1996) *The gender divide performance differences between boys and girls at school.* London: HMSO.

Hill, D. (1994) Initial teacher education and ethnic diversity: cultural diversity and the curriculum. In Verma, G. K. and Pumfrey, P. D. (eds) *Cultural diversity and the curriculum, Volume 4: Cross-curricular lhemes and dimensions in primary schools.* London: Falmer Press.

Hinde, R. A. (1966) *Animal behaviour: a synthesis of ethology and comparative psychology.* London: McGraw-Hill

Holbrook, D. (1964) *English for the rejected.* Cambridge: Cambridge University Press.

Holt, J. (1964) *How children fail.* London: Penguin.

Holtermann, S. (1995) *All our futures: the impact of public expenditure and fiscal policies on Britain's children and young people.* London: Barnardos.

Hughes, S. (1996) *Enchantment in the garden.* Oxford: Bodley Head.

Hughes, T. (1856) *Tom Brown's schooldays.* (reprint 1964) London: Armada.

Hutt, S. J., Tyler, C., Hutt, C. and Christopherson, H. (1989) *Play, exploration and learning.* London: Routledge.

James, A., Jenks, C. and Prout, A. (1998) *Theorizing childhood.* Cambridge: Polity Press.

James, A. and Prout, A. (1990) *Constructing and reconstructing childhood.* London: Falmer Press.

Jenks, C. (1996) *Childhood.* London: Routledge.

Jensen, A. R. (1969) How much can we boost IQ and scholastic achievement. *Harvard Educational Review,* 39: 1–123.

Johnson, P. (1990) *A book of one's own: developing literacy through making books.* London: Hodder and Stoughton.

Jones, R. J. (1997) Deafening silence: telling stories of beginning teachers' understandings of ethnicity. Manchester Metropolitan University: unpub. PhD thesis.

Jordan, B. (1988) What price partnership? Costs and benefits. In James, A. and Scott, D. (eds) *Partnership in probation education training.* London: Central Council for Education and Training in Social Work.

Joshie, H., McCulloch, A., Clark, L., *et al.* (1998) *The outcomes for children of family disruption: evidence from the second generation of the 1958 Birth Cohort study.* Notes of Presentation given at ESRC conference 'Children 5–16 growing into the twenty-first century', January 1998 at Church House, London.

Kamin, L. and Eysenck, H. J. (1981) *Eysenck H. J. versus Kamin L.: intelligence, the battle for the mind.* London: Pan Books.

Kästner, E. (1929) *Emil and the detectives.* (reprinted 1977) London: Puffin.

Kemp, G. (1977) *The turbulent term of Tike Tiler.* London: Faber.

Kempe, C., Silverman, F., Steele, B., Droegemueller, W. and Silver, H. (1962) The battered child syndrome. *Journal of the American Medical Association,* 181: 17–22.

Kerry, T. and Eggleston, J. (1994) The evolution of the topic. In Pollard, A. and Bourne, J. (eds) *Teaching and learning in the primary school.* London: Routledge.

King, M. (1997) *Better world for children? Explorations in morality and authority.* London: Routledge.

Kitamura, S. (1987) *Lily takes a walk.* London: Transworld Picture Corgi.

Koretz, D., Linn, R., Dunbar, S. and Shepherd, L. (1991) The effects of high stakes testing on achievement: preliminary findings about generalization across tests. Paper presented to the AERA/NCME, April 1991, Chicago. Quoted in Gipps, C. V. (1992) *Beyond testing – towards a theory of educational assessment.* (London: Falmer Press): 49.

Lacey, C. (1970) *Hightown Grammar.* Manchester: Manchester University Press.

Lang, A. (1973) *Fifty favourite fairy tales.* Oxford: Bodley Head.

Laslett, P. (1982) Forward, in Rapoport, R. N., Fogarty, M. P. and Rapoport, R. (eds) *Families in Britain.* London: Routledge.

Lee, L. (1952) *Cider with Rosie.* London: Andre Deutsch.

Lefkowitz, M. M. (1976) *Growing up to be violent: longitudinal study of the development of aggression.* London: Pergamon Press.

Light, P. (1986) Context, conservation and conversation. In Richards, M. and Light, P. (eds) *Children of social worlds.* Cambridge: Polity Press.

Lindgrenn, A. (1945) *Pippi Longstocking.* (reprinted 1957) Oxford: Oxford University Press.

Lorenz, K. (1966) *On aggression.* London: Methuen.

Lynch, M. and Roberts, J. (1982) *The consequences of child abuse.* London: Academic Press.

McGarringle, J. and Donaldson, M. (1975) Conservation accidents. *Cognition,* 3: 341–50.

McKee, D. (1980) *Not now, Bernard.* London: Random Century.

McKeown T (1976) The role of medicine – dream, mirage or nemesis. Quoted in Ashton, J. and Seymour, H. (1988) *The new public health: the Liverpool experience.* (Milton Keynes: Open University Press): 6.

Madaus, G. (1988) *The influence of testing on the curriculum.* In Tanner, L. N. (ed.) *Critical issues in curriculum, 87th yearbook of NSSE, part 1.* Chicago: University of Chicago Press.

Maher, P. (1987) *Child abuse, the educational perspective.* Oxford: Blackwell.

Malformation statistics 1991. Series MB3 No7. London: HMSO.

Martin, H. (1972) The child and his development. In Kenyse, C. and Helfer, R. (eds) *Helping the battered child and his family.* Philadelphia: Lippincott.

Mayall, B. (1994) *Children's childhoods observed and experienced.* London: Falmer Press.

Miles, R. (1989) *The women's history of the world.* London: Paladin.

Millar, S. (1968) *The psychology of play.* London: Penguin.

Milne, A. A. (1926) *Winnie the Pooh.* London: Methuen.

Montagu, A. (1976) *Nature of human aggression.* Oxford: Oxford University Press.

Montgomery, L. M. (1908) *Anne of Green Gables.* (reprinted 1964) London: Penguin.

Moyles, J. (1989) *Just playing? The role and status of play in early childhood education.* Milton Keynes: Open University Press.

Mullard, C. (1985) Multiracial education in Britain: from assimilation to cultural pluralism. In Arnot, M. (ed.) *Race and gender: equal opportunities in education.* Oxford: Pergamon Press.

Multi-cultural education. (1981) London: BBC.

Muncie, J. (1995) *Understanding the family.* London: Sage.

Murdock, G. P. (1965) *Social structure.* New York: Free Press.

Murphy, P. (1988) Gender and assessment. *Curriculum*, 9(3): 165–71.

Newbold, D. (1997) Reforming teacher education: innovations in curriculum and partnership. Paper given at NEWI conference, 24–27 March, 1997, Wrexham.

Newell, P. (1995) Respecting children's right to physical integrity. In Franklin, B. (ed.) *The handbook of children's rights comparative policy and practice*. London: Routledge.

Newkirk, T. (1989) *More than stories, the range of children's writing*. Portsmouth: Heinemann Educational Books Inc.

Oakley, A. (1974) *Housewife*. London: Allen Lane.

Office of Population Censuses and Surveys (1991) *Mortality statistics: perinatal and infant mortality. Social and biological factors 1981 and 1990*. London: HMSO.

Office of Population Censuses and Surveys (1994) *1991 census; household and family composition*. London: HMSO

OFSTED (1993a) *Boys and English*. London: HMSO.

OFSTED (1993b) *First class: the standards and quality of education in reception classes*. London: HMSO.

OFSTED (1996) *Exclusions from secondary schools*. London: HMSO.

OFSTED (1999) *Raising the attainment of minority ethnic pupils*. London: HMSO.

Oliver, J. (1985) Successive generations of child maltreatment. *British Journal of Psychiatry*, 147: 484–90.

Opie, I. and Opie, P. (1951) *The Oxford dictionary of nursery rhymes*. Oxford: Oxford University Press.

Opie, I. and Opie, P. (1959) *The lore and language of school children*. Oxford: Oxford University Press.

Opie, I. and Opie, P. (1969) *Children's games in street and playground*. Oxford: Oxford University Press.

Parsons, C. (1996) Permanent exclusions from schools in England in the 1990s: trends, causes and responses. *Children and Society*, 10: 177–86.

Parsons T. (1951) The social structure of the family. In Ashen, R. N. (ed.) *The family: its functions and destiny*. New York: Harper and Row. Quoted in Haralambos, M. and Heald, R. M. (1980) *Sociology themes and perspectives*. (London: Bell and Hyman): 332.

Parton, N. (1985) *The politics of child abuse*. London: Macmillan.

Parton, N., Thorpe, D. and Wattam, C. (1997) *Child protection: risk and moral order*. London: Macmillan.

Perrault, C. (1696) *Complete fairy tales*. (reprinted 1962) London: Longman.

Peyton, K. M. (1970) *Pennington's seventeenth summer*. Oxford: Oxford University Press.

Piaget, J. (1970) Piaget's theory. In Mussen, P. H. (ed.) *Carmichael's manual of child psychology (Volume 1)*. New York: Wiley.

Platt, M. J. and Pharoah, P. O. D (1995) Child health statistical review, 1995. *Archives of Diseases in Childhood*, 73: 541–8.

Pollard, A. (1985) *The social world of the primary school*. London: Holt, Rinehart and Winston.

Pollard, A. and Tann, S. (1993) *Reflective teaching in the primary school*. London: Cassell.

Pollard, A., Broadfoot, P., Croll, P., Osborn, M. and Abbot, D. (1994) *Changing English primary schools? The impact of the Education Reform Act at Key Stage One*. London: Cassell.

Pollock, L. H. (1987) Forgotten children: parent–child relations from 1500 to 1900. Cambridge: Cambridge University Press.

Postman, N. (1983) *The disappearance of childhood: how television is changing children's lives*. London: W. H. Allen.

Powel, B. (1985) Boys, girls and languages in school. London: CILT. Quoted in Cohen M. Is there a space for the achieving girl? In Gipps, C. V. and Murphy, P. F. (1994b) *Equity in the classroom*. London: Falmer Press.

Pyke, N. (1996) Ministers attacked over race research. *Times Educational Supplement*, 3 May.

Rosenthal, R. and Jacobson, L. (1968) *Pygmalian in the classroom*. New York: Holt, Rinehart and Winston.

Ross, T. (1985) *The boy who cried wolf.* London: Random House.

Rousseau, J. J. (1762) *Emile.* (reprinted 1911) London: Dent.

Rowntree, D. (1987) *Assessing students: how shall we know them?* London: Harper and Row.

Salter, B. and Tapper, T. (1981) *Education politics and the State*. London: Grant McIntyre.

Sanger, J., Willson J., Davies, B. and Whittaker, R. (1997) *Young children, videos and computer games, issues for teachers and parents*. London: Falmer Press.

Santrock, J. W. (1990) *Children* (3rd edn). Indianapolis: Brown and Benchmark.

Scaffer, D.R. (1997) *Social and personality development* (2nd edn). Pacific Grove: Brookes Cole Publishing Co.

Scieszka, J. (1989) *The true story of the three little pigs!* London: Penguin.

Scieszka, J. and Smith, L. (1992) *The stinky cheese man and other fairly stupid tales*. London: Penguin.

Scott, J. and Parren, K. (1994) The family album: reflections on personal and family life. In Buck, N., Gershuny, J., Rose, D. and Scott, J. (eds) (1994) *Changing households: the British Household Panel Study 1990–1992*. ESRC Research Centre on Micro-social Change, University of Essex.

Scraton, P. (1997) *Childhood in crisis*. London: UCL Press.

Searle, C. (1998) *None but our words: critical literacy in classroom and community*. Buckingham: Open University Press.

Seedhouse, D. (1996) *Health: the foundations for achievement*. New York: John Wiley.

Sendak, M. (1967) *Where the Wild Things are*. Oxford: Bodley Head.

Shamgar-Handleman, L. (1994) To whom does childhood belong? In Qvortrup, J., Bardy, M., Sgritta, G. and Wintersberger, H. (eds) *Childhood matters: social theory, practice and politics*. Aldershot: Averbury.

Short, G. (1985) Teacher expectation and West-Indian underachievement. *Educational Research*, 27 (2): 95–101.

Short, G. (1991) Children's grasp of controversial issues. In Woodhead, M., Light, P. and Carr, R. (eds) *Growing up in a changing society*. London: Routledge.

Shorter, E. (1977) *Making of the modern family*. London: Fontana.

Smith, C. (1997) Children's rights: have carers abandoned values? *Children and Society*, 11: 3–15.

Smith, M. and Grock, M. (1995) *Normal family sexuality and sexual knowledge in children*. London: Royal College of Psychiatrists/Gorkill Press.

Spear, M. (1996) The influence of halo effects upon teachers' assessments of written work. *Research in Education*, 56: 85–6.

Spencer, H. (1873) *Principles of psychology*. New York: Appleton.

Spencer, J. R. and Flyn, R. (1993) *The evidence of children: the law and the psychology*. London: Blackstone.

Spyri, J. (1881) *Heidi.* (reprinted 1958) London: Dent.

Stainton Rogers, R. and Stainton Rogers, W. (1992) *Stories of childhood: shifting agendas of child concern*. London: Harvester Wheatsheaf.

Steedman, C. (1982) *The tidy house*. London: Virago Press.

Stevenson, R. L. (1883) *Treasure Island*. (reprinted 1985) London: Harrop.

Stowe, H. B. (1852) *Uncle Tom's cabin*. (reprinted 1902) London: Dent.

Swan, J. (1992) *Girls, boys and language*. Oxford: Blackwell.

Taylor, S. (1989) Researching child abuse. In Burgess, R. (ed.) *Investigating society*. London: Longman.

Thompson, F. (1945) *Lark Rise to Candleford*. Oxford: Oxford University Press.

Thorburn, J., Lewis, A. and Shemmings, D. (1995) *Paternalism or partnership? Family involvement in the child protection process*. London: HMSO.

Thorne, B. (1982) Feminist rethinking of the family: an overview. In Thorn, B. and Yallom, M. (eds) *Activating theory*. London: Lawrence and Wishart.

Tinbergen, N. (1968) On war and peace in animals. *Science*, 160: 1411–18.

Tomlinson, S. (1990) *Multicultural education in white schools*. London: Batsford.

Townsend, S. (1982) *The secret diary of Adrian Mole aged $13\frac{3}{4}$* . London: Methuen.

Travis, G. (1998) Future of the family: ministers keep faith in the family. *Guardian*, 30 September, 35.

Trawick-Smith, J. (1997) *Early childhood development. A multicultural perspective*. Upper Saddle River: Prentice Hall.

Troyna, B. (1993) *Racism and education*. Buckingham: Open University Press.

Turnbull, C. (1974) *The Forest People*. London: Cape.

Twain, M. (1876) *Tom Sawyer*. (reprinted 1955) London: Dent.

Twain, M. (1884) *Huckleberry Finn*. (reprinted 1958) London: Dent.

Tyler, S. (1991) Play in relation to the National Curriculum. In Hall, N. and Abbott, L. (eds) *Play in the primary curriculum*. London: Hodder and Stoughton.

United Nations Educational, Scientific and Cultural Organisation *The Four Pillars*. UNESCO online: http://www.unesco.org/delors/fourpil.htm, April 6, 1999.

Utting, D. (1995) *Family and parenthood: supporting child-rearing and preventing break-down*. York: Joseph Rountree Policy Studies Centre.

Van der Post, L. (1962) *The lost world of the Kalhari*. Harmondsworth: Penguin.

Vygotsky, L. S. (1978) Mind and society: the development of higher psychological processes. Cambridge, MA: Harvard University Press.

Vygotsky, L. S. (1987) *Thought and language*. Cambridge, MA: Harvard University Press.

Wetherall, M., Dallos, R. and Cochrane, A. (1994) (eds) *Understanding the family*. London: Sage.

White, J. (1994) Research on English and the teaching of girls. In Gipps, C. V. and Murphy, P. F. (eds) *Equity in the classroom*. London: Falmer Press.

Whitehead, M. (1993) Born again phonics and the nursery rhyme revival. *English in Education*, 27 (3): 42–51.

Williams, J. (1978) *The practical princess and other liberating tales*. London: Hippo.

Wise, G. (1994) The changing family. In Lindsay, B. (ed.) *The child and family. Contemporary issues in child health and care*. London: Baillière Tindall.

Woodroff, C. (1993) *Children, teenagers and health: the key data*. Buckingham: Open University Press.

World Health Organization (1946) *Constitution*. WHO online: http://www:who.org/aboutwho/en/definition. html [cited April 1999].

World Health Organization (1984) *Health promotion: a discussion document on the concept and principles*. Copenhagen: WHO Regional Office for Europe.

Wyse, D. (1998) *Primary writing*. Buckingham: Open University Press.

Index